"If you read just one screenwriting book a year, Howard's book. Howard holds the profession ol many. He understands both the art and the craft building a legacy, which is why most of us write.'

**Mary J. Schirmer**
Screenwriter-Producer, *www.screenplayers.net*

"Houston lays out a fantastic and easy to understand introduction to the future of media in his book. I was blown away by his helpful advice on preparation and building a story world that can expand your reach through multiple platforms and audiences. If you think transmedia is just retelling your same story in different media formats you are going to miss the future."

**Brian Godawa**
Screenwriter, *To End All Wars;* Author, *Hollywood Worldviews*, and
Novelist, *Chronicles of the Nephilim.*

"These transmedia storytelling techniques are invaluable for every type of story. Indeed, Houston Howard's discussion of high concept, and analysis of story setting, are worth the price of admission alone. And there's much, much more. Read on. Write on."

**John L. Geiger**
Co-author, *Creativity & Copyright*

This book is not only an accessible primer for writers, it clearly articulates a process by which professionals can implement transmedia storytelling techniques to elevate their projects. Houston Howard's humorous and enthusiastic vision is a worthy resource for anyone wanting to reach a wider audience with their work."

**Ian Puente**
Vice President of Business Development and General
Counsel at Samuel Goldwyn Films

"As a marketing professional, I found Houston Howard's book a refreshing new approach to storytelling, effective advertising and promotions on just about any level. Advertising is about message delivery and, though its roots are in entertainment, this book explains how to create and deliver those messages to a variety of targets in their own environment. Truly an innovative approach as the industry moves into a more mixed-media environment."

**Jason Hager**
Brand and Marketing Expert, The Manahan Group

"Writing is a bit of inspiration amid a great deal of organized thinking.
Houston Howard's book helps lay the foundation of a rich and enduring narrative over multiple platforms, and lets you focus on the fun parts of crafting your storyworld. It's a rare thing for a writer to share his process. It's even more rare to find a process as comprehensive as Super Story. Read this book!"

**Lindsey Schmitz**
President, Longshadow Productions, Animator

"Written by the humble and personable Houston Howard, this book examines the world of story expansion or as he calls it "Super Story." Storytelling as a passive medium is a thing of the past. For both aspiring creative minds and professionals alike, reading this book will give you the upper hand in this cut throat business. As a film marketing professional, I am confident that the forward thinking in this book will change the way we create, market, and view entertainment. From the script stage, to multi platform distribution, and beyond; do yourself a favor and explore the world that this book has to offer."

**Evan Colfer**
Editor / Film and Marketing Professional

This book is a comprehensive guide to building transmedia worlds that last. From inception and creation to marketing and building communities that will support your franchise in the long-run, this book is an insightful step-by-step guide for anyone looking to tell stories for entertainment or for branding in the 21st century."

**Christine Weitbrecht,**
Brand Consultant and Transmedia Producer, *Thoughts on the T*

"Houston Howard's book is the best introduction to the concept of transmedia storytelling that I have read. Even better, his thoughts for best practice are completely hands-on, readily understandable, and – for us writers – a lot of fun. I've already incorporated some of his ideas into my own current project, and it's better for it. If you only read one new book on cross-platform content creation this year, this should be it."

**Carey Martin**
Screenwriter and professor, Liberty University

"Yes, Houston Howard's book walks you through architecting your world, structuring your narrative, and all that other good stuff. But the best part of this book is that it's so packed with cool ideas, new ways of engaging audiences and exploring stories, it makes you want to quit reading and just go make stuff!"

**Chad Gervich**
Writer/Producer: *Dog With a Blog, After Lately, Wipeout*;
Author: *Small Screen, Big Picture*

"Not only is Houston Howard's book a solid introduction to transmedia storytelling, but also it's a valuable tool to applying it to one's own storytelling. Howard examines how one's screenplay can be a part of a larger canvas and provides an invaluable reference and guide to various levels of narrative storytelling and how to maximize your own world building. An essential guide to any writer looking to create their own fictional mythology. Highly recommended."

**Stefan Blitz**
Editor-in-chief, *Forces of Geek*

"Written in easy-to-understand terms, this book, jus like his previous book, is rooted firmly in 'story' and swerves transmedia as a 'fix all 'approach – recognizing that a gold rush to storytelling on a host of platforms will always fail in the absence of strategy and urges you to roll up your sleeves and start thinking in new ways. Houston doesn't waste time on definitions or debates around 'transmedia', but guides you through removing your story blinkers, stepping outside the confines of your existing storyworld, and helps you see how to make it big — stinkin' big."

**Alison Norrington**
Author, playwright, journalist, and founder of storycentralDIGITAL.

"Howard came and taught my students how to develop a screenplay using the unique writing process outlined in this book. Perhaps the greatest strength of Howard's writing process is that it utilizes a technical approach to developing creative writing. All teachers wrestle with the diversity of the classroom, which makes this writing approach so successful and appealing. Writing came to life in my classroom like never before. Howard's writing process is now a permanent part of my curriculum."

**Cari Rucker**
High School Teacher, Reading Specialist, English Chair

"I was absolutely amazed to see how the creative process Houston Howard sets forth in his boom took my small children's book and rapidly expanded it into a viable franchise without sacrificing its creative integrity. In fact, it actually allowed me to explore areas of my story I didn't even realize were there! If you're a fiction author, you need to read this book."

**Nelson Gassman**
Co-author of *The Sock Circus*

"Finally! This book is a concise resource for how to create media that is focused, well thought out, and marketable. No more 'tid bits' of truths scattered here and there sending you on endless searches and pass/fail experiences. Houston Howard has delivered the mother load of information on what to do, how to do it, and where to take it from here."

**Mark Kudlow**
Veteran screenwriter

"After years of researching, experimenting and flat out guessing, Houston's book has given me answers to unanswered questions and expanded on my own experience and knowledge of creating a marketable product with the story in your head. No more guess work and wasting time and money. You have arrived at the mother load of time saving, money sparing, and sanity salvaging information. I loved reading this book. I only wish I'd read it ten years ago."

**Charity Parenzini**
Writer, Telly Awared-Winning Producer

"With his book, author Houston Howard has provided an everyman's guidebook on how writers can "grow" their story and characters and expand their creative universe. Whether your starting point is a comic book, novel, song, game, television series, play or film script -- Howard provides helpful markers and exercises to map out your project to its fullest potential."

**Kathie Fong Yoneda**
Consultant, workshop leader, author of *The Script Selling Game (2nd edition)*

"People may say that size doesn't matter, but when it comes to your screenplay - big is often times much better. Howard Houston provides you with the needed tools to truly make your story really stinkin' big!"

**Matthew Terry**
Screenwriter, filmmaker, teacher

This book is a vast and comprehensive guide to begin building transmedia worlds that last. The book urges you to to roll up your sleeves and start thinking in new ways that you would've never thought possible. Houston not only gives you the tools to make your story flow but the book passionately empowers you to get off of your couch and begin the creative process and the creative thinking of getting out and doing it for yourself."

**Josh Molina**
Veteran Producer

"I find this book truly inspirational. Early on, Howard writes: "If George Lucas did it and J.K. Rowling did it, then so can we. And so can you. If you have the proper inspiration, a great idea, and you're armed with the right tools, I say chase the giant whale and don't settle for Nemo." When I first began in the film industry, I was focused on one-off stories. Now, I'm all about franchises. This is a great book to get you started!"

**Tom Marcoux**
Screenwriter, Professor

"Before I read and applied the process described in this book, I had a lot of 'primordial story ooze' lying around in notes on my computer and in the recesses of my mind-- about ten years of them. After reading his macro/micro/nano story and fence post concept I was able to convert ten thousand years of world story into something I could actually sit down and write. The process outlined in this book allowed me to take that ooze and put flesh and bone on it so that the story lives and breaths"

**Andrew Nemecz**
Fantasy Author

# YOU'RE GONNA NEED A BIGGER STORY

THE 21ST CENTURY SURVIVAL GUIDE TO NOT JUST WRITING STORES, BUT BUILDING SUPER STORIES

HOUSTON HOWARD

2017

**superstory.works**

To my daughter, Sariah Praise.

At this point, you're nearly three years old and love Darth Vader.
So, here's to me being every bit as cool in your eyes,
but never having to cut off your hand.

# Why you should buy this book.

Yes!

I've somehow managed to ~~manipulate~~ ~~convince~~ inspire you to pick up the book, which these days I take as a small, yet significant, victory. Small victories, they say, pave the road to the Promised Land. I can't remember who said that (possibly C.S. Lewis or Tyrion Lannister) and while I don't necessarily disagree, my preference would be for you to not just pick the book up.

**I would like to you buy it. #realtalk**

Why should you spend a portion of your hard-earned paycheck on this book? Maybe you're trying to decide between this book and another industry book? Or possibly you're considering saving the cash and investing into your burgeoning *Pokemon Go* career. Honestly, you should opt for the book because all the things you'll learn from it are things I wish I would have known when I first began pursuing mainstream entertainment as a career.

You see, I graduated from law school on the East Coast. So, when I moved to Los Angeles to start producing and writing, I had two choices: go to film school and take on *another* $40,000 in student loans or figure out how to do it on my own.

I chose Door Number Two.

For the first couple of years, I read every industry book I could afford. However, I still needed a way to set myself apart from the seemingly 14 zillion uber-talented people trying to break into the industry at the same time. I needed a competitive advantage.

So, I figured out a way to create one.

And you've guessed it... all the secrets, tips, tricks, and strategies are in this book.

## Wait...didn't you already write this book?

No. Well, yes. Kind of.

In 2012, I published my first book entitled *Make Your Story Really Stinkin' Big*, which was, at the time, the first book in the transmedia space that actually dealt with the story side of the model, laying out creative, writer's room strategies for 21st century content creators. It did really well, but, admittedly, wasn't complete. There were strategies we were researching and developing that I didn't feel completely comfortable including in a published manuscript at the time.

I've since developed most of those strategies to a point where I'm confident releasing them to the world. Beyond that, because we're also growing and learning, our creative team has developed entirely new creative strategies in the years since the book's release and, trust me, they can definitely help. Lastly, since 2012, we've also rebranded our creative process from 360° Storyweaving to the much better, easier and simpler **Super Story** process.

So, with a new name and, most importantly, new content, I thought it would be a great opportunity for a new edition. However, instead of calling it *Make Your Story Really Stinkin' Big, Second Edition* we're taking this opportunity to rebrand the book with the Super Story name and use it to launch an entire line of Super Story books written by the various members of our creative team.

If you've already read the previous edition, don't think this is one of those "buy the Super Duper Collector's Edition because it has a different cover, new introduction and updated citation list and that's pretty much it" sort of things. Take comfort in the fact that while much of the book will remain the same, you'll be able to discover a mountain of new and extremely valuable creative strategies with a host of new examples and fresh case studies woven throughout the old and the new content. I mean, just look at the increase in page length.

Frankly, there may actually be too much new content and some very sane people tell me I should split this into two (maybe three) separate books. While the inordinate amount of new content that has been added admittedly makes the book feel a bit like you're holding a brick and drinking from a firehose, I would rather err on the side of giving you too much value and knowledge than making you feel like you've been gypped by a greedy author.

The coolest part, though, is that all this new content has played the role of an alchemist and has turned the original book into something entirely new. In fact, in my humble opinion (or, as the kids say, IMHO), it transforms it from a interesting, thought-provoking book to an interesting, thought-provoking *resource* to which you'll want to keep coming back and mining time and time again. One you'll want to keep close by and pull out as you write your next script, novel, play or game. One that you'll want to keep by your bedside, on top of your Bible — okay, not on top of your Bible.

It's definitely not that good.

But, at the end of the day, it'll definitely be worth your while.

# How to read *this* book.

At this point in your life and at this stage in your career, I presume you know how to read *a* book. However, I thought it would be helpful to give you the lay of the land, just so you know what you're getting into.

**Chapters 1 through 5** of this book are my bricklayers, masons and concrete finishers — working extremely hard to lay an exhaustive and detailed foundation of all the principles surrounding the Super Story approach. These five chapters collectively form the "why" for the rest of the book and help you thoroughly and completely understand the necessity of a Super Story.

If, by chance, you are familiar with transmedia or the basic premise of the Super Story model, feel free to jump straight to **Chapter 6**. Fair warning, though, you may find yourself either questioning the wisdom behind, or being confused by, some of the ideas presented, simply because you missed out on the requisite foundation from the first five chapters. #proceedatyourownrisk

Plus, you may miss some of my well-placed, hilarious jokes...

If the first five chapters are the laborers, **Chapter 6 through 15** are the craftsmen and artisans. This is where you get into the ~~weeds~~ ~~minutiae~~ finer points of development and creation, as well as all the practical steps of actually building a colorful yet robust Super Story.

Once the foundation is laid and the artisans build the structure, **Chapters 16 and 17** bring in the interior designers, who place the finishing touches on your brand new Super Story house.

Finally, **the last two chapters** are simply helpful bonus material you can use as needed. Consider them house warming gifts.

Now that you know what you're getting into...

# Table of Contents

# Foreword.

My name is Steven Mitchell. Steven Long Mitchell to be exact.

But that's not what I'm here to talk to you about.

To save you some time, the cliff notes on my IMDB page tell a tale that describes how I, along with my writing partner, Craig van Sickle, have been fortunate enough to have written, produced and/or directed over 200 hours of entertainment programming. This includes:

- Creating three television series (among which was the NBC cult hit classic *The Pretender*);
- Being the showrunner of four other series;
- Writing and producing numerous movies for cable and broadcast television;
- Writing two feature films (one of which was good enough to keep my name on);
- Writing and Executive Producing the highest rated miniseries in the history of the SyFy channel — a six hour, Emmy-nominated epic called *Tin Man.*

The key word here is *nominated.*

I lost — to Tom Hanks. Not that I'm bitter about it ... at least as far as Tom knows.

But my IMDB stuff is also not what I'm here to talk to you about.

That's because what IMDB doesn't mention is that along the way, I have been blessed to work with some amazing people and incredibly talented, forward-thinking geniuses.

This brings me to what I want to talk about.

And that's Batmen.

Not Bat*man,* Bat*men*; men who are like bats.

Bats can see in the dark with other senses. Batmen can also see in the dark; they can see what others can't even though it's right in front of their faces. Unlike the rest of us who fly around blindly head first into buildings, Bat*men* can see in the dark. Bat*men* are geniuses who actually lead the way.

Two such Bat*men* I want to mention here.

I don't know if this is exactly how it happened, but this is how I picture it: It is the 1970's and George Lucas has just finished writing *Star Wars.* As he types, "*The End,*" he gets a sly grin on his face. His joy is not only because he has written a really great movie, it's because he has created magic that no one can see yet. He has put in motion something no one else knows is even on the pages. Because George can see something others can't yet. An entirely different entertainment landscape, for which he has planted seeds in his epic story, his *Super Story.* We will all watch as it germinates and grows in a way that will change the very face of storytelling forever.

George Lucas is one of the two Bat*men* I have been privileged to work with. He is a genius who sees things others can't, a genius that saw the future through different eyes.

Houston Howard is the same kind of genius, a mind-blowing genius, and his genius is in Super Story. In the new century, Houston caught a glimpse of the future and has been leading the way there since.

I was privileged to be on stage with Houston at a transmedia conference in Canada where we were both speaking. And as he talked I found myself nodding. I had been doing much of what he discussed in his Super Story concept — but I had been flying blindly in the dark bashing my head — and he could see clearly the way forward and the things you need to do to get to the future.

So I read his book.

Then I re-read his book.

It was and remains *the* guidepost through the dark for aspiring content creators as well as established content creators who want to have a future in the entertainment landscape of tomorrow.

I learned more from his book than I did in all of film school at Cal Arts and half of my career.

In fact, until I read his book I couldn't express clearly things I had been doing when creating Super Stories. But Houston has one of those "game-playing, decipher the riddle, solve the mystery, can't rest until I create order out of chaos" minds. One that makes you scream — "Oh, NOW I GET IT!"

Not only can he see in the dark, he can see the future and has designed a treasure map for us all to get there.

I don't know if this is exactly how it happened but it's how I picture it: When Houston typed *The End* when he finished this book, I bet he had a grin on his face just like George Lucas. Houston too can see something others can't yet. An entirely different entertainment landscape, one in which his writing will change the face of storytelling forever.

Had I read this book before I started my career, maybe I would have been able to see in the dark. Maybe I would have been one of the Bat*men.* Maybe I would have taken that Emmy home instead of Tom Hanks — not that I'm bitter about it … as far as Tom knows.

Steven Long Mitchell
Oct 31st, 2016

# Why I decided to write a book.

## I'm a process guy.

I like to know what I'm doing and why I'm doing it, and I'm taking it upon myself to presume I'm not alone.

Much to the frustration and discontent of people around me, I've always questioned things. It's not because I like to buck the proverbial system or that I get some bizarre satisfaction out of hassling people, but rather because I like to discover workflows and then burrow my way to the root to see how they were birthed and why they were even developed in the first place.

Basketball scouts routinely refer to players who have "high basketball IQs," athletes who not only know they have to run off a screen and then make a backdoor cut, but also understand *why* they're doing it. Accordingly, I like to have a "high [input any sort of workflow/process here] IQ."

Likewise, when I encounter a situation where there's no discernible process or workflow, I immediately start implementing one. Maybe it's my board-game design background taking over or my analytical lawyer training kicking in or possibly an innate desire to control everything. Whatever the reason, chaos frustrates me. I have to know how and why, or else I get shifty and weird and it's safe to say that no one likes a guy who's either shifty or weird.

This is why I love listening to Martin Scorsese talk about filmmaking. He breaks down storytelling to a science and can expose all the gears, belts, and wheels that make movies tick. He can take them apart, tell you the "how" and "why" and then put them together again all over the course of a good cup of coffee. When I began seeing films in the same way and then viewing all stories as intricately designed machines, I was ruined forever. It was like in *The Matrix* when Neo first saw the Matrix as all the 0s and 1s; I saw the process, I saw the science — and I fell in love.

So, when I first heard folks like Jeff Gomez and Henry Jenkins spreading (pun intended) the good word about this wonderful concept called *transmedia*, I was excited. As a storyteller, I was immediately drawn to the prospect of applying this storytelling science on a greater narrative scale, and its relevance to today's culture. Accordingly, I had my creative team spend the next year devouring every article, podcast, webinar, and conference devoted to transmedia.

I got the philosophy. I loved the theoretics surrounding it. I was challenged by the high-level intellectualism that came with its application and I was drawn to the narrative possibilities it presented. I was a sponge, soaking up terms like *spreadability*, *hyperdiegesis*, and *intertextuality*. Then one day I woke up and discovered no one had to convince me it was the way to go anymore. I was sold. What started then was an insatiable desire to know how to do it.

So, being a process guy, I started searching for a solid transmedia process, any process actually, but what I initially found were just other creative professionals debating definitions and staying on the theoretical side of transmedia. Remember in *Harry Potter and the Order of the Phoenix* when Dolores Umbridge refused to move beyond theory and Harry asked, "And how is theory supposed to prepare us for what's out there?" Well, Harry, I certainly could relate to this as well.

Don't get me wrong, theory is great. It's what got me hooked to begin with. It's the milk I used to grow from a transmedia infant to a transmedia adult who was ready to leave home for the first time; however, at that point, milk wasn't what I needed. I was hungry. I needed food. I needed process.

Look, I'm sure there were processes out there, but I couldn't find them. I chalk it up to either me not looking hard enough (my wife is convinced that's one my most noticeable character flaws), people not wanting to give away their workflows so as to maintain competitive advantage, or the information simply not being published yet because everything was so new. I would find "how" scraps scattered about — an article about how to construct a story bible, a workshop on how to develop a storyworld, a podcast about building engagement with your audience — but even when I would then burrow to the root of those bits and pieces, I wouldn't make satisfying "why" discoveries.

Transmedia was in an exploration phase where most transmedia professionals and enthusiasts were seeking the same answers, so I completely understood why I was coming up short, though this didn't make it any less frustrating. Most importantly, though, I couldn't find a process that was tailored to fit exactly what I wanted to do.

Basically, I needed a soup-to-nuts process that was replicable, teachable, fit what we did, guided me through the intimidation of the blank page, and actually facilitated the generation of transmedia-viable ideas and outputs.

So, I acted like a Shaker and built one.

That, my friends, leads us to the primary goal of this book: to help equip content creators with all the "how's" and "why's" so they'll have all the tools they need for 21st Century entertainment success.

I assuredly don't think I've developed the singular magic bullet, nor do I think a universalist approach can be applied to any creative industry. I do feel, however, that the Super Story process can fit nicely into a best practices cupboard along with a nice collection of other best practices from other highly talented, creative, and intelligent folks.

## I hate the blank page. It's my enemy.

As writers, it's our mission to defeat the blank page by filling it with a story; however, before most writers begin a project, it just sits there, staring at them, taunting. So, what do they do? They procrastinate. Once they start writing, it's nearly impossible to stop, but before the first words hit the page, they procrastinate as long as humanly possible.

Maybe I'm the only one who thinks this way, but I'd bet dollars to donuts there's a host of content creators who consider the blank page a shapeless and disorienting bully with no borders. I've found, though, that if I have a map to guide me through the Great White Wasteland, I can start the process with confidence and the blank page becomes much less intimidating. I know where the first step is leading me and I know the direction in which I'm headed.

Therefore, the second goal of this book is to help writers and content creators disarm the blank page by giving them a starting point, an end point, and every major checkpoint in between.

Before the Great Westward Expansion, embarking on a cross-country journey was intimidating and dangerous. Today, it's not. Why? Because it's been mapped for us. If I'm taking a road trip, I don't simply step out of my house in Los Angeles, get in the car and drive. I know I'm heading to Cincinnati and that I'll be stopping at the Grand Canyon, Santa Fe, Omaha, and St. Louis on the way. I have tremendous freedom in between those checkpoints, but at least I start the trip with a roadmap in my mind that allows me to budget, prepare, and maybe most importantly, convince others to join me.

## Star Wars is our low bar.

Again, the main reason I began developing my own process was because I needed something tailored to exactly what me and my development team wanted to do creatively and how we were thinking about our projects, and let me warn you now — we're big thinkers. Really big actually. To the point where most people think we're crazy. This, to us, means we're on the right track. It also means that any process we use needs to be scalable to fit our big, crazy vision.

To tell you the truth, I'm kind of obsessed with finding the "big idea," the white whale of any creative industry (especially entertainment). With big ideas, sometimes the thrill of the hunt is every bit as exciting as the joy of the catch. Hunting big Super Story ideas doesn't just involve us sitting there, meditating and then suddenly one big idea appears. Most of the time, we sit down and generate fifty ideas. Maybe a hundred. Sometimes three hundred. From there, we'll take a couple of ideas that are big enough to make us nervous and seem somewhat (if not completely) impossible and start twisting and turning them through our system. It's like working on a Rubix Cube. Twist, turn, twist, turn and before long —

boom — we have an idea that is significant, something that can make a big splash in an over-saturated sea of 21st Century entertainment.

At the end of the day, big ideas get the lion share of attention from audiences, media, bloggers and the like. Big ideas, like a fat man cannonballing into a swimming pool, have the possibility to create waves of change for society. Small ideas can disrupt as well, but not until they grow big enough to become change agents. When it comes to ideas, size does, in fact, matter.

Writers and producers who embody "stinkin' big" mindsets have bold goals and are constantly and consistently pushing the boundaries of what's possible for a singular entertainment brand. This approach requires larger amounts of creativity and brilliance, not dullness. There are quite a few people who can come up with one really creative idea and make it work. Hollywood is filled with thousands. However, the number of people who can conceive something bigger, something bolder, something that can last five generations and beyond — that number is much, much smaller.

If we pitch a Super Story concept and the person to whom we're pitching doesn't get the wide-eyed "these guys are legitimately crazy" look, we didn't think big enough. If it's a small, one-off idea, we're not interested. Why? While big challenges to small thinkers can induce anxiety, small challenges to big thinkers can be equally destructive.

In an idea economy, big thinkers have a tacit advantage over mere-mortal small thinkers. Accordingly, big thinkers need to be challenged. The greater the challenge, the more engaged we as creators become. This attitude is necessary because generational projects don't have easy paths to success. If you want easy, the Super Story process ain't your huckleberry.

I grew up a devoted fan of the *Star Wars* saga. I watched the films, owned the toys, donned the Underroos, played the role-playing game (Second Edition, not the original), and read the expanded-universe novels. Today, I marvel at the fact that the *Star Wars* brand is still making so much money on one idea nearly forty years after inception. Not only is there new content being produced in nearly every medium, there are dozens upon dozens of documentaries produced and books written that analyze every aspect of the franchise. It's astounding how this creative project has not only endured, but has continued to *thrive* over multiple decades.

Lucas has accomplished this by imbedding his idea into not only the entertainment, publishing, and toy industries, but in culture as a whole.

With the *Harry Potter* series, I believe J.K. Rowling has created a similarly enduring work. I'm not just talking about book sales or box-office results. I'm not just talking about how J.K. Rowling is worth a billion dollars because of her franchise. I'm also referring to the massive multi-demographical, worldwide community she's built. The notion that a children's book about a young boy attending a school of wizardry, which was written on an old manual typewriter in Great Britain, now causes adults across the world to argue about what House the Sorting Hat would select for them, is amazing to me. Seriously, to make people that passionate about a piece of fiction is equally rare and awesome. Whether you're a fan of the series is beside the point. The cultural impact it's had is unquestionably remarkable.

Are the accomplishments of Lucas, Rowling, and writers like Tolkien and C.S. Lewis exclusive to them? They created endurable works that have impacted people's lives in ways that 99.9 percent of other creative works haven't, but are they unique in their ability to create works of this nature? Absolutely not.

If George Lucas did it and J.K. Rowling did it, then so can we. And so can you. If you have the proper inspiration, a great idea, and you're armed with the right tools, I say chase the giant whale and don't settle for Nemo. Nemo is cool and all, but Nemo isn't for us (Nemo as in the size of the fish, not the $1.8 billion *Finding Nemo* and *Finding Dory* collectively made at the box office — we would find a way to live with that).

Bottom line: We're going big. We're going for *Star Wars*-sized projects. We want to make J.K. Rowling jealous. We're going for works that are legacy-compliant. If my great-great-grandchildren aren't seeing one of our ideas thriving in their time, then we didn't think big enough.

However, I'm not just saying to dream that big in a "wouldn't that be cool" way. I'm telling you to *plan* that big from the inception of your project. If Lucas can get the results he's achieved and he had to expand the universe on the fly, how much more can we, as informed 21st Century content creators, achieve when we think big and plan accordingly from the gate?

I'm telling you to go ahead and build a 50,000 square-foot house even though you may only use four rooms at first. It's much easier to do that than to keep adding to a two-room starter home. Don't believe me? Dig up some interviews with Damon Lindelof and listen to him talk about how difficult it was to keep expanding *Lost* on the fly when the mysterious island was only designed for the pilot episode. Some people call it eating an elephant one bite at a time. Better that than eating a single cookie and then running out of food.

I know it seems like a lot to take on. You know why it seems like that? Because it's a lot to take on. But you can't expect to create a Super Story that's as big as *Star Wars*, as good as *Lawrence of Arabia,* sells as well as *Harry Potter,* has the meaning of *The Chronicles of Narnia,* enraptures fans as much as *Game of Thrones*, and lasts as long as the *Odyssey* without putting in a healthy amount of old-fashioned sweat equity.

So, how do you plan for something that big?

You follow our Super Story process.

## The honest truth.

Here's the thing — there is no perfect recipe for an Oscar-winning film, a Grammy-winning song, or a best-selling novel. If I could crack that code, I would be a zillionaire, probably win a Nobel prize, and have enough power to somehow avoid LA traffic. So, if you're expecting to find a magic formula for success, you'll be disappointed. Some ideas hit and some ideas don't. Some folks execute and others drop the ball.

Regardless, I'm confident our Super Story process will give you a better *chance* of long-term success, give your project durability, and give you, the content creator, a structure that will help guide you through it all.

Honestly, at the end of the day, it comes down to the fact that it's helped us tremendously. It's guided us, it's challenged us, and has propelled our projects in creative directions we didn't previously think were possible. What this means is there's a good chance it will help you, too.

So, we thought we'd share.

Enjoy.

*Part 1*

# The Approach

THE WORLD HAS CHANGED
I SEE IT IN THE WATER
I FEEL IT IN THE EARTH
I SMELL IT IN THE AIR
MUCH THAT ONCE WAS
IS LOST, FOR NONE NOW
LIVE WHO REMEMBER IT

J.R.R. TOLKIEN

# 1. The times, they are a changin'.

I'm a fan of Bob Dylan and when he sang this in 1964, he was right. In fact, he was right then and even more right (righter?) today. The times have changed, are changing and will continue to keep changing at a breakneck pace for the foreseeable future. Actually, the times are changing so fast that many futurists (seriously, how does one go about getting hired for that job?) are having trouble predicting the future. Back in the old days, it was easy for futurists, and science fiction writers for that matter, to envision and even predict the future generations down the line. Now, they're actually struggling with what the future will look like, primarily because the future is now. Everything they think up feels like it actually happens the next day, which makes casting a longer line into the pond of the future increasingly difficult.

Specifically, Dylan said:

> *Come gather 'round people wherever you roam*
> *And admit that the waters around you have grown*
> *And accept it that soon you'll be drenched to the bone*
> *If your time to you is worth savin'*
> *Then you better start swimmin' or you'll sink like a stone,*
> *For the times they are a' changin'!*

Just how relevant is this for today? If you mention to someone how fast the world is changing, you'll struggle to find anyone who will dispute the claim. Of course, we know that change has always occurred throughout history. However, in the 21st Century, the waters of change are rising around us at a ferocious velocity, without exhibiting even the slightest sign of ebbing.

Just consider the following facts and statistics that show how different of a world we live in compared to the world in which we grew up:

- Right now, about 2 billion people are connected to the Internet. By 2020, more than 4 billion people will be. And so will over 50 billion common, household devices.
- There are five times the number of people learning to speak English in China than in the US.
- India has more honor kids than America has kids.
- In 1992, texting began, but today the daily texts exceed the population of the planet.
- There are roughly 540,000 words in the English language, which is about fives times as many as existed during Shakespeare's time.
- We consume more data in one day than a person was likely to come across in a lifetime in the 18th century.
- There are actually more people on earth who own a cellphone than own a toilet.
- 60 million photos are uploaded to Instagram every day.
- Over 400 hours of video are uploaded to YouTube every sixty seconds — one thousand days of video *every hour.*
- Over 4 billion videos are viewed every day on YouTube, with 70 percent of the traffic actually coming from *outside* of the United States.
- People share 1.3 million pieces of content on Facebook every minute of every day.
- 79 percent of people are using Facebook or Twitter exclusively on their mobile phones.
- Globally, there will more unique information (over 5 exabytes) generated this year than was created in the last 5,000 years.

- The amount of new technical information is doubling every two years, which means that for students starting a four year technical degree, half of what they learn as freshmen will be outdated by the time they are juniors.
- By 2020, a $1,000 computer will have the processing power of the human brain. At this rate, by 2040, a $1,000 computer will have the same computing power as the whole human race combined. #skynet
- NTT Japan has successfully tested a fiber optic cable that pushes 14 trillion bits per second (2,660 CDs or 210 million phone calls per second) down a single strand of fiber, and it's tripling every six months and is expected to do so for the next 15 years.

The Hebrew language has a word "selah," which is a command that means "pause, and think of that." If you were ever to take time to *selah*, it should be after reading that list, especially if you're in the entertainment business. The amount of change is staggering.

Practically, what do these things mean to content creators? They mean we live in a far more global society than ever before. Communication and travel has made it so that the biggest, most expensive Donald Trump wall can't stop the world from connecting in this way. People are not only used to having instantaneous communication with each other, but technology has developed in such a way that people don't just simply and passively consume media anymore.

Today, people nearly *create* as much media as they *consume*.

As more people create, more people consume. This causes more people to create, which causes more people to consume, which causes tech companies to increase capacity and bandwidth, which causes more people to create bigger and better things, which causes more people to consume more bigger and better things, and so on and so on, until we end up in the *Wall-E* future.

Driven mostly by technological progress and global integration, the speed of change is going up and up. Consider how long it took the following things to reach an audience of 500 million:

- Radio: 38 years
- Television: 13 years
- Internet: 4 years
- iPod: 3 years
- Facebook: 2 years
- Apple App Store: 14 days
- "Gangnam Style" Video: 3 days (a billion in only a little over three months)
- *The Force Awakens* Teaser Trailer: 24 hours

Imagine if I wrote a note and asked you to hand deliver it to half a billion people. It would certainly take an unworkable amount of time and, more than likely, be impossible to accomplish. But now, in this hyper-connected world, you can do it in a day.

Selah.

Admittedly, this change hasn't all been positive. Have you spoken to a 13-year-old recently? They're ~~scary~~ ~~weird~~ different because they're growing up in a world that is nearly unrecognizable on a social, geo-political, technological scale.

Consider that in 2015, globally, 50 billion total minutes were spent on Facebook *per day.* This means that the equivalent of 2.9 million years were wasted by Humanity on Facebook *in a single month.* In this light, the future set forth by the creators of *Wall-E* may actually be prescient and is a clue into how we end up getting stuck with the type of politicians and leaders we have in Washington, D.C. #wecandobetter #justsayin'

## Has this changed the entertainment industry?

Because the entire entertainment industry is built around people and their media habits, when people and their media habits change, the entertainment industry is forced to change as well.

Think about it. Back in the dark ages (think the 20th Century), it was exceedingly difficult for anyone to create professional-quality entertainment because access to the industry was difficult to attain. Primarily, the biggest barrier to entry was the extreme cost of the production equipment. Film equipment was extremely specialized, expensive and wasn't available for mass market purchase. In the music industry, recording equipment shared similar obstructive qualities and video games were even more impossible to create independently. This created a funnel which forced anyone who wanted to create entertainment to bow before a handful of corporations (studios, networks, record labels, game publishers, etc.) and present their ideas as tribute. In return for ~~pieces of their souls~~ ~~their first born children~~ a controlling ownership in their projects, the corporations would then grant them use of their equipment which allowed the creators the opportunity to actually create.

Though once the product was created, how were they supposed to get it to an audience? Well, they then had to go to another company (sometimes the same as the first) and in return for ~~the rest of their souls~~ ~~their second born children~~ more control, they would so graciously distribute the produced content to the masses. The result of this model was that there were very few creators and, in turn, very little content created.

Oh, how times have changed.

Today, we have the ability to shoot 4K resolution with our phones. Not only that, we can shoot, edit and distribute a film to digital platforms and, within just a few hours, be in a billion people's pockets. With our laptops, we can record, mix, master and distribute an entire album and almost instantaneously be in a billion people's pockets. There are websites that allow people to create and distribute their own video games for free. We can write a novel, self-publish and be on Amazon or the iBook Store within hours. There are apps that facilitate all of this and even apps that help us create apps.

The studios, the networks, the publishers and the labels have now fallen from "necessary" to "expendable," hence no longer making access a problem. However, in a day where anyone and everyone can make a movie, there are a ton of bad movies. In a day where anyone can cut an album, there are a ton of bad albums. Put quite simply, it has created an over-saturated media market. This is great for consumers (more stuff!), but troublesome for creators.

When I was a kid in the glorious 90's (where's my flannel shirt and *Nirvana* CD?), there were limited entertainment options. Remember, this was pre-Internet, pre-DirectTV, pre-smartphone, which means I was limited to a handful of new video games, a handful of new books, a handful of new movies and a handful of television shows created for the handful of channels to which we had access. Not only did this force me to actually go outside for something other than to catch Poke's and play a part in becoming a normal, functional human being, but it also forced me to simply accept whatever entertainment was available. I mean, I remember watching *The Golden Girls* more often than I care to admit simply because there wasn't any other content to consume.

*The Golden Girls!*

Here's one for you — one of my earliest memories is when television actually used to turn off at midnight.

No, that wasn't a typo.

Way back in the seemingly ancient 1980's, at midnight, all the television shows would turn off, the National Anthem would play and everything would go to color bars until the next morning. Why would a loving God ever allow such horror to exist on earth? Because — brace yourself — there wasn't enough content to fill a 24-hour schedule for 13 channels. And even if there was, people didn't watch television after midnight because that's the time when you were supposed to be asleep.

Oh, how times have changed.

Now, there are thousands of channels of television between satellite, network, cable, and premium. Hundreds of shows and movies on digital platforms such as Netflix, Amazon and Hulu. Thousands of books to be instantly downloaded on your Kindle or iPad. Thousands of video games to be played on your phone, tablet, PC or console. That's not even factoring in the mind-boggling amounts of videos, pictures, tweets, snaps and posts made through social media or the dozens of text messages we get everyday. At any and all times, anyone with a device has instant access to literally thousands, if not millions, of different forms of engaging, mainstream entertainment.

This has caused us to live in an age where we never have to be bored. Think about that. We never have to bored. Ever. What do we do when we're in an elevator for 30 seconds? Hey, that's just enough time for three swipes on my Twitter profile! What about the panic we experience when we go to the toilet and realize we forgot our phones? Honestly, if you are ever actually bored, you're probably in a dangerous situation and you should quickly get yourself to safety.

A showrunner who creates a television show in 2016 doesn't just compete with the other shows on the air like the ~~pansy~~ showrunners in the 90's did. Today, they compete with all the other shows on the air *and* every show ever made because they're all available 24 hours a day. Trust me, if you put a television show on the air, you better believe you're still competing with *The Fresh Prince of Bel Air* for the ninety minutes a day my wife can watch television. It's the same with filmmakers and authors and game publishers and music producers.

To put it into perspective, let's say you have the biggest and best burrito stand on your street. Then one day, over 10,000 small burrito stand competitors open shop next to you. What would happen? Would you spend more to market? Would you create flavors nobody else could emulate? How would you keep the business going?

All of this impacts the economic concept of Supply and Demand. Basically, within a free market (God bless America), the law of Supply and Demand states that when the demand of a product exceeds the available supply, the supplier of the product will increase the price of the product because it has become more valuable in the marketplace. Not only that, the suppliers have no incentive to either drop the price or increase the quality. If, conversely, the supply begins to exceed the demand, the suppliers will still try to produce more goods, but those consuming the goods will find the product less attractive and purchase less because the price is too high. Now the market creates incentive (and more realistically, necessity) for the supplier to actually *decrease* the price while also *increasing* the quality.

Up until now, the demand was always greater than supply, which caused the gods on the mountain (read: the studios/labels/networks/publishers) to simply slop down whatever sub-par product they wanted and we, the content-starved peasants, would grovel and humbly accept it. Now, my friends, we live in an era where the supply of entertainment is so high it's stunning, which has created the leverage in the marketplace to shift away from the big companies to, for the first time, the audience/consumer. Now, audiences say:

> *"Hello, Mr. Studio. Understand that I'm no longer going to just automatically watch your movie. If you want me to watch it, you'll have to make it really, really, really, really good, deliver it on the devices I'm most comfortable with, and engage me the way I want before, during and after the film. Now, you have to fight for my mind, fight for my eyes, fight for my ears, fight for my heart and fight for my mouth. Oh, by the way, if you don't, at best I'll just wait and rip your movie from a torrent and watch it for free. If I'm in a particularly good mood that day, I'll just go engage the 8,000 other forms of entertainment I have access to right at that very second and forget your film ever existed. At worst, I'll create a Twitter mob that will tank your movie even before it premieres. Why? Because I can."*
>
> #savage

As if it couldn't get any worse, the abundance of entertainment has also sophisticated the audiences by desensitizing them to simple, more basic forms of storytelling. Plainly put, the days of *Matlock*-style storytelling are over. In an era where audiences are used to extreme amounts of multi-tasking, interacting with multiple devices more fluidly than should be possible and consuming, dissecting and connecting hundreds of pieces of content every day, it simply takes more to excite and entertain them than ever before.

They want A plots, B plots, C plots, D plots, all heavily serialized, evoking events from previous episodes, while making references to an array of minor and major characters. Moreover, they demand the existence of ongoing mysteries, convoluted chronologies, all working together to create elaborate webs of references. They demand films to be more serialized and television to be more cinematic. They demand gaming elements in novels and greater storytelling in games. And, to think, it was hard enough to create a film/show/game/book *before* this hyper-sophistication. It makes creators want to scream in frustration at them like Maximus screams at the stunned audience in the film, *Gladiator*, "Are you not entertained!? Are you not entertained!?"

However, the opportunities are massive for those storytellers who can meet these demands. It's funny (not haha funny, interesting funny) because I hear people claim the acceleration of media has caused people's attention spans to shrink below that of a goldfish. I don't think that's necessarily true. I just think it's *harder* to engage and entertain. I say this because the same people they say can't focus on one thing for one second are the same people who can watch ten hours of *House of Cards* in a single weekend. The same people who can marathon seven *Star Wars* films leading up the release of the upcoming chapter of the saga. This means the capacity for focus and devotion are there, we just have to know and understand the strategies that will allow us to connect in meaningful, 21st Century ways.

## Yeah, but how has it affected *my* industry?

### Let's talk television.

Television, in my opinion, is the most exciting, maybe perfect storytelling medium in existence right now. Original content created for premium and digital platforms such as Netflix, Amazon, Hulu and HBO Go has ushered in a wildly exciting era of television narrative. Up until now, television has been the writers' medium and, because of its visual capabilities, film has been the directors' medium. However, now seasons of shows such as *Game of Thrones, Daredevil* or *House of Cards* are essentially created as 10-hour movies, marrying the deep, complex narratives of television with the visual spectacle and cinematic photography of features ("Battle of the Bastards" anyone?).

However, these shows have started to act like amazing drugs, not just through addiction, but also by building our "tolerance" for narrative sophistication and eye-popping visuals. Speaking for myself (even though I know I'm not alone), after binging through the grandeur of a veritable 57-hour *Boardwalk Empire* movie, I find it very difficult to ever go back to regular, network television. It seems too basic and simple. I admit, I've been spoiled and the fact that I've been spoiled means these digital and premium shows have raised the bar for any other showrunner to engage me as a consumer and fan.

We can quibble about the precise chronology, but programs that were exceptionally innovative in their storytelling in the 1990s (*Seinfeld, The X-Files, Buffy the Vampire Slayer*) appear more in line with narrative norms of the 2000s. And many of their innovations — season-long narrative arcs or single episodes that feature markedly unusual storytelling devices — seem almost simple and formulaic today.

In his book, *Complex TV*, Jason Mitten discusses the desensitization of television audiences:

> *"In 2011, one of the year's most popular new network programs,* Revenge, *opened its pilot with a party scene that climaxes with a murder. It then flashed back five months to chart how the narrative arrived at this climactic point, a major event that would only be reached in the season's 15th episode, with the rest of the pilot incorporating voice-over narration and multiple flashbacks to various time frames. What was most remarkable about this pilot was how unremarkable it was — critics and fans found this style of complex storytelling commonplace and undistinguished, generally classifying the series as a decent "prime time soap" or belittling it as a "guilty pleasure." … Narrative complexity has suffused television to the degree that* Revenge's *temporally fractured narrative technique can go relatively and, sadly, unnoticed…"*

This phenomenon is equal parts exciting for the audience and mind-numbingly frustrating for television executives, creators and writers.

However, the changes in audience sophistication, television technology and audience media habits have not only changed the way the narratives themselves are created, but also changed the most important aspect of the television industry — the money.

Here are a few changes that are symptomatic of the major shifts under-cutting the television industry today:

- **Change**: Television viewing is down 10 percent from last season. **Takeaway**: With an over-abundance of entertainment options, people are simply watching less television overall.

- **Change**: 20 percent of "TV" time is done on digital devices. **Takeaway**: More and more people are watching "tv" on their phones, iPads and computers. What's interesting about this is that "television" is actually the box in your living room. So, what do you call it when you watch "tv" on your phone? Episodic content? Digital episodics? Who knows?

- **Change**: Broadband subscribers topped cable subscribers for the first time. **Takeaway**: I'm actually surprised this change took as long as it did to manifest. I mean, if you only had enough money to pay your internet bill or your DirectTV bill, what would you pay? Internet, of course. Why? Because you can still watch "tv" online even if your DirectTV turns your service off.
- **Change**: Netflix topped 60 million subscribers globally. **Takeaway**: On-Demand, subscription-based, time-shifting services are dominant in the television landscape right now and Netflix looms over them all. People like to watch what they want, when they want and for less than $10 a month, it's a no-brainer.
- **Change**: This year, upfronts were down 10 percent for networks, 6 percent for cable. **Takeaway**: With more eyes moving away from traditional television and going to more diversified, fractured digital platforms, the value of the advertisements on traditional television decrease. Right now, one 30-second spot on Fox in primetime runs roughly $350,000. This isn't the production budget of the commercial, it's simply for a 30-second hole that airs *one time* and then is gone forever. Brands are increasingly making the decision that investing that much money into advertising on a platform people are increasingly abandoning for digital is simply ~~utter insanity~~ ~~bananas~~ too risky. Even the people who are still watching broadcast TV will more than likely just DVR through the commercial or check their phone while it plays. If that's the case, why not spend your money elsewhere?

The last change is the most significant because the less money brands pour into upfronts (which is where the networks make 75 percent of the ad revenue for the year), the less money the networks have to spend. The less money the networks have to spend, the less television shows they pick up, the less they pay creators, the less they devote to their show budgets and the less the shows can pay their writers and their gaffers. All of a sudden the omelets in craft services turn into bagels, then into donuts, then into Red Vines. And when you start cutting back on craft services, people begin freaking out.

It's interesting because narratively the product television is currently creating has never been better. Couple that with the fact there are over 400 scripted series being developed right now and more outlets for more scripted content than ever before and it seems like television is hitting on all cylinders. However, as the eyeballs of the audience begin to migrate to other platforms, which, in turn, impacts the advertising revenue it generates, the economic uncertainty surrounding the industry has, unfortunately, never been higher.

## Let's talk about film.

As the Oscars approach their 90th year, we have to begin wondering how long it will be before nominated films begin to include movies not made for the silver screen, but for second screens, mobile screens, or even virtual reality screens. Looking at the recent Golden Globe Award winners, this seems to be closer than we may think. The online series, *Transparent*, became the first digital series to ever win a best series award while Jeffrey Tambor won the award for best actor as well. With so many films being produced every year, I'm sure the film industry will follow suit.

As with the other industries, the film industry is trying to bake a cake with a bad recipe. When you have a spoonful of cheap labor, a pinch of inexpensive production technology and a teaspoon of efficient distribution mixed with an average of 40,000 independent movies flooding the market each year, the value of the individual product is decreased because of more competition between cheaply produced, comparable goods.

In the past, studios controlled distribution which provided immunity from outside competition. So even if you made a movie, the odds were good it would never get into the mainstream market. But the internet has forever changed this. Now, every year, we're hit with a tsunami of movies, which in turn, create nearly insurmountable competition for filmmakers.

Focusing for the moment on the independent film market, Steven Soderbergh (the Oscar-winning director of *Ocean's Eleven, Erin Brockovich, Traffic* and over 40 other films ranging from no budget to micro-budget to shoestring budget to low budget to mid budget to big budget) has spoken at length about his disillusionment with independent film making. The reason for his discontentment is centered upon the fact that getting investment capital is increasingly becoming more and more difficult. The reason the investment pool is drying up? The numbers are no longer making sense.

According to Soderbergh, there is so much competition in the film market (including studio and independent) that just to be a tiny blip on the radar of audiences, you need to spend at least $35 million in domestic P&A (prints and advertising — basically, your film's marketing) and at least $35 million in international P&A just to make audiences aware you even exist.

Let's say you have a $5 million production budget. Because you only recoup P&A at a rate of 50 cents on the dollar, your break even for the film ends up being a whopping $145 million ($5 million to pay off production budget plus $140 million to pay off the P&A at 50 cents on the dollar). That's what an average American can earn over the course of nearly three thousand years.

Imagine going up to an investor and saying, "So, I have this great $5 million script. You're going to love it. If you will invest $5 million to cover production, all we have to do is make $145 million and you get all your money back." Does that make business sense to anyone?

Bueller?

It definitely doesn't make sense to me and it's making less and less sense to potential investors around the world. The only alternative is to cut back or eliminate your P&A budget, but then you're almost certainly dooming your project for financial failure because no one will know your project even exists in the groundswell of an over-saturated entertainment market. That, honestly, is probably riskier than jumping off the P&A cliff.

This is why studios don't like to make anything but $150 million comic book movies. Think about it. They pour $100 million into production, $100 million in domestic P&A and $100 million in international P&A to create a $550 million breakeven. The amount of $100 million films that make $550 million are much more than the number of $5 million that make $145 million. They're simply playing the odds — very, very high stakes odds.

So, while the cost of producing films is decreasing, the cost of creating awareness with an audience is increasing which destroys equilibrium in the business plan for your independent film. To think that it wasn't too long ago the independent film industry had a burgeoning production and distribution model; however, today that model has completely disappeared. There are only mega-budgets (movies made for $150 million dollars and up) and micro-budgets (movies made for under a million, often far under a million). There's nothing in between. — well, almost nothing. Even the movies that make it through no man's land — the movies made between $5 million to $20 million — are largely anomalies (i.e. movies by a handful of auteur directors, like the Andersons — Wes and Paul Thomas — who cemented their careers when indies were being regularly funded).

Quite simply, until the business of filmmaking can begin to skew the risk analysis back toward the other direction and make investment sense to a high net worth individual, finding significant amounts of investment capital will remain a rare and difficult feat.

"But what about *Veronica Mars*," you shout defiantly. "That was funded through Kickstarter! This will save the indies!"

True, that was a great feat and while crowdfunding sites like Kickstarter and GoFundMe may be attractive alternatives for filmmakers since they don't require a financially sound breakeven analysis, I would temper your crowd-sourcing expectations.

Over 90 percent of the projects funded through crowdfunding sites are funded for less than $50,000 (99 percent at less than $100,000) and film projects aren't even in the top five of projects funded. It's true (and awesome) that *Veronica Mars,* an IP that was established in the marketplace with 64 television episodes over three seasons, had novel spinoffs and a web mini-series that collectively created a cult fan following, was able to raise $5 million. Good for them! However, mere-mortal independent films, without the massive pre-awareness of *Veronica Mars,* on average, raise about $16,000 through crowdfunding sites. So, while it may be possible to crowdfund for some sort of a budget, it's definitely a significant drop from where serious independent filmmakers are used to operating and creating.

"Heck, since the independent scene stinks," you smirk. "I'll just make studio movies for the rest of my life!"

Well, hold your horses, Tonto. The studio system may not be the wisest pool to dive into either. Increasingly, a small number of movies are making the lion's share of the box office money. Simultaneously, the industry is witnessing a meteoric rate of flops. Case in point, *Alice Through the Looking Glass*, the follow-up to Tim Burton's 2010 Lewis Carroll adaptation, made less in total than its predecessor made *in a single day*, which is a 73 percent decline between the two films. *Looking Glass* actually became the first sequel to earn $200 million less domestic than its studio predecessor.

*Looking Glass* isn't alone, though. Movies as diverse as *The Divergent Series: Allegiant*, *Huntsman: Winter's War*, *Gods of Egypt*, *Jane Got a Gun*, *Zoolander 2*, and *Whiskey Tango Foxtrot* have all tanked at the box office in 2016. Even though it opened in 2,333 theaters across the country, Zac Efron's EDM movie, *We Are Your Friends*, had the fourth-worst opening weekend ever for a movie of its size. It didn't have time to wallow in its failure because in the next month, two movies — Jon Chu's remake of *Jem and the Holograms* and Bill Murray-starring *Rock the Kasbah* — earned a respective $570 and $758 per theater it was showing. This means that less than six people attended each showtime in each theater.

Less. Than. Six.

Think about that. Major studio releases were playing to six people. In fact, in 2015, forty-one movies ended their runs as box office bombs, a 28 percent increase over the years prior. Ungodly amounts of money, state of the art technology, famous directors and superstars are being thrown at these movies and still, the studios simply hope and pray they have one or two films over-perform and make up for their increasing list of flops.

Even though flops and failures have always been a part of the Hollywood P&L sheet, George Lucas and Steven Spielberg (a couple of guys who know a thing or two about making studio films) say that because of the increase in production costs and the obscene amounts of money it takes to market films, the studios have moved into extremely precarious financial positions. Why? Because even though you may think all the studios have giant vats of Scrooge McDuck money, unfortunately they don't.

Which leads us to Hollywood's dirty little secret: the studios debt-finance their movies. Meaning they take out loans. Really big loans. From the banks. Just like you and me.

This means that bloated costs to make and market movies cause these loans to get bigger and bigger and bigger and bigger, which, according to Lucas and Spielberg, have created a Hollywood bubble. Like the Housing Bubble that burst in 2008, the studios are becoming over-extended with debt. Spielberg and Lucas predict that it'll simply take six flops in one year, without having a film over-perform, to disrupt the model. Once a studio loses that amount of money without having a safety net, the banks will cut off their financing and call in their loans. Without the money to pay back the debt, the studios will be forced to move into bankruptcy.

If the historic flops of *John Carter* and *The Lone Ranger* would have happened to any studio other than Disney, it would have closed up shop for good. We've already seen it happen with a mini-major like Relativity Media and without ticket price restructuring ($150 a ticket, which the exhibitors will never do), Spielberg and Lucas predict a dim, dark future for the studio system.

## Let's talk about music.

No industry has been more volatile over the past decade than the music industry. From Napster to the iTunes Store to Spotify, the way consumers consume and interact with music has changed dramatically. As with the other industries, there is more access to more music than ever before in history. People love music — they just don't want to pay for it. Instead, they want to rent it from Spotify, Pandora or Apple Music, all of which have pretty miserable artist shares. Analog dollars to digital dimes to streaming pennies, as they say. All of this results in musicians having a harder time than ever.

The record industry that once nurtured them has shrunk dramatically. CD sales are drying up rapidly and internet royalties are not making up the difference. Record labels now have smaller budgets so they need to run a tighter ship. They are often under-staffed in most areas and tend to struggle to keep up with the workload. As a result, they find it difficult to deal with the pressures placed upon them by the artists and their management teams who are constantly pushing for success. This, unfortunately, means the amount of support available from the record label to the artist is limited.

The amount of support they do offer typically does not suffice for the artists. Therefore, they need to ensure they have good, strong management and a solid team around them to make up the support the record labels lack. Certain things the record labels used to take care of now need to be done in-house by the artist's team. Things like building a social media presence and promoting yourself on YouTube need to be managed internally before seeking the help of the labels.

As with television and film, a great product — a hit song — is harder than ever to produce because of the sophistication of the audience. Back in the day, the Motown and Tin Pan Alley writers only had to write one killer hook to make a hit. Now, because listeners give a radio station, on average, seven seconds before changing the channel, a song needs a new "high" all the time. According to Jay Brown, a co-founder of Jay Z's Roc Nation label, "It's not enough to have one hook anymore. You've got to have a hook in the intro, a hook in the pre, a hook in the chorus, and a hook in the bridge, too."

To show you just how much as changed in the industry, consider that in 1997, Elton John sold 33 million copies of the hit record, "Candle in the Wind," his tribute to the recently deceased Princess Diana. His artist share of the those sales was $37.5 million. Not a bad year at the office. In 2015, OMI had over twice the amount of streams that Elton John had sales — 71.4 million streams. This should mean he should make twice the money, right? I applaud your optimism, but sadly it's wrong. His artist share of 71.4 million streams, even though he reached over twice the amount of people, was right around $129,000. That is the average salary of an IT manager and not what you would expect from the top-streamed song of the year. Also, more than likely, that $129K simply went toward paying off his record label advance, which means he probably never even saw it. Regardless, that's a 99.7 percent drop in profit, despite a 216 percent increase in reach.

And don't even get me started on the ~~despicable~~ ~~underhanded~~ "creative" accounting by the record labels when it comes to paying their artists. Because they're making less money themselves, they're dolling out lower advances, still making artists pay for the production of the album from those advances, signing them to 360 deals that allow them to take a piece of everything the artists ever do and force the artists on the road for nine months out of the year.

Waylon Jennings and Willie Nelson once warned mothers to not let their babies grow up to be cowboys; maybe now they should warn them not to go into the music business.

## Let's talk about video games.

I was fortunate enough to grow up in the first video game generation. I was four years old when the original NES was released and had a much different relationship with video games than children have today. For the first few years, we only owned a small handful of games — *Super Mario Bros, Mike Tyson's Punch Out,* and *Legend of Zelda* immediately come to mind. Later, my brother and I talked our parents into adding *Bases Loaded* and *Rad Racer* to the collection. Throw in *Castlevania* and *Double Dragon* that I received as a birthday presents and those were the seven games I played over and over and over and over and over. There weren't expansion packs, I couldn't save data and when I lost I had to start over (I still retain the emotional scarring this caused me as a child and, today, wonder how game publishers could possibly be so sadistic).

Even though kids are typically young and stupid and don't quite appreciate the value of the things they own, in the early 80's I absolutely understood the value of my NES. In 1983, the NES was $299, which if you adjust for inflation, is like spending $727 on a console today. I understood that coming from a lower middle class family meant that if I didn't take care of my console, there wouldn't be another. Not only that, but the games weren't cheap either, so I better enjoy them because there probably weren't going to be any others outside of Christmas — if I was ~~lucky~~ blessed.

Oh, how times have changed.

Fast forward to today and we see most gamers on Steam owning what they call "piles of shame." These are hundreds upon hundreds of games in their libraries that go untouched, uninstalled and unplayed (Pixar movie in the making perhaps?). There's even a SteamShame website that actually calculates how many games they've yet to play.

Even the games players actually engage with, they're not actually finishing. About halfway through, they lose interest and jump into yet another game where they'll do the same. The appetite for gaming is there, which has upped the ante to make a game that can actually engage gamers all the way through, but now there's been an over-saturation of the market which has driven the financial and emotional value of games down.

Which brings us back to the early 80's.

In the first half of the decade, the video game industry crashed. Revenues peaked around $3.2 billion in 1983 and then dropped to $100 million in 1985. This caused massive shockwaves through the industry and caused many companies to file bankruptcy, including Atari. While there were many reasons for the crash, the primary reason was obvious — an over saturation of the market.

Sound familiar?

Consider these facts:

- **In 1990**, the average retail cost of a console game was $50 (which, inflated for today's market, is about $94 in 2016 money). **In 2016**, the average retail cost of a console game is, interestingly enough, $50. This means that there's been a 53 percent decrease in cost, which is great for the consumer!

- **In 1990**, the average cost to produce a console game was approximately $800,000. **In 2016**, the average cost to produce a console game is — wait for it — $28 million. In fact, Lucasfilm actually spent upwards of $500 million creating the *Knights of the Old Republic* game (holy Jar Jar Binks!). So, while there's been a 53 percent *decrease* in retail cost, there's been a 3500% *increase* in production cost. If you're in the business of making video games, those numbers are going the wrong way.

- **In 1995**, 95 console games were released. **Contrast that with 2016**, where 300 console games were released. But that's not even the worst part — there are over 500 mobile games released *every single day* through the various app stores and download sites.

So, like with the other industries discussed, a massive supply is dwarfing demand, which is driving down value, retail cost and most importantly revenue. However, at the same time, fans are still demanding more features, high quality and faster turnaround times between versions, all of which are driving up production costs for developers and publishers.

Speaking from personal experience, I've had an iPhone ever since it came out and continue to own an Xbox to this day. In that time, I've never actually paid for a mobile game. I download and play free ones up until they try to make me pay for something (can you believe the nerve?) and then what do I do? I delete it and, with a few swipes and pokes, download another free one. Every couple years, I update my version of *Madden* and *NBA 2K* for my Xbox, which means that within a time period where tens of thousands of games have been created, I've only paid for maybe six. Oh, don't get me wrong, I've played tons, but have only actually spent maybe $300 in total.

Listen, I recognize I'm part of the problem for creators. But as a consumer, this isn't a problem at all. This is great!

Sure, it's great for consumers, but seeing how the conditions are mimicking the crash of the 80's, it's not sustainable for creators.

## Dude, you're really being a downer.

I'm honestly not trying to be a downer and I'm certainly not trying to get you to rethink you career choice. People still love entertainment! Stories still work! Entertainment is being consumed at a level never before experienced in human history and if you have stories you want to tell, there has never been as much access to the industry or as many platforms in which to tell them.

I'm simply trying to play the role of the 21st century Bob Dylan and let you know how, in fact, the times are changing. Remember what he said:

> *Come gather 'round people where ever you roam*
> *And* ***admit*** *that the waters around you have grown*
> *And* ***accept it*** *that soon you'll be drenched to the bone*
> *If your time to you is worth savin'*
> ***Then you better start swimmin' or you'll sink like a stone,***
> ***For the times they are a' changin'!***

Just like with addiction, you can't be helped until you admit there's a problem. We, as creators/writers/producers, need to open our eyes and accept the entertainment world for what it is — over-saturated, volatile, and most importantly, completely different than it was even a decade ago. If we don't, we'll sink like stones.

Why, then, do we think we create the same way we did twenty, ten or even five years ago? The Bible teaches that to have an advantage in war, we have to understand the times in which we live. That's the key. Understand the times and adapt to a new model that fits that time.

So, based on the times, we need a model that can:

- Lower the churn rates of audience;
- Engage audiences in a different, meaningful way;
- Hedge investments for investors and backers;
- Diversify and compound revenue; *and*
- Decrease audience friction, which is any reason they won't do something (price, complexity, interest level, cultural norms, etc.).

Wouldn't it be nice if there was a way to create entertainment that checked all of these boxes?

Never fear.

Super Story is here.

YESTERDAY'S HOME RUNS DON'T WIN TODAY'S GAMES

BABE RUTH

# 2. A new way forward.

I know, I know — the last chapter was obnoxiously long.

So, to bring balance to the Force, I'll make this one extremely short.

By now, you should recognize the need for a new way forward; a means to successfully navigate an ever-changing 21st marketplace. If you don't recognize it, I would suggest re-reading the aforementioned obnoxiously long chapter.

If you're with me and recognize the industry is negatively becoming stacked against creators in favor of consumers, let's start talking about this new way forward.

Let's talk about Super Story.

## What is this so-called Super Story?

Before you say anything, let me assure you a Super Story isn't a story about super heroes, *per se*. So, if you're not into all the Marvel stuff (although you should watch *Daredevil* on Netflix because it's awesome) and don't care for the DC Multiverse, you'll be just fine.

A Super Story is much bigger, more dynamic and more robust than any one genre. In fact, it's so dynamic and robust, we feel that all great messages deserve a Super Story.

Essentially, there's story and then there's Super Story. If you just want to tell a story, go find Robert McKee. If you want your story to survive in an age of distraction and become bigger than you've ever imagined, you're going to need a bigger story — you're going to need a Super Story.

In 1977, two movies with similar subject matter, similar budgets and similar target markets were released. *Close Encounters of the Third Kind* did well and was just a really good movie. *Star Wars*, however, became a $50 billion brand. What's the difference? While I'll deconstruct specific creative decisions later in the book, on a broad level, *Close Encounters of the Third Kind* is a story, but *Star Wars* is a Super Story.

*That* is what we do at my company, One 3 Creative.

We want to actually and authentically connect to people in today's world. Yes, the same people who are distracted by screens, overwhelmed by data, tempted by an ocean of entertainment at their finger tips and are connected to the entire world with amazing machinery that fits in their pockets. Unfortunately, an entertainment brand built around a single, simple story will find it difficult to do just that.

The changing world has given consumers enormous power and storytellers a choice: adapt a 21st century strategy or become a veritable dinosaur — and not in an awesome "I can eat people and step on things" dinosaur way, but a very bad "you fade away and disappear, never to be heard from again" dinosaur way.

I'm telling you, you need a Super Story in order to survive in this crazy environment. You need to think big from inception, start building a brand from day one, and create in a way that no matter where people turn or what kind of media they consume, your Super Story is there — ready to be told in a meaningful, 21st century way.

At the end of the day, a Super Story allows you to:

- Grow an engaged and active fandom;
- Extend the life of your project;
- Build a bigger, more sustainable brand;
- Generate additional revenue; *and*
- Tap additional markets and demographics.

Honestly, the bullet train is leaving the station and those not onboard will be left behind to watch their competitors seize the future.

Don't say I didn't warn you.

## What's the recipe for a Super Story?

I'll go into mind-numbing depth soon enough, but essentially a Super Story is made up of:

- Transmedia storytelling principles;
- Powerful emotional connection with the audience that communicates a meaningful truth; *and*
- Online and offline community building and outreach.

You put all three of those things together and you're on your way to creating something robust, meaningful, engaging, sustainable, timeless and tailor-made for the 21st Century marketplace.

So, let's deconstruct all of these elements and see how to best utilize them.

See, I told you this chapter would be short. :)

TELL ME THE FACTS
AND I'LL LEARN
TELL ME THE TRUTH
AND I'LL BELIEVE
BUT TELL ME A STORY
AND IT WILL LIVE
IN MY HEART FOREVER

NATIVE AMERICAN PROVERB

# 3. Transmedi-huh?

## What it's not.

The first (and largest part) of the Super Story conversation is the exploitation and utilization of transmedia storytelling principles when developing your narrative architecture. If we were building a car, the transmedia principles would consist of all the parts and hardware we need to build the machine — the gears, pistons, axels, chassis, pumps, belts, ball joints and carburetors.

You may or may not have heard of the term "transmedia." Chances are you haven't. And even if you have, you've probably heard it used incorrectly or have some unfortunate misconceptions of what it actually is. At its broadest level, *transmedia is the art of telling a story across a variety of mediums and platforms in a way that forms a cohesive whole and creates an entirely new experience for the audience.* However, when discussing transmedia principles, I don't like to start with what it is. I actually like to begin discussing transmedia by outlining what it's not.

### Transmedia is not multimedia.

If you only take one thing from this book, let this be it.

Multimedia is telling the same story over and over again in multiple mediums — the *Twilight* books become the *Twilight* movies that become the *Twilight* game that become the *Twilight* graphic novel. At every touchpoint in the franchise, you receive the same plot, just presented in a new and different way. This model has been the bedrock of the entertainment franchises since the 1980's when rights-holders sought out commercial exploitation across a range of mediums and by a variety of industries for merchandising purposes. However, in the 21st century, the traditional multimedia franchise has begun to generate ever-diminishing results. The reason being that in an age where consumers are surrounded by new, original content at all times, when given the choice between paying for a new story or a story they've already experienced (albeit in a different medium), they're opting for new every time.

Why eat leftovers when you can have a new, fresh meal?

Transmedia is what creates that fresh meal.

## Transmedia is not digital.

I hear people say all the time, "I understand transmedia because I create for the digital space!" Digital media can (and should) be included in your overall transmedia plan, but just because you create digital assets doesn't mean you're using transmedia at all. In fact, you can have a completely analog transmedia project and, conversely, a completely digital, non-transmedia project.

## Transmedia is not virtual reality.

For years, virtual reality has been predicted as the next big thing in entertainment and it appears the Chosen One has finally arrived. Every day, it seems, there are more virtual reality providers and more affordable platforms becoming widely available to consumers. Like it or not, VR is coming to market like a new rich kid at school — in a cool, brash, flamboyant way, but not knowing exactly how to fit in yet.

It has become the darling to dance with for most transmedia professionals, and like digital, virtual reality content can be included in your overall transmedia strategy. However, just because you create content for VR doesn't mean you're engaging in transmedia at all. You're simply engaging in VR.

## Transmedia is not cool marketing.

This seems to be an extremely common misconception people have about transmedia. Even so far to say it was invented by marketers as a way to, well, market things. Let me just say that while transmedia can (and should be) used as a tool by marketers (check out our Super Story book on branding!) and while all good transmedia should inherently market, transmedia is much, much bigger than a simple marketing label.

And it wasn't invited by marketers.

It was invented by Jesus, but I'll talk about that later.

## Transmedia is not merchandising.

"What about me? My movie has action figures and trucker hats. That means I do transmedia, right?" Not necessarily. If done properly, your overall transmedia plan can (and should) include merchandising. In fact, the rights-holders to Slinky approached my company about developing a Super Story blueprint so Slinky could be built into an empire much like Legos, with merchandising being a large component of their profitability projections. In fact, one of the producers, pining for ubiquity, said to me, "I even want Slinky shower curtains!"

I had to let him know that having a shower curtain with a Slinky logo or a Slinky character on it isn't transmedia; it's licensing. However, with the right approach he could, in fact, transmediate his merchandise — even a shower curtain. What's the difference?

A transmediated shower curtain is where we reserve part of the epic Slinky story just for the shower curtain; a part that's important, that you can only find on the shower curtain and that reveals something significant about the story, the world or one of the characters. It still has the logo and maybe a character, but now it's part of the narrative tapestry we're weaving for the franchise. Let's not stop there, though. When you download the Slinky app and then hold it up to the shower curtain, an augmented reality map appears (gasp — sorcery!), which is the key to mastering and unlocking your mobile game, which itself extends the story found in the feature film.

The other is just a shower curtain with a logo. See the difference?

When I explained this to the Slinky guy, he stared at me wide-eyed and simply said, "Oh, okay. Yeah, I'll take that instead."

So, while you can weave merchandising into your transmedia plan, just because you merchandize doesn't necessarily mean you are taking advantage of a transmedia opportunity.

## Transmedia is not big sci-fi movies.

I'm a nerd and love big sci-fi movies, but I'll be the first one to tell you that just because you're a big sci-fi movie doesn't mean you're optimized for transmedia expansion. Conversely, if you want to use transmedia, don't think your story needs to be an epic space opera. While there have been sci-fi properties that have used transmedia principles well, I personally think if you don't have a big sci-fi story, it's even *more* necessary to employ a transmedia strategy.

## Transmedia is not extending the *experience.*

Extending the "experience" can be a transmedia trap because it feels like it should be transmedia. Leave the whole "if it feels right" standard of right and wrong behind with your college experimentation, because transmedia should always extend the *story*, not just an *experience.*

Theme park attractions are a great example of this. *Cars Land* at Disney California Adventure takes you into Radiator Springs and extends the experience of the *Cars* franchise. You are now inside Radiator Springs, which is cool, but it isn't transmedia. Why? Because the *story* of *Cars* isn't extended into the park. Fans don't learn anything new about the movie, the characters or the storyworld which makes it simply a novelty experience. If, however, the fans could explore a part of Radiator Springs you can't see in the movies or cartoons, and actually learn new and valuable information, the *Cars* attraction would not only extend the experience of the franchise, but also become a *necessary* part of the overall narrative tapestry.

## So, what is it?

Again, at its broadest level, transmedia is the art of using a variety of mediums and platforms to create both a cohesive eco-system of entertainment as well as an entirely new experience for the audience. It's also definitely more than just a current entertainment buzzword. It actually dates back centuries, but with today's democratization of media and convergence of technology, it has been thrust into the forefront of today's mainstream storytelling conversation.

Remember when I said Jesus invented transmedia? What I was referring to was that the Bible itself was one of the earliest forms of transmedia, since before it was translated into English, the only way people could consume it in its entirety was through a multitude of channels and a variety of media over a period of time — hymns, sermons, stained glass windows, morality plays, etc. So, while the whole "Jesus inventing it" thing was tongue-in-cheek, transmedia does have its roots in the original Super Story.

Another historical example of transmedia is found when examining the works of old dead German guys. Specifically, the works of Richard Wagner. He was a German composer, theatre director and conductor best known for his late 19th century operas. His operas were noted for being wildly complex, with intricate harmonies and progressive orchestration. He was also known for utilizing the libretto of the opera in innovative ways. Say there was a part of his opera where, in the story, there were a thousand people standing on a volcano tossing babies into the lava in order to satisfy some pagan ritual. Well, even though that would be awesome for the story, that would be extremely difficult (if not impossible), extremely expensive and extremely dangerous to stage, which means that most directors would cut or skip it altogether.

Wagner, though, understood the power of transmedia.

When the opera would get to that particular part of the story, the lights were cut from the stage, but the orchestra continued to play. In the libretto, the story continued and people would read about the volcano/baby bit and once they were finished, the lights would come back on and the story would pick up right after the volcano. Therefore, the way Wagner arranged it, the story went from stage, to libretto, back to stage in a coordinated, valuable and meaningful way. In this model, the story wasn't *just* delivered through the opera. The entirety of the story was opera *plus* libretto.

Because he employed these types of strategies, Wagner referred to himself as "the architect of all media." He would draft a blueprint for specialists to both follow and execute, and his own planning was always done three and fourth dimensionally. He didn't call it transmedia, though. He actually called it "*gesamkunstwerk.*"

So, if you think transmedia is a funny word, it actually could be much, much worse.

## The official-*ish* definition.

Quite a few people may recoil at the heading of this section, because the "true" definition of what transmedia is seems to still be a point of contention in certain creative communities. I actually was invited to a summit of transmedia thought leaders a few years ago and we were tasked with trying to develop a definition of the space that encompassed all the different types of projects being created under the banner. Within just a couple of hours, the summit devolved into a gigantic nerd fight and ended up making my list of Top 25 most miserable days on Earth.

So, that being said, let's look at some of the most recognized contributions to the transmedia definitional conversation and distill it down to the common denominators.

In 2007, the PGA (Producers Guild of America not the Professional Golfers Association) ratified an actual Transmedia Producer credit. This was a significant moment for the transmedia space, because one of the major entertainment industries officially recognized, validated and legitimized the art of telling stories across multiple mediums for the mainstream. In its code of credits, the PGA roughly (though imperfectly) defines a Transmedia Narrative as one that:

- Has at least three storylines;
- Is in at least three mediums/platforms;
- Exists in one narrative universe; *and*
- Has no repurposing.

While people can quibble with some aspects of this definition, to stay industry compliant, you'll need to follow this list.

Others have defined transmedia as a collection of narrative components transmitted via numerous media and communication platforms which, when woven together by the audience, results in a richer and deeper story than any of its individual components.

Henry Jenkins, an American media scholar, USC professor and trusty transmedia expert, has expanded on the definition of transmedia by saying that it is:

> *"A process where integral elements of a fiction get dispersed systematically across multiple delivery channels for the purpose of creating a unified and coordinated entertainment experience. Ideally, each medium makes its own unique contribution to the unfolding of the story."*

His definition expands on some really vital elements, such as the fact that transmedia is, at its core, a strategy — a purposeful, systematic, process-driven strategy. In other words, it's not platforms, it's not technology, it's an entertainment game plan that is, in no way, accidental, haphazard, *ad hoc* or left to chance.

Moreover, when employing a transmedia strategy, you need to make sure you create an eco-system of entertainment that is unified and coordinated across the multiple mediums and platforms. When you don't, you create continuity errors that will frustrate your audience. For example, when I was a kid, I loved He-Man and the whole *Masters of the Universe* franchise. Seven-year-old Houston was a dedicated fan of the *He-Man* animated series and also a fan of the action figures. At the time, all the action figures came packaged with mini-comics that told stories of the particular characters. For a while, these mini-comics told new and different side adventures that weren't covered in the cartoons; however, with the introduction of a character named Hordak, the mini-comics began to diverge from the continuity of the animated series.

When I purchased the actual He-Man action figure, the mini-comic showed him as simply a powerful savage who lives in the jungles of Eternia until he ventures out to protect Castle Grayskull from the evil forces seeking its power. However, when I watched the cartoon, He-Man's character is completely different. In the cartoon, He-Man is the alter ego of Prince Adam, the son of Eternia's king and an astronaut from Earth, who transforms into He-Man by entering a magical cave.

Wait...what?

Mini-comic? Just a barbarian. Cartoon? Magical, transforming son of an astronaut king. Not only that, but in the mini-comics, Teela is the biological daughter of Man-At-Arms. In the animated series, though, she's not his biological daughter at all, but a clone created by Skeletor.

Seven-year-old Houston *hated* this. #thestrugglewasreal

Granted, they were different stories in different mediums (so not technically multimedia), but they weren't unified and coordinated, which created continuity breaks and frustration for the audience. It actually bugged me to the point that I had to choose between the cartoon and the comics because I didn't feel they were part of the same continuity.

Looking back on this as an adult, I can now diagnose the breakdown occurred as a flaw in the licensing model Mattel utilized. They licensed the rights to do the animated series to Filmation and the rights to produce the comics to DC Comics, neither of which were creatively working in association with one another. The only connective piece between the two companies was Mattel itself and they weren't coordinating the content because they were just a toy company, not content creators. Because of the lack of coordination and unification, there was a fracture of the continuity and, because the fans couldn't seamlessly travel between mediums/platforms, there was ultimately a fracturing of the fanbase itself.

You would think Mattel would have learned its lesson, but a few years ago my company was called in to look at *Monster High*, one of their most financially successful brands. While the brand as a whole had done well (at the time it was a $500 million a year brand, second only behind *Barbie*), it was, at the time, experiencing creative growing pains. From the beginning, Mattel had rightly conceived of the project as transmedia and launched it as a web series, teen books, comics and a cartoon. They initially managed it internally, but once it grew to a certain point, they fell back to a licensing model and granted the rights to exploit the story in the other mediums to outside organizations. We were specifically called upon because they were experiencing a fracturing in their fan base; the fans of the books didn't watch the cartoon and the fans of the cartoon didn't read the book. They couldn't pinpoint the reason, but it was obvious to us.

The concept behind *Monster High* is the kids of famous monsters go to high school; Dracula's son, the Wolfman's daughter, etc. In the cartoon, no one knew the kids were actually monsters and they, and their monster parents, kept it as a closely held secret. However, in the books, the kids were openly monsters and it wasn't a secret at all.

Thirty-year-old Houston was equally as frustrated at Mattel as seven-year-old Houston was.

Because there was no one coordinating the story content across mediums and platforms and between licensees and other rights holders, they were experiencing significant breaks in the continuity and, as a result, fan frustration. Of course the fans of the books weren't watching the cartoon! Even though the concept was the same, it was essentially a different story universe altogether. Fans like stories to fit snugly together and make sense in a larger narrative tapestry, but if you don't make an effort to unify and coordinate the content across platforms, you'll force your fans to choose favorites between fractured storylines and never truly maximize your IP's creative potential.

## The cornerstones of transmedia.

Taking all of these transmedia principles and doing inventory on the basic points of agreement, we can now take a step back and boil it down to the most universally recognized transmedia elements.

### Multiple mediums and platforms.

Creating in multiple mediums and deploying in multiple platforms is fundamental to a transmedia project.

To stress the importance of designing stories imbued with *multi-modality*, transmedia thought-leader, Henry Jenkins, helped coin the phrase: "If it doesn't spread, it's dead." Multi-modality is just a fancy-pants way of saying in this day and age, we need to design stories that can be effectively and meaningfully spread into multiple mediums in order to be successful.

Essentially, to compete in today's marketplace our projects need to be like dandelions, whose seeds scatter in all directions when the wind blows, in order to create value and expand consumer awareness by dispersing the content across many potential points of contact.

It's great to have six movies that all impact each other in valuable ways, but if they're all films, it's not transmedia. It's just a cool film series.

Michael Moorcock's *The Eternal Champion* book series that consists of 15 volumes is outstanding dark-fantasy literature, but because it consists of all bound novels, it's not transmedia. Likewise, it's amazing how *Arrow, The Flash, Supergirl* and *Legends of Tomorrow* all crossover into each other and fit together as a shared television universe, but it's not transmedia because it's all simply live-action television.

When I refer to multiple mediums and platforms, I'm referring to any way to tell and experience a story. This can include films, television, comics, video games, music, stage plays, novels, virtual reality, augmented reality, interpretive dance, card games, apps, escape rooms, social media, comic strips, poems, animation, short stories, tattoos, spoken word and so on and so on and so on. Later in the book, you'll find a gigantic list that shows just how many ways there are to tell a story and create new experiences for audiences, but, right now just know that there are soooooooo many options for storytellers to exploit.

Remember, to be industry-compliant, you need *at least* three. I have no idea why they ended up deciding on three, but three is the magic PGA number for whatever reason. However, three storylines in three mediums/platforms is only the *minimum.* In fact, when my creative team breaks a Super Story, we always start with seven.

## Story expansion, not adaptation.

Remember, transmedia is not multimedia because multimedia is rooted in adaptation. And, like Batman and Joker, Holmes and Moriarty and Darkwing Duck vs. NegaDuck (man, that was a serious feud), transmedia is the sworn arch-enemy of adaptation. Adaptation is repurposing the same story, while in a transmedia model, *you never want to tell the same story twice.*

Instead of the story of your book becoming the story of your film, that becomes the story of your young adult comic that becomes the story of your console game, transmedia would actually extend the story. In this model, the story of your book sets up the entirely new story of your film, which impacts and seeds interest into the new story of your comic, which has a new story that then informs you on how to beat the entirely new story in your console game.

When you are wondering if something is or isn't transmedia, ask yourself these two questions:

1. Does it shift mediums?
2. Does it extend the story?

If you can answer "yes" to both of those questions, it will almost always be considered transmedia.

As I mentioned previously, I'm a big fan of *Star Wars*. When I was a kid, my mom bought me the novelization of the original trilogy. I loved to read and loved *Star Wars* and there was nothing else to do (supply and demand and all that), so of course I read it. It was good, but I already knew the story because it was the same story from the movies.

Then one glorious day, my mom brought home a different book, *Star Wars: Tales of the Bounty Hunters*. In *The Empire Strikes Back*, there's a scene where Darth Vader is addressing a group of bounty hunters and commissioning them to go out and capture Han Solo. We know from the movie that Boba Fett is the bounty hunter who's successful, but we never see what happened to the rest of those bounty hunters — in fact, we never see them again.

Unless you read this book.

It was a collection of short stories from a variety of authors with each short story following a different bounty hunter as he went out to find Han Solo and the gang. It dealt with their adventures, subsequent failures and how they ended up crossing paths in various ways. This, my friends, was something altogether different than the novelization of the original trilogy.

This was new *Star Wars* stuff!

It was in a different medium and platform (printed short story anthology rather than film), so the first question is a clear "yes." Did it extend the story? Absolutely! This is the reason it was so mind-blowing to me. This was information I couldn't get anywhere else and continued the story of the movie without having to shoot one extra frame of film. Since the two questions are both answered in the affirmative, you know it is, indeed, solid transmedia design.

What about in 2005 when the rapper Mike Jones put these lyrics in his song, "Back Then"?

*They used to love to diss me,*
*Now they rush to hug and kiss me now*
*They telling all they friends when I leave*
*How they miss me now*
***281-330-8004***
*Hit Mike Jones up on the low*
*'Cause Mike Jones about to blow*

When you dialed the phone number, you actually got Mike Jones' voicemail. Transmedia? It is, in fact, shifting mediums (song to phone/voicemail) so the answer to the first question is a solid "yes." However, this doesn't extend the story. When you call the number, you didn't learn more about the song, about Mike or about what Mike was talking about. You received no new information, which means the answer to the second question is "no," even though it seems cool.

Cool, in my experience, is a dangerous transmedia trap. This is because cool doesn't necessarily equate to transmedia. There are thousands of cool projects and innovations in the marketplace worthy of our time and money, but don't employ transmedia principles in any way.

But *selah* on this nugget of eternal wisdom: *while cool doesn't equal transmedia, transmedia should always equal cool.*

## Additive comprehension.

Recall for a minute how Henry Jenkins posited that in a transmedia narrative, "each medium [ideally] makes its own *unique contribution* to the unfolding of the story." This unique contribution is something called *Additive Comprehension*, which literally means "increasing your understanding about something."

Sure, it's a clunky phrase, but it's wildly important to a Super Story and a transmedia narrative as a whole because Additive Comprehension *creates the incentive for the audience to travel* to your various stories. Not only that, but when you heavily incentivize audience migration from story to story, you also increase the potential of them purchasing your stories and subsequently building a loyal fan community. Getting people to buy your products and then transforming them from consumers to fans is, obviously, the cornerstone of any profitable, sustainable business. And I like profit. (Capitalism for the win!)

What then keeps consumers from purchasing a product?

The dreaded *friction* enemy.

Friction is a psychological resistance to a consumer doing what you want her to do (e.g., buy the book, buy the movie ticket, download the content), brought upon by a number of factors. These factors may include high prices, difficulty in locating the product, confusion, aggravation, boredom, lack of quality, or even social stigma.

To make matters worse, designing a rich transmedia franchise will inherently bring about even more potential for friction because you're not just asking a consumer to simply purchase the book or download a song. Rather, you're asking them to purchase the book, then watch the movie, then download the song, then search for the web series on their phones, then visit a website and so on. With each additional step, the friction actually increases.

While nearly impossible to *completely* eliminate friction, your goal is to minimize it as much as possible. Note that I said it's *your* goal as a content creator. Don't push this off to a marketing team or to some people who may be more business-minded. You, as the writer and creator, can do wonders in defeating the dreaded, evil, snarling, trolling friction beast.

How?

Incentivize, incentivize, incentivize and incentivize a zillion times over.

I'm not talking about coming up with gimmicky BOGO schemes. I'm talking about incentivizing creatively through story and essentially ~~bribing~~ rewarding them with new, valuable story information. You need to incentivize your audience so much that they *want* to travel from story to story and platform to platform. You need to get them drooling (not literally — that would be gross) for the next component and have a burning desire to search, explore and mine all of your stories for more and more and even more.

You accomplish this through making your stuff really, really good (which should be a given) *and* by building Additive Comprehension into every single component of your Super Story. And when I say every single one, I mean every single one.

Game designer Neil Young actually coined the term Additive Comprehension to refer to the ways each new text adds a new piece of information, which forces us to revise our understanding of the fiction as a whole. To put it simply, building in Additive Comprehension means that *every story in your project needs to include and communicate something new, valuable and unique about your project that can't be found in any other story.* The very fact that it can't be found in any other story is what actually makes it a *unique* contribution.

In a true transmedia rollout, there's no such thing as a urtext, a central place that holds all the information about your project. If someone wants to learn everything about your project, she'll have to experience all of your stories. Thus, the incentive for exploring from story to story.

In *The Matrix* franchise, you can't learn everything about the concept and the world simply by watching the movies. Rather, you have to collect key bits of information conveyed through three live action films, a series of animated shorts, two collections of comic book stories, and several video games. The movies may show the awesome Neo fight scenes, but if you want to see how exactly the machines took over, you have to go watch *The Animatrix* digital shorts, because that's the only place you can actually find that information.

If you can hook the audience, they'll want to travel to other stories (taking the time and paying the money to do so) because they'll want to learn more about the world, the characters, and the concept in which they've invested themselves.

The *Twilight* books, however, communicate the same information as the films, which communicate the same information as the graphic novels. So, as a casual fan, where's my incentive to continue to pay for the same information simply adapted to a different medium?

Again, every single story you write needs to communicate something new, fresh, unique, interesting, and original so as to incentivize fans to support it financially. Think of it as an "Oh, snap!" moment for your fans — they learn something so significant that it makes them open their eyes wide and physically exclaim. Think of it like a *Sixth Sense*-esk plot twist or a major, significant revelation.

For example, I'm not a huge comic book guy. I like them and I'll read them occasionally, but I'm not a "line up every Wednesday and have boxes stacked up all over my house to the point that my wife wants to divorce me" kind of comic fan. When Marvel began their new line of official *Star Wars* comics, one my comic nerd friends contacted me and asked me if I had read *Star Wars #7*. I politely explained to my friend that, despite being a *Star Wars* aficionado, I hadn't read it and then I laid out the aforementioned reasons. Too much friction for me. He then proceeded to tell me that *Star Wars #7* introduces readers to [**spoiler alert**] Han Solo's wife.

Wuuuuuuuuuuuuuut?

I've read every *Star Wars* novel, seen all the movies, played the video games, the roleplaying games, done it all and never, ever does anything even hint at Han Solo having a wife.

"Well, buddy, I hate it break it to you," my friend says, "but you meet her in *Star Wars #7.*"

If I could have found that information in a book or a movie, I would have just gone there. However, the only place I could find Han Solo's wife was in *Star Wars #7,* which meant that week, I not only read *Star Wars #7,* but also the six issues leading up to it.

And there she was: Han Solo's *black* wife. Yes, Han Solo married a black girl. Which is not only unexpected, but awesome.

Oh snap, indeed.

Lucasfilm created not just one, but seven new transactions from someone who wouldn't have purchased one single comic. They accomplished this not by having amazing art (which they had) or amazing writers (which they did — Jason Aaron is my favorite). They accomplished it by baiting me with valuable information that I could only find in one place.

Think of Additive Comprehension as if you're drawing a treasure map for your fans. The path may have them cross the sea, land on the rocky beach, cross the treacherous mountains, slog through the swamp and brave the scary volcano and then, and only then, will they find the "X." What's the deciding factor on whether they'll make the journey?

What's in it for them or, in other words, what are they going to find in the treasure chest?

If there's only $20 in the treasure chest, the journey isn't worth it and the friction will keep them home. But if there's a $100 million worth of gold in the treasure chest, all of a sudden that volcano doesn't seem as scary and the rocky beach suddenly has a great view and seems like a nice place to vacation in the Fall. Maybe you don't get everyone to make the journey, but you get quite a bit more than you did previously. Now, if you put a Mew, Mewtwo, Moltres, Zapdos, Articuno and Ditto in the chest, every *Pokemon Go* player in the free world would be there no matter what (but only if there's Wi-Fi).

As long as you incentivize migration and *always* reward it with valuable Additive Comprehension, your project will take on a breathtaking synergy with fans migrating from story to story with amazing ease. Be warned, though, if you bait them with the promise of Additive Comprehension and they open the proverbial chest only to find something not valuable, you'll damage your trust and reputation with the audience and it will be more difficult to get them to travel moving forward. Always, always, always come through for your fans.

One project my company is working on now is a standalone concept album that extends the world of *The Pretender* television show. When we began the project, we asked Steven Long Mitchell (the co-creator of the show, as well as a principle partner of One 3 Creative) to give us a list of questions to which the fanbase has always wanted answers. He gave us ten to twenty big reveals and a couple very significant, "Luke, I am your father" reveals for *The Pretender*-verse. In our ramp-up to the drop of the album, we're going to be marketing directly to the fanbase and letting them know there's something extremely valuable for them in the treasure chest. This should lessen the friction between traveling from a television show to a musical concept album. However, once we put the word out, we better come through with the value.

It's worthy to note that, technically, Additive Comprehension isn't a requirement for a PGA Transmedia Producer credit. Nevertheless, increasing purchase transactions and engagement by incentivizing and rewarding migration is simply good business. Since we all want our businesses to be financially solvent and want entertainment to continue to be more than a hobby, Additive Comprehension has become a cornerstone of transmedia philosophy and, in turn, a cornerstone of the entire Super Story process.

## Storyworlds.

Along with three different storylines being present in a transmedia project, the PGA requires all of those storylines to be united in "one narrative universe." The concept of a narrative universe is what I call a "Storyworld" and a Storyworld is very different than a story.

The difference between a Storyworld and a story is the difference between your house and that one time your brother-in-law caught your house on fire trying to deep fry a turkey for Thanksgiving. Storyworlds are places and stories are interesting, amazing things that happen in those places.

For example, we know the *story* of *The Matrix* is Neo accepting his destiny as the Chosen One and waging war against the Machines with Morpheus and the other cast of characters. However, the *Storyworld* is a future earth where machines have taken over and put humans in a weird VR environment so they can use them as energy sources. We know the story of *Harry Potter*, Harry's rise as a wizard and ultimate vanquishing of Voldemort. However, the Storyworld of *Harry Potter* is where that story takes place, which is The Wizarding World, an alternate dimension of our world where wizards exist.

The reason Storyworlds are so important is they are the elements that reveal and/or create the story potential for the rest of your IP. When you identify the Storyworld of *The Matrix*, you recognize that the IP is actually much bigger than just Neo and Morpheus and there are thousands of other characters and stories to exploit. By elevating *Harry Potter* beyond just Harry and identifying The Wizarding World, you now see Harry's story is just one really good story in a much bigger world. In *Star Wars: A New Hope,* when Obi-Wan and Luke Skywalker leave Tatooine, Obi-Wan tells Luke, "You've taken your first step into a larger world." He's literally telling Luke (and the audience) the Storyworld of *Star Wars* (a galaxy far, far away) is much bigger than Luke Skywalker.

Since I love metaphors and analogies, I want you to think of your stories as oranges. Your oranges are your products and you need to sell them to create profit. If you were to carry the oranges yourself, you'd probably be able to carry a few, but if you wanted to really increase your sales and your profit potential you'll need to carry more oranges. What you need is a box. With a box, you carry multiple oranges at the same time. Plus, the bigger the box, the more oranges you'll have to sell. The more oranges you have to sell, the more profit potential your business has. Your Storyworld is the box for your stories.

Granted, Storyworlds don't always have to be as big as a galaxy or an alternate dimension. In fact, the television show, *Deadwood,* has a wildly vibrant Storyworld and it is only four square miles in total. Whether your Storyworld is a huge box like *Star* Wars or a smaller box like *Deadwood,* a fantasy box like *Middle Earth* or a gritty, inner city box like Baltimore is for *The Wire,* it's still the box for all the story oranges in your IP and one of the most important, fundamental aspects of a transmedia project.

## You end up with a different project.

Not only is *The Matrix* a great example of a Storyworld, but it's a fantastic case study for the other transmedia cornerstones as well. When they created *The Matrix*, the Wachowski ~~brothers~~ sisters conceived of the entire IP as transmedia project from the beginning.

As I mentioned previously, most people think of *The Matrix* as simply three feature films; however, the entirety of *The Matrix* story was told over feature films, books, animated shorts, console games, comics, short stories and a massive multiplayer online game. In fact, the Wachowskis told Warner Bros. the only way they would let them produce the features was if they maintained the integrity of the transmedia principles built into the DNA of the franchise.

Personally, one of my favorite components of the franchise is *The Animatrix*, which is a compilation of nine animated short films that detail the backstory of *The Matrix* universe. In regards to great Additive Comprehension, two films on the compilation, "The Second Renaissance Part I" and "The Second Renaissance Part II," show how the original war between man and machines began and what led the machines to create the Matrix itself. That's not discussed in the films and you can't learn it in the comics or games; the only place you can find that information is by watching *The Animatrix.*

My favorite short film on the compilation is actually "The Final Flight of the Osiris." It's a beautifully animated film that deals with two characters not named Neo or Morpheus. Their ship is called the *Osiris* and as they try to evade a group of Sentinels, they end up on the surface of the earth. When they are on the surface, they not only see thousands of Sentinels digging and drilling into the ground, but where they are digging is directly over Zion — the last refuge of Humanity. They know they have to warn Zion, so they turn and run, but the Sentinels see them and pursue. The captain, Thaddeus, orders a transmission be recorded and the woman, Jue, decides to hack into the Matrix and drop the recording. Jue, now in the Matrix, makes it to a mailbox and hides the transmission inside. Soon after, the Sentinels destroy the Osiris, and inside the Matrix, Jue drops dead hoping the data eventually makes it to Zion.

It's a great little short film, but the coolest part is what happened after the short film was released.

When the *Enter the Matrix* video game was released for Playstation, one of the first missions you're given as a player is to use two new characters, Ghost and Nairobi, make your way to a mailbox and retrieve a transmission that was dropped there and return it to Zion. If you didn't see *The Animatrix,* this holds up as simply a fun mission in the game. If you did, however, see *The Animatrix,* it now has more meaning because you realize the transmission you're retrieving is the one dropped by Jue in the "The Final Flight of the Osiris."

But the fun doesn't stop there!

One of the early scenes in *The Matrix: Revolutions* feature film is the council of Zion all watching a screen playing, you guessed it, the last transmission of the Osiris. If you hadn't watched *The Animatrix* or played the *Enter the Matrix* video game, you're still able to make sense of this scene and it stands alone in the context of the film. However, if you had experienced one or both of the other stories, now you're watching this film in an entirely new way.

Not only that, but if you recall the epic freeway chase scene in *The Matrix: Reloaded,* you were probably dazzled by the frenetic and beautiful way that sequence was shot. However, when the Playstation game was released almost a year after the film was out of theaters, the players realized if they went back to the freeway chase scene and paused it in certain places, the billboards actually contained cheat codes that allowed the players to better play the game itself.

Do you see how this is different than the *Twilight* books that became the *Twilight* movies that became the *Twilight* everything else?

The Wachowski's truly created something outstanding and, a decade or so later, still stands the test of time. Given that we have hundreds of more tools and platforms at our disposal than the Wachowski's had at theirs, how much further can we go? The opportunities are there and the principles have been defined. The only remaining question is whether you are willing to put them to use to create something more valuable, more meaningful, more sustainable and more engaging for your fans?

I SUPPOSE IT IS TEMPTING IF THE ONLY TOOL YOU HAVE IS A HAMMER, TO TREAT EVERYTHING AS IF IT WERE A NAIL

ABRAHAM H. MASLOW

# 4. Styles of transmedia.

## Understanding the tools in the toolbox.

When transmedia first began creeping into the mainstream entertainment landscape, there was no particular creative blueprint for creators to follow. The entire space was steeped heavily in experimentation and, thus, a wide variety of stylistic interpretations emerged in a short amount of time. Some projects were interactive, some were participatory, some were rooted in gaming, some digital, some were derivations of traditional projects and some were a little mix of everything. To certain practitioners, the diversity was exciting. To others, it was an opportunity to bicker about who was wrong and who was right, who was a transmedia "purist" and who wasn't.

I have no interest in such debates.

Today, these debates still exist, but I, for one, have always been an advocate that all the different styles and interpretations have a place at the table because they all have different strengths and weaknesses. If you understand each style's strength and weakness, you'll know when to utilize all the variations for maximum creative impact. With this perspective, the different styles of transmedia become like different tools in a toolbox — all to be used in very specific circumstances that are tailored to their inherent strengths.

Think of it like this: if you want to drive a nail in a wall and you decide to use a flathead screwdriver, you're not going to have much success. However, just because the nail didn't move, doesn't mean there's anything wrong with the tool itself. You were just using it at the wrong time and were trying to fix a problem the tool was never meant to fix.

## Coast to coast.

Essentially, the two main styles of transmedia can be broken down to West Coast Transmedia and East Coast Transmedia. Even though this sounds like some vicious transmedia rapper battle, the origin of these terms are actually quite innocent (though it would be cool to be the Suge Knight of transmedia). Broadly speaking, there are more films shot on the west coast and more television shot on the east coast. During the first couple of years transmedia was being heavily experimented with, people started applying transmedia differently when using it in conjunction with a film than people did when using it in conjunction with a television show. Thus, it became known as West Coast Transmedia and East Coast Transmedia. Despite the fact that in today's market, West Coast Transmedia strategies can easily be employed on television shows and East Coast Transmedia strategies can easily be used on a film, the monikers continue to stick.

So, what is the main distinction between the two? From a very high, Google Earth level, West Coast Transmedia is used to *expand and stretch* an IP into multiple stories, whereas East Coast Transmedia is used to *drill down and deepen* the experience of one individual story.

## West coast bound.

West Coast Transmedia is when highly connected, standalone stories created and deployed in a variety of mediums and platforms work together to drive revenue. West Coast Transmedia is the cooler, more capable, "why can't you be more like him?" first cousin of a traditional franchise. The most important characteristics of West Coast Transmedia, though, is the stories are *independent* and can *standalone,* which create the potential to generate revenue. Additionally, West Coast Transmedia components are typically released in more expensive, resource-intensive, traditional mediums and platforms.

Think of West Coast Transmedia like a photo mosaic; independent, standalone photos that, when placed together, create a much larger picture. At any point, you can pull out how ever many photos you want and experience them completely autonomously from one another. If you miss a few, it doesn't affect the experience of the others; however, because they create a larger picture, you're incentivized to look at them all. In the same way, with West Coast Transmedia, you should be able to individually examine any component and it be a complete, comprehensible piece;

however, when you put it with the other West Coast components, a much larger whole and story unfolds.

To give a better understanding of how this style works, let's take a look at some current projects that are using West Coast Transmedia in some very effective ways.

- **Marvel**: Since the launch of their cinematic universe (MCU), Marvel has been operating on all cylinders when it comes to West Coast Transmedia. They have released feature films from *Iron Man, Captain America, Thor, Hulk, Guardians of the Galaxy* and *Ant Man* to its crossover *Avenger* films and now the *Civil War* crossovers. They launched tie-in broadcast television with *Agents of Shield* to *Agent Carter* and digital television with *Daredevil, Jessica Jones, Luke Cage, Iron Fist* and *Punisher.* The five digital shows all share the focused storyworld of Hells Kitchen (while the rest deal with mainly New York City) and will then crossover into *The Defenders* mini-series. Additionally, they have one-shot and short run comic tie-ins that go along with the MCU continuity, as well as cartoons that are also considered canon.

  This is considered West Coast Transmedia because you can watch the *Iron Man* films without watching *Agents of Shield* and *Iron Man* can stand alone as an independent experience. You can watch *Daredevil* without seeing the *Avengers* films. You can read the comics without seeing anything else and the comics can stand alone. However, when you put them all together, it's a much more valuable picture of the storyworld and a more rewarding experience for the fans. Moreover, the stories expand into a variety of mediums and they're all strong and independent enough to drive revenue into the IP.

- ***Star Wars***: Just like with Marvel, Disney is releasing textbook examples of West Coast Transmedia with the new and improved *Star Wars* rollout. From the Skywalker saga films, to the standalone anthology films, to the *Star Wars Rebels* cartoon to the comic books to adult and young adult novels to video games and even to the *Lego Star Wars* cartoons, *Star Wars* already has an impressively rich narrative tapestry just a few short years into the Disney-era of the brand. This is thanks to the fabled Story Group, a team of storytellers who have been entrusted with coordinating all the content under a unified vision for the IP. However, before Disney purchased Lucasfilm for $4 Billion, the *Star Wars* IP was already being expanded using West Coast Transmedia via the Expanded Universe. For years, Lucasfilm released coordinated novels, video games, roleplaying games, comics, short stories and even ill-fated holiday specials. Many of these components actually had some of the best *Star Wars* storytelling to date (I'm looking at you Zahn novel trilogy and *Knights of the Old Republic* video game). Much to the fans chagrin, however, Disney decided to give the Expanded Universe content with the tag of "Legends," which means they officially moved it out of the *Star Wars* canon, but have reserved the right to move parts back in when needed. However, the fans (myself included) have found it fun and exciting to see which parts of the old EU are getting "called up to the big leagues" and being folded into the new canon, such as Grand Admiral Thrawn getting "called up" to *Star Wars: Rebels* and having a standalone novel devoted to him.

This is considered West Coast Transmedia because you can see the films without reading the novels or read the novels without playing the video games. Each piece can be parsed out or experienced in the context of everything else. However, because of the Additive Comprehension you find in each element, such as how did the Rebels steal the plans to the Death Star (watch *Rogue One*) or how did Han and Chewie capture the Rathtars in *The Force Awakens* (check out the *Legos* cartoon), you're incentivized to explore them all. When you do, you'll find a much bigger, more meaningful picture appearing.

For example, the novel *Star Wars Battlefront: Twilight Company*, focuses on a team of rebel "Marines" who fight in the trenches and on the front lines of the various intergalactic conflicts. This is the same group of soldiers you play in the Battle of Jakku map in the *Star Wars Battlefront* video game. At the end of that battle, you (as the soldiers) destroy a Star Destroyer, which crashes into the sand. That Star Destroyer is the ship that appears in

*The Force Awakens* as the ship that Rey plucks for parts and actually flies through during a chase sequence later in the film. Like *The Matrix* example we discussed earlier, all of these can be experienced alone, but when you put all the experiences together, it's a much better experience for the fans.

- ***Harry Potter:*** The *Harry Potter* series didn't actually start as transmedia. In fact, because it was adapted from books into films and I've already established that transmedia is the sworn arch enemy of adaptation, is this disqualifying? No. While the franchise began as multimedia, once the IP moved into films, the transmedia aspects of the project began to appear.

  As an aside, a project that starts as multimedia and then, at some point, begins to be transmedia, is called *Chewy Transmedia.* Likewise, a project that begins as transmedia from inception is called *Hard Transmedia* and a project that never intends to be transmedia, but whose fans and licensors create un-canonized extensions is called *Soft Transmedia.* I'm not sure why those are the names, but they are.

  *Harry Potter* is a great example of Chewy Transmedia because once it was adapted into films, it was extended into the *Pottermore* digital experience (ten thousand extra pages of *Harry Potter* material about things and characters besides Harry), the *Harry Potter and the Cursed Child* two-part stage plays and now the *Fantastic Beasts and Where to Find Them* spin-off films.

  This is an example of West Coast Transmedia because you can read the books and not see the stage plays and the books standalone. You can watch the plays and read the books, but never experience *Pottermore* or watch the spin-off movies and still enjoy them. Each one is an independently enjoyable experience where you don't *need* the other components, but you are incentivized to experience them because when you do you have a more meaningful experience.

- ***The Chronicles of Riddick***: After the debut of the critically-acclaimed film, *Pitch Black,* the *Chronicles of Riddick* IP latched ahold of a rabid fanbase and has grown into a substantial West Coast Transmedia project. In fact, within the IP, they have released three feature films, an animated feature, console video games, a novel series, motion comics, a mobile game and an upcoming television series dealing with an underground system of bounty hunters. All of these can standalone and generate revenue and while it's not a necessity to experience them all, you're incentivized to so because of a broader experience.

- ***Assassin's Creed***: Over the past three years, this franchise has been growing and expanding at a rapid pace. Set in a Storyworld that is the stage for a centuries-old struggle between the Assassins and the Templars, this IP launched as a console game. Since its launch, it has grown into a nine-part game series with no signs of slowing down. Beyond their console games, however, they have an entire novel series, comic and graphic novel series, three digital features, a mobile game, a feature film and another feature already in pre-production.

  This is West Coast Transmedia because every touchpoint tells an independent, standalone story that could be experienced by itself and still be enjoyable. However, because they never tell the same story twice, you're heavily incentivized to explore and experience all the stories to form a bigger picture of the storyworld. And, because all the components are standalone, independently enjoyable experiences, they can all drive revenue into the IP.

- ***World of Warcraft***: While not as broad as *Assassin's* Creed, *World of Warcraft* is a recent example of West Coast Transmedia. Launching as a an extremely popular Massive Multiplayer Online Game, the project has extended into mobile games, a feature film and a line of beautifully-drawn prequel comics entitled, *The Bonds of Brotherhood.*

  Again, standalone stories, generating revenue, yada yada yada… (did I just "yada" transmedia?)

- ***The Walking Dead***: This is another example of chewy West Coast Transmedia since the project was adapted into television from a comic series. However, once it became a hit show, the transmedia went wild. Not only did they launch a spinoff television show that explores an entirely new part of the storyworld (which isn't itself transmedia, but is really cool), they also launched a tremendous line of TellTale mobile games that explore the backstory of characters as well as other mobile games that introduce entirely new characters. Additionally, they have a series of standalone novels and even tabletop board games that continue to expand the story and the storyworld.

- ***24***: Moving out of the sci-fi/fantasy/post-apocalyptic genres, the action franchise, *24*, has actually had a nice West Coast Transmedia spread. It began as an hour-long drama series that simulated "real time," with an entire season taking place over the course of one day. From that, they released a mobile mini-series following a different set of counter terrorism agents entitled *24: Mobile,* a broadcast mini-series, *The Rookie: CTU* web series that explores an entirely new set of agents and is being relaunched as a broadcast series that follows an entirely new cast.

  Because the creative decision was made to have the different touchpoints follow new and different CTU agents, it makes it easier for them to stand alone and be independently enjoyable as West Coast Transmedia.

- ***Fight Club:*** While not as expansive as some of the other West Coast Transmedia examples, *Fight Club* has actually been extended in a valuable way using the same principles. In addition the feature film (which was adapted from a book, so this is Chewy Transmedia), a series of comic books were launched that follow the character Tyler Durden, made famous by Brad Pitt. In the comics, you find information about Tyler Durden that *completely* changes the way you see the movie, which makes it a perfect example of Additive Comprehension (I won't spoil it for you — go read it). Additionally, David Fincher has announced a rock opera, which will be done in association with Trent Reznor from Nine Inch Nails and continue to extend the *Fight Club* story in a valuable way.

- ***Veronica Mars:*** Teen dramas can use West Coast Transmedia principles as much as the sci-fi/fantasy epics. *Veronica Mars* is a teen noir mystery drama that was launched as a television series in 2004. After it was cancelled, the creators maintained their fanbase (the Cloud Watchers) and were able to, as previously discussed, launch a standalone feature film that was financed through Kickstarter. From there, the project extended into mystery novels and even into a digital spinoff series for the CW's digital content website, *CW Seed.* All standalone, all generating revenue.
- **Kevin Smith's Viewaskewniverse***:* Getting about as far away from sci-fi fantasy with epic scopes and generational Storyworlds as one can get, even Kevin Smith's indy opus to New Jersey has employed solid West Coast Transmedia principles. First was the Jersey Film Series — *Clerks, Mallrats, Chasing Amy, Dogma, Jay and Silent Bob Strike Back,* and *Clerks II.* They then produced a short series of standalone comic books, digital shorts, an actual *Clerks* cartoon and have announced a live action television series that extends the story of *Mallrats,* roughly titled *Mallbrats.* Smith has also said he would love to continue the story of *Clerks,* but not as another film, rather as a stage play, which would be amazing.

From extending something as big as a galaxy far, far away to a mere Quick Stop in New Jersey, West Coast Transmedia is a valuable tool to come up with multiple, standalone products and truly exploit the large story potential for your IP.

Just so we're clear, the major advantages of West Coast Transmedia consist of the following benefits:

- Creates multiple points of entry into an IP;
- Generates revenue from multiple streams; *and*
- Takes advantage of a cross-marketing synergy between the stories because they're all connected in some way.

However, while it has definite benefits (most of which is where you make your money), West Coast Transmedia also has some distinct disadvantages, such as:

- Because the components are typically rooted in traditional mediums and platforms, the individual experiences aren't very innovative;
- Due to higher cost of production for traditional mediums and platforms, West Coast Transmedia components are slower to market, which creates large gaps of time when the IP isn't engaging a fan base; *and*
- If there are quite a few components spread out in the marketplace, it's difficult to maintain continuity and make sure everyone finds everything. This ultimately increases the risk for audience fracture.

Looking at West Coast Transmedia as a tool in the toolbox, the times you want to reach in the toolbox to put it to use are when you want to:

- Generate revenue (your investors, underwriters and bosses will thank you);
- Tap and engage a variety of demographics; *and*
- Extend the life of the IP.

## East coast love.

In real life, we all know the West Coast is the best coast. Let's be honest, the weather is near perfect, the coffee is better, you can hike, surf and ski all in the same day and this is where Joe made his first trade. Sure, we have earthquakes, fires and a quasi-socialist state government, but I feel like those simply offset hurricanes, tornadoes and snow. Yep, West Coast is definitely the best coast.

However, from a transmedia perspective, even though it's where you make your money in your transmedia plan, West Coast Transmedia isn't necessarily preferable to East Coast Transmedia. The devil may lie to you and tell you it is, but just know that it's simply a different tool with different strengths.

Whereas a West Coast Transmedia story can exist independently and doesn't rely on any other story for a complete, enjoyable experience, an East Coast Transmedia story *extends (or innovates) the experience* of another story (typically in low cost, easy to produce mediums and platforms), but are *dependent* on the other story for context, meaning and understanding. With West Coast Transmedia, the stories work together like a photo mosaic, but even though it paints a broader, more meaningful picture together you can still pull out an individual photo and enjoy it by itself. An East Coast Transmedia extension, though, is more like a puzzle piece to where it has no value unless attached to something else.

For example, the First Edition of *Make Your Story Really Stinkin' Big* had ten chapters. If I decided to do a bonus eleventh chapter, I would need it in a different medium to be considered transmedia. Therefore, I could simply shift it to a YouTube video of me explaining the concepts found in Chapter 11. Since it's in a different medium and extends the story in a valuable way, the book plus the YouTube video work together to form the entirety of the experience — good transmedia so far. But is it West Coast Transmedia or East Coast Transmedia?

If a reader never saw the YouTube video and only had read the book, the book and its ten chapters would still make sense and stand alone. This means the book itself is a West Coast component. However, without reading the first ten chapters of the book, the YouTube video explaining Chapter 11 won't make sense at all. Because the video is *dependent* on the book for context and meaning, the video itself is considered the East Coast Extension of the West Coast book.

However, as good East Coast Transmedia should do, the video extends the experience of the book in a valuable way. In other words, even though you're finished with the book, you're not finished with the experience because there's a video to watch that keeps it going. The video doesn't launch an entirely new product like West Coast Transmedia, it just *extends* the experience of an existing one (in this case the book).

Keep this in mind, though: while a West Coast story is a whole, complete story, an East Coast story is just a slice of that larger story. Consequently, because East Coast stories are just story slices, they are very difficult to understand by themselves and, thus, monetize. While it's not impossible (I'll discuss how to monetize an East Coast Extension later in the book), it's traditionally difficult since people typically don't like to pay for slices of experiences that don't make sense unless you pay for something else.

You may be wondering why you should waste your time developing East Coast Transmedia stories if they don't makes sense on their own and you typically don't make money off of them. The answer is that what you sacrifice in standalone context and overall revenue generation, you gain in *fan engagement.*

West Coast Transmedia is typically ported in larger, more traditional mediums and platforms that, while they have good revenue potential, they are also more resource-intensive and take a much longer time to get to market. For example, if you wanted to make a feature film and started pre-production tomorrow, it wouldn't see the light of day for two years. Which means that while the film may be great when it premiers, there is going to be a large period of time where you're not actually engaging with your fanbase.

This is where East Coast Transmedia thrives.

Because they are typically low cost and ported in mediums and platforms that are easier to produce, East Coast Transmedia can not only extend the experience of a West Coast story, but allow you to engage with your fan base in a valuable way while the larger components are being developed.

For example, the cult *CW* show, *Gossip Girl*, utilized a simple, yet effective East Coast Extension. In addition to the weekly, hour-long drama that uses the mysterious, ongoing narration of someone only known as Gossip Girl, the show also launched a fictional blog, penned in the voice of the show's anonymous narrator. Between episodes, the blog would feature character background information fans didn't get from the show, additional narratives, interactive maps, still photos, and seeds for future storylines. If fans never saw the blog, the broadcast show can still be enjoyed, which means it can stand alone and is a West Coast component of the overall *Gossip Girl* IP.

If someone didn't watch the show, however, the blog won't make sense. Character background information is no longer special if you don't know the characters to begin with. Interactive maps are meaningless if you don't first know the Storyworld. Seeding future storylines is pointless if the harvest of those storylines on the show are never seen. Therefore, because the blog is *dependent* on the television show for context, meaning and understanding, the blog would be considered an East Coast Extension of the West Coast show.

Its value, though, comes in the fact the blog gave the fans more, meaningful *Gossip Girl* throughout week — without the showrunners having to shoot one extra minute of television. Through East Coast Transmedia, the showrunners were able to continually engage the fanbase and, consequently, turn a one-hour experience into a week-long experience. Granted, *The CW* wasn't making money off the blog, but it was still valuable in so far as it kept the audience consistently engaged with the brand and the story.

Another great example of East Coast Transmedia is the aforementioned *Star Wars: Tales of the Bounty Hunters.* You can watch *The Empire Strikes Back* and it be an enjoyable, standalone experience. This means that the movie is a West Coast component of the *Star Wars* IP. However, if you didn't see the movie and, consequently, didn't see the scene where Darth Vader commissions the bounty hunters to find Han Solo, the book of short stories loses all of its value, meaning and context. This means that it's dependent and, thus, an East Coast Extension of the film, *The Empire Strikes Back.*

In review, the big takeaways from the differences between West Coast Transmedia and East Coast Transmedia are: West Coast, independent — East Coast, dependent. Looking, though, at East Coast Transmedia as a tool in the toolbox, the times when you want to reach in the toolbox to put it to use is when you want to:

- Engage fans in a low cost, easy-to-produce way; *and*
- Extend or innovate a West Coast experience.

Don't be so quick to celebrate your understanding of the difference between West Coast and East Coast Transmedia, because I'm going to go one level deeper. There are actually two different types of East Coast Transmedia, with the major distinction coming in your decision of whether to *extend* or *innovate* the West Coast component.

Using the tool analogy again, think of East Coast Transmedia like a screwdriver. Screw drivers, in general, accomplish the same thing — driving screws. However, looking more closely at the tool, you realize there are flathead screwdrivers and Phillips-head screwdrivers. Even though, they're both screwdrivers, they are designed slightly differently, which means you need to understand the differences to know the best time to use them.

## Let's *extend* the experience.

The first type of East Coast Transmedia is called Dispersed East Coast Transmedia and is where you use a dependent story in a different medium and platform to *extend* the experience of a West Coast component. The key for Dispersed East Coast Transmedia, however, is that the story extension is experienced in a different medium or platform *before or after* the West Coast story — not *during.*

At this point, mild confusion may set in.

Trust me when I say that mild confusion is a perfectly normal byproduct. Horrible, anger-inducing confusion that leads to you returning this book for a full refund and unfollowing me on Twitter is not normal, though. If you're experiencing the latter, just go back and re-read this chapter before you make any rash decisions that may or may not impact my meager Twitter (@houston_howard) following.

Actually, the examples given so far in this chapter concerning East Coast Transmedia — YouTube video, *Gossip Girl, Star Wars: Tales of the Bounty Hunters,* etc. — have all been illustrations of *Dispersed* East Coast Transmedia. However, to give you a better understanding, here are a handful of other Dispersed East Coast Transmedia examples:

- ***Dawson's Creek***: The tween television drama *Dawson's Creek* about the fictional lives of a close-knit group of friends beginning in high school and continuing in college may be an older example (it dates back to — gasp — 2003!), but it's still an effective one. In addition to the broadcast show, they also had a website that was "Dawson's Desktop," the personal computer of Dawson Leery. During the week and between episodes, you could go to the website and read the emails Dawson would send and receive. It was a simple, yet effective way, to give you added depth into storylines that were taking place in the show and also a way to seed storylines for future episodes. For example, Dawson received his early acceptance into USC via email, well before it was revealed in the Season 4 finale.

  If you watched the show and didn't experience the website, the show would still hold up as an enjoyable experience. This means the show is a West Coast component of the *Dawson's Creek* IP. If you didn't watch the show, however, Dawson's Desktop website wouldn't mean anything and wouldn't make sense. Who's Dawson and why does he have a creek? Because it relies on the show for context and meaning, the website is an East Coast Extension of the West Coast television show.

Moreover, because you experienced the website between episodes and not simultaneous to the show itself (you weren't reading the emails on the website *while* you were watching the show), this would be considered Dispersed East Coast Transmedia. Again, it's experienced in a different medium or platform *before or after* the West Coast story and extends the experience of the West Coast story in a valuable way. Instead of just a weekly, one-hour experience, *Dawson's Creek* became a multi-hour, or even week-long, experience for the fans of the IP.

- ***Star Wars: Rebels***: While the cartoon *Star Wars: Rebels* is a West Coast component of the *Star Wars* IP, it actually has a handful of East Coast Extensions itself. First, there is *Star Wars Rebels: Recon Missions*, which is a mobile game that extends the story of the cartoon by allowing players to further explore locations set up in the cartoon. If you weren't watching the cartoon and didn't know the characters or the locations, the value and meaning behind the mobile game is severely diminished, which means the game operates as an East Coast Extension of the West Coast cartoon.

  Additionally, a book titled, *Star Wars Rebels: Rebel Journal* was published and is marketed as the actual journal of the main character in the cartoon. It looks as if it's written in his handwriting and gives his perspective and further insights into himself, other characters and even on issues not discussed in the cartoon. A similar book was also published and titled, *Sabine's Sketchbook.* This book was marketed as the sketchbook of another character in the cartoon, who is a graffiti artist. In the same vein as the journal, you see Sabine's artwork as well as some of her notes, thoughts and insights about various things in the show. Both the journal and sketchbook also tip the fans off on each character's respective romantic feelings for each other, which is something not explored yet in the cartoon. Without the West Coast cartoon, you wouldn't know who these characters were and, thus, wouldn't care about their books. This means the books are dependent on the West Coast story for context and meaning, making them East Coast Extensions of the West Coast cartoon.

Because the mobile game and the two books aren't experienced while you're watching the cartoon (but rather between episodes or between even seasons), they would all be considered Dispersed East Coast Transmedia. They all extend the experience of the *Star Wars: Rebels* cartoon and cause it to go from a half hour experience with gaps between engagement to a much longer, continuous experience across multiple mediums.

- ***Independence Day: Resurgence***: While the recent sci-fi film, *Independence Day: Resurgence,* didn't quite have the box office splash of the original (behold, the power of Will Smith), they did have a good example of Dispersed East Coast Transmedia. Because the original film was released in 1996 and the sequel was released in 2016, a 20 year gap of narrative time was created. To bridge that gap, an interactive website, *The War of 1996: United We Survive*, was launched and allowed fans to explore everything that happened around the world in the 20 years since the aliens invaded. For example, it's discovered the world has united in global cooperation, there is a base on the moon, and everyone has iPhones integrated with alien technology. Most importantly, the fans discover why Will Smith's character doesn't appear in the new film; he dies while testing an alien aircraft.

  Without the website, the films can stand alone and be enjoyed by the audience, which means the films are West Coast components. Without the films, the website is stripped of its context and meaning, which means the website is an East Coast Extension of the films. This is an example of Dispersed East Coast Transmedia because the website extends the experience of the films by using a different medium and platform and is to be experienced *after* the first film and *before* the second film; not *during*.

- ***Twilight: The Short Second Life of Bree Tanner***: Before the film adaptation of *Twilight: Eclipse* was released, it was leaked that the film was going to introduce a new character who didn't appear in the previous novels. Collectively, the Twihards groaned in frustration because there was no way, in their minds, that a Hollywood screenwriter could ever conceive of a character worthy of Stephanie Meyer's teen vampire opus. Meyer, however, used a Dispersed East Coast Extension of the films as a way to pacify their concerns. She wrote and released *The Short Second Life of Bree Tanner*, which was a digital novella that introduced you to the character, gave her backstory, showed how she became a vampire and ultimately explained how she ends being a part of the evil vampire army in the *Twilight: Eclipse* film.

  The films can stand alone, which means if you never read the digital novella, the films would still make sense and be enjoyable to an audience. The films, therefore, are West Coast components of the IP. While the digital novella extended the experience of the films, without *Twilight: New Moon* or *Twilight: Eclipse* bookending it, it has no context or meaning. This means the digital novella is an East Coast Extension of the West Coast films. Because the East Coast novella was designed to be read after *Twilight: New Moon* and before *Twilight: Eclipse* (not during), this would be considered another example of Dispersed East Coast Transmedia.

Are you still hanging in there? Trust me, this will all actually click into place very soon.

- ***Grand Theft Auto Five***: The most recent iteration of the open world action-adventure video game published by Rockstar Games, *Grand Theft Auto V* employed a great example of Dispersed East Coast Transmedia. In addition to their console game, they also released a mobile game through their *iFruit* App entitled, *Chop the Dog*. Chop is Franklin's canine sidekick in *Grand Theft Auto V*. Look after him well in the "Chop the Dog" game and you will reap the benefits when playing as the character Franklin in *Grand Theft Auto V*. Moreover, in the same app, you can play the fake Stock Market, which is a great way to make (and lose) money you can then spend in the console game experience. Not only can you make the money, but the share price of the stocks in the app can be influenced by the player in the console game. For example by showing loyalty to a particular brand or by engaging in corporate espionage in the console game, the share prices in the app will change.

The console game is the West Coast component because it can stand alone apart from the mobile game. Because the mobile game derives its context and meaning from the console game, the mobile game is the East Coast Extension. It's Dispersed East Coast Transmedia because the Stock Market and *Chop the Dog* are meant to be played outside of the console game experience (as opposed to during). It thereby extends the experience for the console game by allowing players to continue playing in the GTA sandbox even while they're away from their Xbox or PS4.

- **Taylor Swift's *Blank Space Experience***: Film, television and gaming aren't the only industries that can benefit from the engagement created by Dispersed East Coast Transmedia. In fact, Big Machine Records utilized the tactic when they released Taylor Swift's record, "Blank Space." The song and accompanying music video tell the story of the ill-fated relationship of a mega-rich, yet unstable, young woman and a young man she brings to her uber-mansion. The mansion is the sole location of the video, which shows the couple both happy and fighting in various parts of it — both inside and out. In conjunction with the song and video, they also released the *American Express Unstaged: Taylor Swift Experience,* which is a companion app that creates a 360° experience for the song.

The app allows the users to follow Swift and her love interest throughout many rooms of the mansion as they dance or fight or kiss, etc. The user gets to explore rooms of the mansion that aren't explored in the music video and go on a veritable "choose-your-own-adventure" experience throughout the mansion. Finally, the users can discover over sixty hidden narrative clues around the mansion that give more insight into Taylor Swift's character, her love interest, previous relationships, etc. In fact, the app actually won the 2015 Emmy for Original Interactive Program, which is cool.

Because the song and the music video can stand alone and don't rely on the app for meaning and context, the song and the video create the West Coast component of the IP. Without the song/video, however, the app wouldn't make sense, which means it's dependent on the song/video for context and meaning. This makes the app the East Coast Extension of the West Coast song. It's Dispersed East Coast Transmedia because you experience the app *after* you listen to the song as a way to extend the experience of the song. Through the app, Big Machine was able to extend a three and a half minute experience into a multi-hour experience, and without having to create any more music.

- ***Interstellar:*** In the film *Interstellar*, Cooper leaves his daughter to find a new home in space, but his mission wasn't the first to try and locate a hospitable planet. Before Cooper, NASA's first attempt was the Lazarus missions led by Dr. Mann. So what happened to Mann on the other side of the wormhole? Christopher Nolan teamed with award-winning comic-book artist Sean Gordon Murphy to tell Mann's story in the digital comic, *Absolute Zero*.

  The movie can stand alone without the comic, but without the movie setting up the reason why they need to find another planet, the comic doesn't make sense. This means the movie is a West Coast component and the comic is an East Coast Extension. It's a Dispersed East Coast Extension because you read it *after* you see the movie and, when you do, the experience of the movie is extended beyond just three hours.

- ***The Walking Dead - Torn Apart*:** In the pilot of *The Walking Dead* television show, Rick Grimes encounters a zombie, affectionately known to the fanbase as "Bicycle Girl," who has been cut in half and is slowly crawling across a field with just its decrepit arms. At the beginning of the episode, Rick is frightened by the zombie, but by the end of the pilot, he returns with his giant Rick Grimes gun to handle his zombie-killing business. By this time, Bicycle Girl has only made it another twenty yards or so across the field, so Rick walks up and pulls out his gun. However, before he fires, he says, "I'm sorry this happened to you."

  I've always loved that moment of the show, because it made it seem like this was a humanitarian mercy-killing rather than just trite zombie eradication. By doing this, it elevates the zombies from just monsters to actual ex-persons who have pasts, families, who had hopes and dreams — just like us. It drives home the point that the zombie-apocalypse is not just a tragedy for those who still have to live in the world, but for the dead as well.

  AMC recognized this as an opportunity and launched a six-part web series entitled, *The Walking Dead: Torn Apart*, that explores the backstory of Bicycle Girl, whose name is actually Hannah. The story follows her as the zombie-apocalypse begins and she tries every way possible to keep her two children safe. At the end of the web series, a helicopter hovering over the neighborhood announces to any survivors to make their way to the concession stand at the park, where they are evacuating refugees. Hannah and her children leave on foot in an attempt to get there, but Hannah is bitten along the way. After she is bitten, Hannah hands a pistol to her daughter and tells her and her brother to run to safety at the concession stand. After the kids run away, she gives herself up to the walkers as a diversion, is devoured and torn in half. The last shot is of her waking up as a walker and then starting to pull herself along the ground. That's where we meet her in the pilot.

With this new comprehension, though, I re-watched the pilot and saw it differently. I realized that Hannah is pulling herself in that direction because that's the direction her children ran — she was just going after her kids. She was not only physically torn apart by zombies, but she was also torn apart from her children. That's base human drama appearing in a zombie show and is what actually sold me on the entire franchise.

If you watched the pilot of *The Walking Dead* without seeing this web series, the pilot would still stand alone, making the show a West Coast component. However, because the web series solely centers on the backstory of a character introduced in the pilot, I would argue that everything special about the web series is dependent on the pilot for context and meaning. This would make it an East Coast Extension of the West Coast show. Because you watch it *after* you watch the pilot and it actually *extends* the experience of the show well after the episodes are finished, it is considered Dispersed East Coast Transmedia.

- ***Fear the Walking Dead - Flight 462***: Based on the success of the *Torn Apart* series with *The Walking Dead*, AMC upped the ante with *Flight 462*, a 16-part web series that extends the story of spinoff series, *Fear the Walking Dead*. While *Fear the Walking Dead* is set in Los Angeles when the zombie-apocalypse begins, *Flight 462* takes place in a commercial airplane after it takes off from LAX. Because the characters have been in the airport and then 30,000 feet in the air, they don't know the world has gotten crazier than a bag of raccoons. Over the course of the series, the plane and the lives of its passengers are put in jeopardy once they discover an infected traveler. The plane eventually crashes and the web series crosses over with Season 2 of *Fear the Walking Dead*, with one of the web-series characters joining the television show's cast.

Like with *Torn Apart* and *The Walking Dead*, if you watched the show and not the web-series, the show still makes sense and is enjoyable. This means the show is a West Coat component of *The Walking Dead* IP. The *Flight 462* web series, however, is completely built around the dramatic irony of the characters not knowing what's happening on the ground. If the fans had been watching *Fear the Walking Dead*, they now knew more than the characters, thus creating the tension of the series and the dramatic irony. Without watching the show, the fans are just as confused as the characters and it's definitely not as interesting. Therefore, I would categorize this as being dependent on the show for value, context and meaning, making it an East Coast Extension of the West Coast show. It's Dispersed East Coast Transmedia because you don't watch the web series while you're watching the show; you watch it *in between* the episodes and allow it to actually *extend* the experience of the television show itself.

- ***Better Call Saul* - Detective Abbasi's Case Notes**: In the sixth episode of the first season of *Better Call Saul*, Jimmy McGill's client, Mike, is being interrogated by two detectives from Philadelphia, Sanders and Abbasi. Every time Mike answers a question, Detective Abbasi scratches notes into his tiny notepad. Mike, just like the audience, wants to see what's in the notepad, so he has Jimmy create a diversion that allows him to swipe the notepad. Mike finally sees what's in the notepad, but the audience never does. AMC (who is extremely hip to transmedia principles) saw an opportunity and created an interactive website that allows the audience to actually read Detective Abbasi's case notes from the notepad. While doing so, the audience then discovers the real reason the detectives are questioning Mike.

If you never read what was in the notepad, the show still makes sense and is enjoyable. This means that it's standalone and, thus, a West Coast component. Without the show, however, a fan would have no idea why they are supposed to rifle through an interactive notebook. Who's Detective Abbasi? Who's Mike? This means the notebook is dependent on the show for context and meaning, making the interactive notebook an East Coast Extension of the West Coast show. Because you experience the interactive notebook *after* you watch the episode and because it *extends* the experience of the episode after the episode ends, this would be considered an example of Dispersed East Coast transmedia.

The keys for Dispersed East Coast Transmedia, again, are that a story in a different medium or platform:

- Is dependent on the West Coast story for context, meaning, understanding and value; *and*
- Extends the story of the West Coast story by being experienced *before or after* — not *during*.

## Let's *innovate* the experience.

Just as Dispersed East Coast Transmedia extends the experience of a West Coast story after it ends, Converged East Coast Transmedia *innovates* the West Coast experience and makes it feel like a West Coast experience you've never had before. It accomplishes this by shifting a piece (or pieces) of the story into different mediums and having the audience experience it *during* the West Coast experience.

As with any East Coast story, the Converged East Coast Extensions are dependent on the West Coast for context and meaning and typically don't drive extra revenue. At the end of the day, the only meaningful difference between Converged East Coast and Diverged East Coast is simply a difference in timing.

To give you a better understanding and illustrate how Converged East Coast Transmedia is used in practice, here are a handful of examples:

- **Rides.tv - *Dirty Work*:** *Dirty Work* is an Emmy Award-winning digital comedy series produced by

Fourth Wall Studios (an LA-based transmedia studio that received a $200 million investment from the richest man in Los Angeles). The show follows the comedic adventures of three Los Angelenos working in the crime scene clean up business. When fans visited the Rides.tv website, they would enter their email addresses and phone numbers on a splash page. Then, when they would watch the digital series, their devices were pulled into the experience. When characters would send each other text messages, the fans would receive the texts on their own phones. When the characters' boss would email them, the fans would receive the email in their own inboxes. When the characters would call other people, the fans' phones would ring and they would only be able to hear the conversation through their own phones.

The fans did have the option of watching the digital series on "lite" mode, which would eliminate the calls, emails and texts from the experience, which proves the digital series can stand alone and is the West Coast component. However, if the fans weren't watching the show and just received random text messages, phone calls and emails from characters they didn't know, their transmedia experience would have quickly transformed into spam. Because the story information communicated through the texts, calls and emails (note the different mediums) is dependent on the show for context and meaning, those extensions are considered East Coast Extensions of the West Coast digital series.

Moreover, since the East Coast Extensions occur *while* the fans watch the show, they are Converged East Coast Extensions. If the fans received the calls, texts or emails after an episode ended and it would help bridge the gap during the week until the next episode, the experience of the West Coast component would be extended and the extensions would be Dispersed East Coast. However, because all the extensions begin when the episode starts and stop when the episode ends, they are considered Converged East Coast Extensions. Again, it's simply a matter of timing.

The benefit of Converged East Coast Extensions is when you layer the extensions into the West Coast experience itself, the experience feels very fresh and new. While you may have watched a digital series before, a digital series where you receive phone calls, text messages and emails from the characters suddenly feels like a digital series you've never experienced before. Behold, the coolness and innovation that comes along with Converged East Coast Transmedia.

- ***Fear the Walking Dead:*** In addition to their aforementioned Dispersed East Coast web series, *Flight 462*, AMC also incorporated a Converged East Coast Extension into the show. If fans used the Shazam app (best known for its music identification capabilities but has since expanded its integrations) during the pilot, "bonus" content was unlocked on their phones. For example, there is a scene in the pilot where the main characters are stuck in traffic on an LA freeway (welcome to my world everyone) due to an incident that is taking place on an off-ramp. While they see the flashing lights of police cars and ambulances, as well as a group of people recording something on their cell phones, the characters are too far back to really see what is going on. When gunfire erupts, they speed off in a different direction.

  If the fans used the Shazam app during that scene, their phones would have pulled up the up-close video footage from the group of people who were recording the incident on their phones. On their television, the fans would have watched the characters stuck in traffic, but on their phones they would have been able to watch the actual incident, which was one of the first, true zombie encounters.

  The show stands alone without the mobile app, which means the show is the West Coast component. If you're not watching the show, the content on the mobile app doesn't make sense, which means the mobile app is an East Coast Extension. It's Converged East Coast Transmedia because the mobile app experience takes place *during* the experience of the West Coast television show. Instead of extending the episode after it ends, the Converged East Coast Extension makes it feel like you're watching an entirely new, innovative type of television show.

- **John Lennon: *The Bermuda Tapes:*** This is an interactive app that tells the story of John Lennon's life-changing journey sailing through a mid-Atlantic storm to Bermuda in June 1980, the profound creative discovery during his time on the island and the artistic collaboration from abroad with wife Yoko Ono at home in New York. The app integrates Lennon's demo tapes recorded in Bermuda, while converging them with innovative game play and also intimate documentary storytelling.

  With this project, the music can stand alone (you could play the songs on the radio or Apple Music and they would still work as good songs), which means the demo songs would be considered the West Coast component. The other aspects of the app, the interactive game, the photography, plays off the content of the songs, which is why I would categorize all the other aspects of the app as East Coast Extensions. They're Converged East Coast extensions because they take place *during* the experience of the West Coast songs (you listen to the songs while you're doing everything else).

- ***Grand Theft Auto Five***: While most video gamers are accustomed to playing a game and then, separately, referencing a game manual or wiki, Rockstar Games cleverly turned the GTAV game manual into a Converged East Coast experience. They released a massive (over-100-page) free digital app for smartphones, tablets as well as desktops called *Grand Theft Auto V: The Manual.* The official manual app has everything from essential and practical Game Controls, Features and Credits info, to a tour through the activities and local shops and brands in the game –

and best yet, a special digital version of the game map to zoom in and explore with an interactive legend to browse neighborhoods and points of interest all over the entire world of Los Santos and Blaine County. Without the game, the manual is worthless, which means the game is West Coast and the manual is East Coast. It's Converged East Coast, because the interactive map is meant to be used *while* you're playing the game so as to track progress, reveal proximity to important items, etc.

- ***Skrillex Quest***: As a way to innovate the experience of listening to his album, the artist Skrillex created the video game *Skrillex Quest.* A homage to games from the old NES days, the game sent a sword-wielding player into an NES cartridge to explore a kingdom glitched by dust on the game's contacts. It's essentially hack and slash combat against glitchy cubes combined with *Zelda*-style dungeon exploration for a good, nostalgia-fueled time. However, as they played, the fans could listen to the new *Skrillex* album. In fact, the story of the game is actually based on the lyrics of the song and when you beat a level, the players can then listen to the next song.

  Because you need the lyrics of the songs to help win the game, the game itself can't stand alone and would be an East Coast Extension of the West Coast music (the songs could stand alone on the radio, Spotify, etc.). It's Converged East Coast Transmedia because you play the game *as* you're listening to the music and, in turn, it feels like an innovative way to listen to an album.

In conclusion, the keys for Converged East Coast Transmedia, again, are that a story in a different medium or platform:

- Is dependent on the West Coast story for context, meaning, understanding and value; *and*
- *Innovates* the story of the West Coast story by being experienced *during* the West Coast experience — not *before or after.*

Again, think of Converged and Dispersed East Coast as two different types of screwdrivers. With Dispersed East Coast, what you lose in innovation, you gain in extending the experience for the audience. With Converged East Coast, what you lose in extending the experience, you gain in innovation. It all depends on the particular situation you find yourself in and what specific problem you're trying to solve.

As I mentioned, few years ago, everything was mushed together under one big "transmedia" label. But, as with any industry, as the space and practice matures, terminology and definitions emerge as a way for practitioners to better understand when, how and why to implement particular solutions. I'm sure carpenters are glad at some point someone said, "Instead of just saying 'tools', this will be a hammer, this will be a flathead screwdriver and this will be a table saw or ban saw."

In my opinion, so many transmedia failures can be attributed to practitioners trying to use transmedia principles, but using the wrong tool in the toolbox at the wrong time.

How do you know which transmedia tool to use?

- If you want to drive revenue and different demographics, use West Coast Transmedia.
- If you want to extend a West Coast experience for the audience, you should use Dispersed East Coast Transmedia.
- If you want to innovate a West Coast experience, you should use Converged East Coast Transmedia.

Or, if you're creating a Super Story, use them all.

# IF YOU DON'T HAVE A COMPETITIVE ADVANTAGE, DON'T COMPETE

JACK WELCH

# 5. Why Super Story?

## Basic value propositions.

After ripping apart the transmedia principles, which are the first (and most dense) part of a Super Story, you're probably asking yourself what you've gotten yourself into. You may be questioning your purchase decision and possibly even be considering setting the book aside because it makes your brain hurt.

Don't quit now. Your brain already hurts and you're already tired, so you may as well finish and get a reward from it.

Rewards! That's it!

Let's talk about rewards to keep you going!

What are the rewards you get from a Super Story? Let me take a step back and spend ~~the next hundred pages~~ this chapter outlining the specific business reasons you should adopt this model. I call these *value propositions*, some people call them unique selling propositions, but whatever you call them, know that I've had to use them in every pitch I've ever had whether it was with investors, film producers, networks, labels or brand managers.

You see, people don't like to change their ways. In fact they will come up with as many crazy objections as they can think of in order to prolong their stagnation because, hey, at least stagnation is safe and familiar. The value propositions in this chapter are the reasons we are evangelistic about the Super Story model. Not only that, but they are the strategies you use to overcome objections and actually convince people of this amazing, new way forward.

So, why build a Super Story?

## You get happier, well-fed fans.

True fans are the lifeblood of any entertainment brand and are the key component in establishing leverage and influence in the entertainment industry. The reason studios reboot everything or solely focus on creating comic book or young adult movies isn't because they have a passion for those stories or a burning desire to see them revived for this generation. The actual reason is much simpler than that. It's because those particular IP's have established fanbases, which make $100 million investments more secure and, in a risk-averse industry, security is a very good thing.

Fans, you see, are the key.

When I say "fans," I'm not talking about your gaggle of Instagram followers. I'm talking about people who buy your stuff and support your brand. When you have fans, you have power. Maybe not evil super villain power, but the next best thing — brand power. When Taylor Swift published her open letter to Tim Cook, the CEO of Apple, concerning her objection about Apple not paying artist royalties for the three month trial of Apple Music, Apple reversed its decision within just a couple of days. Did Taylor Swift change the business plan of the most profitable corporation in the history of planet earth because she had such an eloquent argument? Of course not. Apple changed course because Taylor Swift has a giant army of "Swifties" that ~~creepily~~ ~~obsessively~~ loyally support her brand. That, my friends, proves the power of a fanbase.

This may seem obvious, but far too many writers and producers don't fully understand it. If they did, they would do everything in their power to make their fans happy because a happy fanbase is a supportive fanbase and a supportive fanbase is a fanbase that buys their stuff. Granted, keeping your fanbase happy is easier said than done. In fact, later in the book, I'll go over a handful of specific fan community strategies you can implement in your project.

Better yet, you would be remiss if you didn't pick up Steve Mitchell's book on fandoms that he wrote with Jacci Olson (a fandom guru) titled, *The Awesome Power of Fandoms: A How-To Guide to Engage, Grow, and Unleash Global Franchise Fanbases.* It's the gold standard on how to practically grow and maintain a supportive community of not just fans, but actual motivated, mobilized brand evangelists.

Generally speaking, the way you make your fans happy is giving them more of what made them fans to begin with — *more story*. At first, this seems easy, until you realize just how much the entertainment appetite of audiences has increased over the past few years. According to a recent report, on any given day, millennials in the United States spend about nine hours using media for their enjoyment. Compare that to the 1980's, which was only about two hours a day, and you see just how much the entertainment appetite has increased. That's more time than they typically spend sleeping, working and spending time with their parents, teachers or significant others. And the nine hours is *in addition to* using media at school, for their homework or for work, so, in reality, the total daily hours of media consumption are actually more than nine.

The entertainment appetite of this generation of fans and how much they need to consume to stay happy is, honestly, mind-boggling.

They consume, they want more, they consume, they want more, they consume, they want more. This reminds me of Ryback, a WWE wrestler, who after his matches chants (along with the crowd), "Feed me more! Feed me more!" This is how modern audiences are — and I totally understand it. Recently, I binged through the entire series of *Game of Thrones* over the course of a month. That means in a month, I spent almost two full work-weeks doing nothing but watching *Game of Thrones* and what do you think my reaction was when I finally ran out of episodes?

I wanted more!

More *Game of Thrones* is what I was craving, even after a massive 71 hour meal. Like a stoner on a midnight fridge raid, I started hunting for more food. I found all the behind the scenes specials and commentaries and fed on them. Then, I found more food in the *After the Thrones* talk show and went back and watched all of them. I still wasn't satisfied so I continued to forage and found a series of animated videos that cover the insanely complex history and mythology of Westeros. Yes, more food! Because I'm a fan of *Game of Thrones* I simply wanted more and more *Game of Thrones* — and that's a compliment to the *GoT* brand!

Here's a practical suggestion: in the most positive way possible, take care of your fans like you would a dog. First, understand that I love dogs. My wife, Courtney, and I have two dogs and consider ourselves dog *parents* as opposed to dog *owners.* Yes, we're weird dog people who treat our dogs like furry children rather than mere canines. So, when I compare fans to dogs, it's actually a high compliment.

One of the first lessons I learned when I got my first dog as a child (RIP Buford) is that I had to feed my dog every day, no matter what. My parents told me if I stopped feeding my dog or went too long between meals, at best he would go somewhere else for food. If I went far too long without feeding him, he would die. At worst, though, he may turn primal and turn me into a Ramsay Bolton-style dish.

So, I fed my dog.

Interestingly enough, as I would feed him, I would watch him grow. As he grew from a puppy to a mature dog, predictably, I actually had to feed him *more* food because his appetite had grown as well. The big takeaway: it's important to always feed your dog, because if you do, it will love you and proudly stay by your side as it grows — but you're never going to be able to stop feeding it.

Fanbases are similar. The more you feed them, the more they grow. The more they grow, the bigger the appetite, and so on. This means you have to feed them more and more and more and more, which, in turn, also means you have to create more and more and more and more story content to use as food.

But, here's the catch: if you're a filmmaker, you can't shoot films all the time. It's too expensive, difficult and production cycles take too long. It's the same if you're a television producer or a video game publisher or a book author. This means if you can't constantly feed them with your area of speciality, you'll need to reach in the ice box and find some other sources of food.

A Super Story is the most nourishing, filling, healthy yet delicious meal you can ever feed a fan. A meal they enjoy at the time and yet remember forever. A meal that they'll tell their friends and family about. A meal that isn't just one simple course, but a combination of appetizers, multiple main courses, baskets of bread, desserts, take home boxes, mints and everything in between. It's grandma's Sunday dinner one day and the coolest, trendiest hipster restaurant the next.

When you feed them a Super Story, you'll start to see your fanbase become bigger and happier and ultimately more supportive of your overall entertainment brand.

Now, I have to go get something to eat…

## You'll cultivate a bigger, more diverse fanbase.

There used to be a major push in Hollywood to chase the "four quadrant picture," which is a movie or a show that will appeal to everyone (all four quadrants — males, females, young and old). Examples of these rare and precious projects are *Star Wars, The Wizard of Oz, Toy Story, Lord of the Rings, Harry Potter, Jaws,* and *Shrek.* Taylor Swift, Bon Jovi and Michael Jackson are great examples of four quadrant music artists. *Seinfeld, The Pretender, Breaking Bad, Game of Thrones, Survivor, Big Bang Theory* and *American Idol* are four-quadrant television shows. A four-quadrant hit is what every executive dreams about every time their head hits the pillow. These projects have the biggest fanbases because their fanbases aren't just made up of one type of fan — they're made up of everyone. It's the Holy Grail, the sweet spot, the blue ribbon and the homecoming queen all wrapped into just one story.

However, despite the fact Pixar seems to have a magic four-quadrant formula (we'll discuss that later), four-quadrant stories are historically very difficult to intentionally engineer. This is because old guys love war and history, young guys like sex, violence and fart jokes, young girls like romance and older women like mystery and intrigue. This makes it very difficult to create one story that checks all of those boxes and thereby appeals to all of those markets.

Modern entertainment philosophy is very much resigned to the fact you can't really *engineer* a four-quadrant story and to try and do so is folly and a waste of time and resources. And I get it. When I hear a writer say their story is "for everyone," which means men, women, teens, tweens, children, puppies and everything in between, my first instinct is to roll my eyes (in my mind of course, actually rolling my eyes would be rude) and label the writer as an amateur. It's now recommended for the writer to focus on a single, defined target market and create for that market. Once the writer engages the target market, the eternal hope is to catch lighting-in-a-bottle and watch as the project is elevated to all four-quadrants organically.

Realistically, you can't build a good business plan premised on the expectation of becoming the next Michael Jackson or creating the next *Seinfeld.* In success, you may become as big (or bigger) than Michael Jackson and your show may end up dwarfing *Seinfeld,* but it's very difficult to plan for it. This is why it's recommended that you focus on a specific target market and hope for the best.

To be clear, a target market is a specific group of people you have determined to be part of your customer base. These projections are based on demographic studies and market research done with various sample groups. This means you typically need to do more than five minutes of solid Googling.

When a producer approaches you and tells you their story is targeted to a "faith-based audience" or "children ages 2 to 7" or "childless, high net worth, career women," the story sounds more focused and, most likely, better-prepared for the marketplace. Because the producer has a good understanding of his target audience, all future advertising, marketing language and trailers can be created with that target market in mind. Honestly, it's very difficult to argue against writing for a target market and against the fact that not trying to engineer a four-quadrant story is the safest, most prudent business approach when actually creating traditional entertainment projects.

And I agree. In a age where everyone can tailor their entertainment consumption to fit their exact taste, stories should be created more like sniper rifles than grenades. This means the stories should be focused on one or two specific target markets with the understanding they more than likely won't reach other demographic quadrants.

However, the downside of targeting a faith-based audience is once the fanbase is developed, it's primarily going to be made up of Christians. The downside of targeting children 2 to 7 is your fanbase will be made up of only children 2 to 7. What about all the other quadrants that you're not targeting? Their money spends the same as everyone else's. Their eyeballs are just as valuable to advertisers and sponsors. Do we just ignore them?

The short answer is, no.

We go after them. #nodemoleftbehind

## The four-quadrant storyworld.

Wait — didn't I just convince you *not* to try to engineer a four-quadrant story and to simply focus on a specific target market?

If you don't mind me answering my own question, yes that's exactly what I said. I said to not and try to engineer a four-quadrant *story*. I never said not to engineer a four-quadrant *storyworld or IP*. Those concepts are inherently very different.

Think of your IP like a house.

If the goal is to get people inside the house, the most traditional way is to simply open the front door; however, there are many other entry points as well. You could open the windows, the garage door, the backdoor and even the chimney, thereby giving people more opportunities to enter the house. Not only do you give people more options whereby they can choose the point of entry they're most comfortable with (Santa only uses chimneys), but you also allow the house to fill up quicker because multiple people will simultaneously use multiple points of entry. This actually increases the chances of your ultimate success.

For example, if you're a filmmaker and your film is in the theater, my mom will not see it. She thinks the movies are too expensive, too loud and she hates crowds. Sorry, but she's not coming through your front door. She may gladly enter your house, though, if you give her a way she's comfortable with, such as television or books. All you have to do is open a window or a garage door and you'll ultimately have her as part of your project's fandom.

Therefore, instead of expecting a single story to carry the burden of reaching every demographic, a Super Story employs a series of focused stories that each target one (or potentially two) different demographics and are intertwined within the same storyworld. For example, one story may be an *As Good As It Gets*-ish film targeting older men and women. Another story may be a *Grand Theft Auto* type video game targeting young men and another may be a web series targeting young girls in the vein of *The Lizzy Bennet Diaries.* All of these stories can be connected, thrive in the same storyworld and be part of one IP.

In this case, one story doesn't have to bear the burden of connecting with all four quadrants, but all four quadrants are targeted and tapped regardless. You get the benefit of focusing and targeting your individual projects, but you still get the benefit of a four quadrant story, which is a bigger fanbase representative of all walks of life.

Yes, a Super Story allows you to have your cake and eat it too.

And one last note about having a diverse fanbase...

Diversity is an important topic in entertainment right now, with most of the focus understandably going toward ensuring there is diversity on screen and even behind the camera. However, in addition to diversifying projects above the line, below the line and within the story itself, it's also good to create diversity in your fanbases. Because entertainment is a powerful and effective mechanism to bring people together, if a project attracts a diverse set of fans, the entertainment can now be used as a cross-cultural bridge.

Sure, you may be a socialist and I may be a capitalist and, granted, we may not be able to discuss politics right now, but we both love *The Walking Dead* so you can't be *all* bad, right?

Super Stories can be powerful ways to bring all walks of life together and at least give them something to talk about that doesn't cause them to troll or flame each other on Facebook.

## Everyone doesn't like everything.

I hate to break it to you, but not everyone is going to love your comic book. Not everyone will love your hip-hop album or virtual reality experience. Not everyone will think you've written the Great American Novel and not everyone will fall in love with your film like people did with *The Wizard of Oz.*

And that's okay.

People are different and, thus, like different things. #GodBlessAmerica

It's as simple as that and instead of complaining about it, you need to embrace it and plan accordingly.

Some people love movies, some people love comics, some people love video games, some people are avid readers and love to curl up with a good book, and to some people, television reigns supreme. In the same way, there are some people who don't go to the movies or who don't have cable to watch television. There are some people who hate reading books and would rather simply listen to music or play a tabletop board game.

Given this fact (and, yes, I'm going ahead and declaring this to be fact), is it possible to create the magic bullet film or book or game that can break down all the barriers set up by factors like age, culture, political persuasion, interests, and gender?

I hate to burst your bubble, but don't plan on it.

If you figure it out, congratulations. Try not to spend your bazillion dollars in one place. But to everyone else, don't just open one door into your house and pray for a miracle. Instead, actually embrace the fact that everyone doesn't like everything and plan accordingly.

On second thought, it never hurts to always pray for a miracle, so be sure to keep that part up regardless.

**Perfect spaghetti sauces.**

Enter Howard Moskowitz — a short and round man in his sixties who most often wears huge gold-rimmed glasses, and is a market researcher and psycho-physicist who single-handedly innovated the burgeoning spaghetti sauce industry.

While working for Pepsi in the '70s, he was tasked with figuring out the perfect amount of sweetener for a can of Diet Pepsi. Pepsi knew anything below 8% sweetness was not sweet enough and anything over 12% was too sweet, so Howard took the most logical approach. He whipped up experimental batches of Diet Pepsi with every possible sweetness percentage — 8%, 8.25%, 8.5%, 8.75% — all the way up to 12%. He tested all the batches on hundreds of people to see what batch was the most popular. Easy enough, right?

Wrong.

There was no clear victor because the data was all over the place. And then it hit him — finding the perfect sweetness for Diet Pepsi is just as impossible as catching the Easter Bunny. Why?

Because neither exists.

In the mid-'80s, he was contracted by the Campbell Soup Company, who was in the spaghetti sauce business. They owned Prego and were going up against the industry giant, Ragú, and desperately wanted to come up with the perfect spaghetti sauce. However, when Howard came into the picture, he brought with him the fascinating concept of, what he called, *plural perfection.*

Openly declaring there was no such thing as the perfect spaghetti *sauce*, only the perfect spaghetti *sauces*, Howard designed over forty variations of spaghetti sauce that differed in every conceivable way — spiciness, sweetness, thickness, etc. When he charted what his focus groups liked, he saw everyone had a slightly different definition of what the perfect spaghetti sauce was. So, in the age when all spaghetti sauce was thin and blended, Howard talked the Campbell Soup Company into developing multiple kinds, including the then-unheard-of "extra chunky" brand. Not only did he find everyone liked something different, he also discovered once someone found a style she liked, she was more apt to then try variations she wouldn't try before. The whole study ended up being extraordinarily successful.

Today, it's difficult to appreciate how innovative this approach was to the food industry because now when we go to the grocery store, we see fifty variations of spaghetti sauce instead of just one kind. However, before Howard's innovation, the food industry was on the eternal search for human universals.

So, how does this apply to Super Stories?

If we know people like different things (which includes not only tone and genre, but also platforms and mediums), we should stop trying to push them out of their comfort zones. Instead, as twenty-first-century producers, we need to pull them into the project through doors/windows/platforms/mediums they're most comfortable with, understanding that once we meet them where their interests lie, they'll be more apt to cross over into other mediums. This will be especially true when we incentivize them to do so with both Additive Comprehension and Dynamic Connections.

Years ago, I had two family-related incidents that illustrated this concept of plural perfection beautifully.

When we were designing a Super Story project called *Fury*, we started with a board game, which we exhibited at a trade show in order to connect with a manufacturer. While at the trade show, we were approached by a production company that commissioned us to develop our board game into a feature film script. We happily complied and wrote the film script in a way that extended the story of the board game. Ultimately, the production company passed on the script because it ended up being too expensive for them to produce.

After they passed, we were able to place the script at Fox, who gave us a whole page of rewrite notes we needed to implement to make the script Fox-compliant. One of the many notes we received concerned a minor character named Macy. Toward the end of the script, you find out that Macy isn't who she says she is. In fact, you find out Macy isn't even her real name, though you never actually find out her real name. For the executives at Fox, Macy's identity, including her real name, was a point of interest and much-desired information, so they asked us to include it in a rewrite of the script.

Ultimately, once we added in all the rest of the notes, we couldn't figure out how to include her backstory and stay within our targeted page length. Most writers may stress about this quandary, but we recognized it as a Super Story opportunity. We decided to produce a Katy Perry-esk pop song from Macy's perspective that revealed her backstory, her true identity, and, yes, her real name. At this point, the song plus the feature film plus the board game all worked together to tell the complete, epic story of *Fury.*

Let's go back to the board game trade show for a second. If you've ever been to a board game trade show or convention, you're probably a nerdy white guy. Why? Because the tabletop board game industry is almost solely driven by the nerdy white guy demographic.

This is important because one of my business partners is black and, at the time, had a seventeen-year-old son. With his Beats headphones and his pointy hair, this kid was too-cool-for-school and nearly the exact opposite of everyone who makes up the board game demographic. Which is why, unfortunately, he outright rejected me when I tried to get him play the *Fury* board game. In fact, I tried to get him to play it multiple times and he would reject me every, single time. He simply refused to play my nerdy, white guy board game.

Friction.

At the time, he also said he wanted to go to film school to learn to be a director. Knowing that, I would encourage him to start reading feature film scripts since you can't be a great director until you truly understand stories on a script level. I encouraged him to start by reading our *Fury* script since he already had some familiarity with the overall concept. He actually took the script, but, being a seventeen-year-old, he didn't want to take the three hours to read it.

Still friction, but at least we're one step closer.

At his core, though, he was a music lover (he wanted to go to film school to be a *music video* director) so when we produced the song about Macy's character, he approached me about listening to it. Already, there had been a role reversal because I was no longer trying to convince him of anything. Instead, he was now pursuing me for something. I eventually let him listen to the song and, because he latched on to the character's backstory (which we left on a cliffhanger), he walked up and asked,

"Hey, I love this song, but what ends up happening to this girl?"

I told him he had to read the feature film script to find out and you know what? That night he went and read the entire thing.

But it didn't stop there because that weekend our families went on vacation and the kid ended up playing the board game multiple times.

Behold, the power of Super Stories.

We could have said we were going to create a board game everyone would love, would unite all races, creeds, religions, ages and genders and be a shining example of a four-quadrant game. Honestly, that would have been unrealistic. Alternatively, we could have said we were only going to target nerdy white guys and ignore the young, urban market. That, however, would have been bad business.

Instead, we simply went to where the young urban consumer was and opened an entry point into the project that was relevant to him. Once the story hooked him, we then incentivized him enough to cross over and do something he refused to do previously. We let him in the house a different way and once he was in, we were able to move him from room to room.

Pretty darn cool, in my opinion.

Another early Super Story lesson included by nephew and my dad. My nephew, who was thirteen-years-old at the time, was a pure video game kid. He would play for hours and hours a day and hardly every read a book. My dad, at the time, was a 63-year-old retired railroader who, after retirement, became a pastor. If you want to talk to my dad, you talk about one of four things: the Bible, Church history, Cincinnati Reds baseball or University of Kentucky basketball. If you try to talk to my dad about anything else, he'll be polite to you, but you'll never *actually talk* to my dad. Clearly, my dad and my nephew were very different people who represented very different demographics.

For Christmas one year, we were at my parent's house and my nephew received *Assassin's Creed III* as a gift. In case you don't remember, *Assassin's Creed III* is set in Boston during the American Revolution and is wildly historically accurate (outside of the time-traveling assassins, of course). Excited, he tore it open, threw it into the Xbox and wasted no time in assassinating every single person in sight.

I could see my dad's brow furling as he watched my nephew hack and slash his way through Revolutionary War Boston. Eventually, though, my nephew butchered his way through the entire city to ultimately arrive at the local church. When he went inside the church and approached the pastor, I was fully expecting the annual Howard blowup to commence. By this time, though, my nephew had progressed from just murdering everyone outright, to talking with them, mining them for all their information and after having learned everything he needed, driving his sword through their hearts.

When my nephew began speaking to the pastor, my dad interjected with, "Wait! He's a real guy!" Honestly, that was preferable to what I thought he would scream, so I explained to my dad how all the *Assassin's Creed* games are wildly historically accurate and developed by hipster historians. Suddenly excited, he took us into his office and pulled out an old, musty book about Church history.

Opening this book, he actually found a passage about this pastor. The pastor, apparently, was a member of a group called The Black Robed Regiment, who were influential clergymen who promoted American independence and supported the military struggle against Britain. By encouraging the Patriot cause, those ministers helped muster critical support among members of their congregation and actually had higher bounties on their heads than Thomas Jefferson or George Washington. King George thought if he could kill these pastors, he could kill the Revolution because he would have simultaneously killed morale. It was an interesting piece of history of which I wasn't aware and allowed us to avoid the annual Howard blowup (that happened a couple of days later for other, unrelated reasons).

The most interesting part of the story, however, happened the next day when I came over to my dad's house to watch a UK basketball game. I go into his study, thinking I would find him, but instead found my nephew — reading that old, musty Church history book. The operative word there is that he was *reading*. Listen, I bequeathed this kid all my *Star Wars* novels thinking it would inspire him to read more, but he never even picked up one of them. So, you can imagine my surprise when I find him reading this history book. When I asked him what was doing, he simply told me he was "working" and to leave him alone. I quickly surmised he was, essentially, looking for "cheat codes." Once it dawned on him the people in the game were actually real, historical figures, he thought if he learned more about those people, he would actually be able to play the game better.

It was brilliant strategy, actually.

Stepping away to allow him room to "work," I walked into the living room to turn on the basketball game, only to find my dad playing

*Assassin's Creed.* Here was a man who had played a video game maybe one time in his entire life playing Xbox, trying to find that church.

The psychology of what was going on in the Howard household that day was fascinating because what neither my dad nor my nephew realized was they were both operating in the same storyworld — Revolutionary War Boston — but had entered through two different points of entry. My nephew entered through violent, open-world video game. My dad, however, entered through an old, musty history book. But once they were both in the proverbial house, they crossed and began doing things they wouldn't have done from the outset.

A few years later, I was speaking at a conference and the *Assassin's Creed* team from Ubisoft was there. So, I made sure I hunted them down and told them this story — which they loved. I told them, though, while they were expertly tapping the thirteen-year-old market, they were missing out on the 63-year-old pastor market. They laughed, but I was being serious.

Since they're weird hipster historians and they already know the history, why not actually write a legitimate history book that older men would love. However, when they write it, make sure they do it with the video game in mind so they can actually put unique information about people and places that, if you read and apply it, you can actually play the game better. Then, you'll get all the thirteen-year-olds demanding for their parents to buy them the book because they'll want to master the game. And what self-respecting parent isn't going to buy these kids a history book if they ask for it?

Conversely, you'll get older men who will get the book because it's a legitimate history book. But when they read it, they can be incentivized to get the game. For example, while they're reading about the Battle of Lexington and Concord, the book will let them know if they experience the game, they can also experience the same battle from 63 different perspectives and actually see firsthand what lead up to the first shot being fired. Even if the older men don't run out and buy an Xbox, maybe they buy a copy for their kids or grandkids and sit next to them as they play it. At worst, you've created a nice grandfather-grandkid moment (which is good for the world) and either way you get the extra transaction. Not only that, but the *Assassin's Creed* fanbase would be made up of not only thirteen-year-olds, but also older folks as well, making the fanbase bigger, more diverse and ultimately more robust.

The Ubisoft guys just stared at me and said, "Wow. I don't think we could do that." When I asked why, they simply said, "Because we're just video game guys."

And therein lies the problem.

To create Super Stories, you not only have to look at your projects differently, but you need to look at yourself differently as well.

When you embrace this very simple concept of using multiple, targeted stories to open different points of entry into your IP and design your Super Stories to be a four quadrant storyworld, you'll be amazed at how much bigger and diverse your fanbases will become.

## You'll generate *compounding* revenue.

Ancillary or additional revenue streams have become part and parcel with what is known as the entertainment multimedia franchise. This traditionally means a movie spawns additional revenue opportunities beyond what is directly generated by the movie. The additional revenue sources are typically produced by the parent company licensing the right to make and sell the additional product to outside firms. Examples of these other sources of revenue include, but aren't limited to, video games, toys, action figures, cartoons, comics, etc.

Multiple revenue streams are actually important in any sustainable business, entertainment or not. They provide a time-tested way for an owner to reduce risk and allow a more predictable cash flow from a variety of sources, rather than relying on a single, traditional product or service. When multiple revenue streams are created, franchisees have the ability to reach the same loyal customer more often and with more touch points.

However, as we discussed previously, the traditional multimedia franchise has been suffering in today's over-saturated entertainment environment because people increasingly don't want repurposed content. Notably, Kathy Franklin, the President of Franchise Development of Lightstorm Entertainment (James Cameron's production house) said they've had to completely rethink their franchise strategies because the old model of franchising is only producing diminishing returns.

This is causing more and more producers and franchise developers to continue to create multiple revenue streams for financial sustainability, but do so in a way that extends the story at every touchpoint rather than adapting their content. This significantly changes the traditional franchise because it simultaneously disrupts the traditional licensing model that is a foundational aspect of the modern franchise. Now, producers have to not only license the right to produce the ancillary product, but also create, coordinate and control the new story content that will be included in that product. Admittedly, this requires producers to be more involved and creative during the licensing process, but the benefits will greatly outweigh the increased work.

Every time you create another revenue stream in a different medium and platform, you will naturally attract a new demographic. For example, in 2012, Vertigo, an imprint of DC, produced a comic book series adapting the film *Django Unchained.* While using the same story as the film didn't extend the experience for the fans of the film, it did open the story of Django to comic book fans who may have not seen it, and simultaneously created another source of revenue for the IP.

Now you have film fans and comic book fans entering into the house through different doors, thereby creating two revenue sources instead of just one. This is great, but you haven't incentivized either group to travel to the other product. What you're left with is two sources of revenue and, without incentive to travel, simply two transactions (movie ticket and comic sale).

In 2014, however, Quentin Tarantino wrote a comic book follow-up to *Django Unchained* titled, *Django/Zorro,* that extends the story of Django and crosses his character over with iconic character, Zorro. When that series was released through Dynamite and DC Entertainment, it created an extended experience and additional revenue-driving product for *Django* fans to buy and enjoy. Additionally, it opened another door into the house and, like the adapted comic, made the IP accessible to comic fans who possibly hadn't seen the film. So, at this point, the benefits are the same as an adapted comic — two sources of revenue, two transactions (movie ticket and comic sale) and two ways into the house.

However, because the comic extends the film, the film fans are now incentivized to migrate to the comic. Conversely, because the film extends the comic for the fans that enter the IP through that door, the comic fans are incentivized to migrate to the film. Now, you have two sources of revenue, two ways into the house, but because we've incentivized migration, there are now *four* transactions.

Four transactions are better than two.

If you added a third component that extends the story, say a video game, you would have three sources of revenue, three ways into the house, but because we've incentivized migration, there are now *nine* transactions (comic fans buy comic, see movie and buy video game; movie fans see movie, buy comic and buy video game; video game fans buy game, see movie and buy comic).

Nine transactions are better than four.

If you added a fourth component, you would create four revenue streams, four ways into the house and *sixteen* transactions (I'll leave all the math equations to you).

As you can see, the Super Story model begins to exponentially increase the revenue potential of your project. The result will be your project immediately becoming more attractive to any underwriter (angel investors, studios, labels, etc.) worth her salt, because revenue potential and ROI is a primary factor in an investment decision.

No, it's not sorcery, it's simply the power of a Super Story.

## Your project will have a longer shelf life.

Even if you are blessed to have one of the few traditional entertainment projects that actually makes money, the shelf life (and therefore revenue life) of traditional entertainment is shockingly short. Typically, the average shelf life of a film is two to four years. For a video game, it's three to five years. For an album, it's one to two years. Even with streaming and other digital after-market platforms helping make projects "evergreen," it's difficult to ever describe traditional entertainment projects as long term investments.

From an investment stand point, long term investments tend to exhibit lower volatility than short term investments. The longer your investment, the more likely you will be able to weather low market periods. Investments with higher short-term volatility risk (such as entertainment) tend to have higher returns over the long term.

In order words, when you invest in a traditional entertainment project that has a short revenue life, you have to hit the market at exactly the right time. Any shift in the economy, the news, and even the weather can impact the revenue intake of a project when it drops or premieres. Just ask anyone whose film was set to premiere during the week of September 11th, 2001. Or ask Kevin Smith how the split of "Bennifer" and the subsequent epic flop of *Gigli* negatively affected his (much better) Ben Affleck vehicle, *Jersey Girl.* If the entertainment market suddenly becomes volatile for any reason and the project in which you invested is negatively affected, it's going to be very difficult for your investment to recover.

Moreover, as an aside, putting your money in long-term rather than short-term investments also provides tax advantages on capital gains. Often long-term gains are taxed at rates below your income tax bracket. Short-term gains, on the other hand, are actually taxed as regular income.

The trick, then, is somehow (**cough** Super Story **cough**) turning entertainment into a long term investment. Accomplishing this will be wildly attractive to investors, studios, publishers, and anyone who has a financial stake in entertainment projects.

In a recent Wired.com article, "The Force Will Always Be With Us," Kathleen Kennedy was quoted as saying:

> *"New movies won't just be sequels. That's not the way the transnational entertainment business works anymore. Forget finite sequences; now it's about the* ***infinite series****. If everything works out for Disney ... you will probably not live to see the last* Star Wars *movie. It's the* ***forever franchise****."*

Why wouldn't a studio want to invest in an IP that can generate revenue over 20 or 30 years, rather than a one-off IP that could possibly generate revenue for two? Wouldn't a book publisher rather invest in an IP that can possibly generate revenue for a decade as opposed to a year or two? The overall entertainment game is now, in fact, becoming a long-term investment game.

For example, *The Pretender* television series was cancelled in 2001. Ultimately, Steve Mitchell and his writing partner Craig Van Sickle, finished off the series with two made-for-TV movies. Typically, when a show is cancelled, the IP dies and everyone moves on to another project. However, viewing themselves as IP managers rather than simply television writers, Steve and Craig decided to simply shift *The Pretender* IP into other mediums and platforms. In fact, they began publishing *The Pretender* novels. Then, they created graphic novels. Then, they wrote spin-off novels. Now, they're producing an original concept album and an animated mini-feature. Because they've fed their fanbase over the years, they're now in discussions about bringing it back as another series and potentially a feature.

Ultimately, by using Super Story principles and using sound multi-platform strategy, they extended *The Pretender's* shelf life (and revenue potential) by fifteen years and counting.

In the same way, the *Murder She Wrote* IP has generated twenty years worth of revenue through novels, *after* the show was cancelled in the mid-90's. After *Firefly* was ~~screwed~~ cancelled by Fox after only eleven episodes, Joss Whedon shifted the franchise into single-issue comic books, then into a feature and now into graphic novels — extending the shelf life of the IP, and its revenue potential, by nearly fifteen years.

It really comes down to the fact that fifteen years of revenue is better than two. Twenty is better than fifteen. Forty years of revenue is better than twenty. It's better for fans, it's better for investors, both of which is better for 21st century creators — which is you.

Here's the catch though — not every story has the innate ability to shift into other mediums and become a forever franchise, just like not every car has the ability to be competitive in a NASCAR race.

Do you want a forever franchise that entices investors and underwriters with long term revenue potential and continues to feed a fanbase over the course of decades?

If so, you're reading the right book.

## You can help engineer success.

Traditionally, in the top-down model of entertainment, stories are handed down from the holy and exalted media conglomerates in exactly one medium of their choosing. This medium is, effectively, the only door through which fans can access this Storyworld. It's presumed all fans, no matter what their interests or habits are, will all want to go through the same door.

If enough fans squeeze through this one, single door, the "suits" (as Billy Walsh would say) will consider gracing us with a sequel or an adaptation into another medium (two new doors into the Storyworld), both of which are more than likely going to be worse than the initial offering. If not enough fans squeeze through the door, the future doors will never materialize because the suits will say there are not enough fans to justify the risk.

Now, I'll be the first to admit that, for the most part, projects fail because the content simply stinks. However, it would be a logical fallacy to presume that everything that fails financially does so because the content isn't good. It could be due to creative timing, market shifts, the economy, poor marketing, or bad casting. However, it could also simply be because the suits at the studios or publishing houses didn't open enough doors and create enough entry points for potential fans to enter into the IP.

While it *feels right* to claim that it's too risky to release ancillary material when you don't even know if the core product will be a success, that line of thinking is actually a riskier proposition.

If a studio is making a film, they drop $80 million dollars into creating something new and then hope and pray millions of people show up at the theater on the same weekend. If they show up, success! If they don't, we lose our money.

I know the studios like to think of themselves as risk-averse, but, to me, that seems like they're rolling the dice. Big, expensive dice.

Think about why studios and networks are committed to rebooting and adapting pre-existing content into films. It's not that they hate original content and love comic books, it's that they love *pre-awareness* more. Fans' pre-awareness of a story hedges the investment into the story itself and takes some of the pressure off a film's marketing efforts.

This means pre-awareness is the key in the equation because it makes the whole project less risky and gives it a better chance of success. Honestly, if you want to develop original content, this is great news for you. All you need is pre-awareness and you'll be good!

How, though, do you establish pre-awareness?

As previously discussed, if you start making a film today, it most likely won't see the light of day for two years and your investors won't see a dime for over three, probably four (if ever). When I released my first book through the publisher, it took over a year for it to land in *Barnes & Noble* — not including the time it took for me to write it.

Instead of just sitting idly by during that time, begin to employ a Super Story strategy and start releasing low-cost, fast-to-market extensions of the IP. This will begin to introduce the IP to the audience and allow you to start building your fanbase well before your larger release finally drops. Then, when it's time for all the fans to show up at the theater on the same weekend, there's a greater chance they will because you've invested in creating pre-awareness in a meaningful, story-based way (as opposed to just traditional marketing).

Not only that, but depending on what your initial releases are, you could actually start paying your investors while they're waiting on the film to become profitable. Investors love little nuggets like this!

My company actually had a series of meetings with Overbrook Entertainment a few months following *After Earth*'s flop at the box office. When the film was released, they actually deployed some great and effective extensions of the film, including a mobile game, original music and a series of young adult books. However, when the film flopped based on its first couple of weekends, they wanted to scrap the entire IP. But there was only one problem — the extensions actually continued to sell extremely well.

Eight months after the flop of the film, their young adult novels and music continued to build and cultivate a young fanbase. This was a fanbase that simply didn't show for the film (probably because it was marketed to older Will Smith fans despite him not being the lead character), but ended up coming into (and loving) the IP through different points of entry.

My question to them was why they didn't release the novels, music and mobile games during the lead up to the film? If they would have, they would have built pre-awareness over a two year period and cultivated a young fanbase that would have actually shown up on those first two weekends at the theater.

So, instead of waiting for success to employ a Super Story strategy, use a Super Story strategy to actually help *engineer* success.

## You can build a better brand.

Whether you like it or not, every time you publish a book, release a film or drop an album, you're launching a new brand. The only question that remains is whether the brand is going to suck.

I actually wrote another book with Chris Hoffman, our branding specialist at One 3 Creative, called *Super Story — Super Brand.* In the book, we completely deconstruct the traditional way brands are formed and how they typically communicate their brand messages. Then, we rebuild the entire branding process with the Super Story model. Whereas the book you're reading now is more entertainment-centric, *Super Story — Super Brand* is specifically targeted to branding and marketing professionals who are completely outside of the entertainment industry.

But whether you're creating entertainment, brands apply to anyone who is releasing anything to the market. Traditionally, writers and producers have been great at creating the entertainment, but very poor at launching, building and sustaining a brand. They write their books, make their movies, or launch their games and then after initial fanfare, they're off to the next project, allowing the brand they launched with their project to languish and die. Because of this, I'm a huge advocate of producers and content creators building entertainment brands like entrepreneurs build consumer brands. When they do, the entertainment brand is much more poised for 21st century success and long-term sustainability.

In fact, there are so many things that make sense in entertainment that, when you go outside the Hollywood bubble, don't make sense in the consumer world at all. For example, in the consumer world, the more expensive it is to produce a product, the more expensive the price is for the consumer. The reason a Maserati costs $80,000 more to purchase than a Toyota is because of a much higher cost of production. In the entertainment world, though, I could make a movie for $150 million and someone else could make a movie for $30,000, yet the consumer pays $12 for a ticket to both.

That denies the normal rule of business and economics.

Another aspect of consumer brands that differs from the way entertainment brands operate is in the area of product diversification. A product diversification strategy is a form of business development where businesses diversify their product range by modifying existing products or adding new products to the range. The strategy provides opportunities to grow the business by increasing sales to existing customers or entering new markets (new entry points into the entertainment house).

Think about it.

Imagine for a second I went to an angel investor and asked for an infusion of investment capital for my new shoe store venture. I tell the investor I plan to sell size 10, grey, Chuck Taylors for men — and that's it.

Does that make sense? Of course not.

Predictably, the investor would question my ~~sanity~~ venture (and the potential investment) primarily because I would be cutting off viable markets and focusing too much on a single demographic. Why not have different sizes? Different colors? What if someone doesn't like Chuck Taylors? Can I add running shoes, tennis shoes, dress shoes, or boots? Can I have women's shoes? Children's shoes? What about socks? Why not a purse to go with the shoes? Maybe even sunglasses? In the realm of consumer brands, product diversification makes sound, business sense because it opens the brand up to a broader customer base and, hence, higher revenue potential.

So, why does it make sense for a film producer to simply walk around with a independent film targeted to the LGBTQ community? Or an author to just have a single novel targeted to middle age house wives? It's the same as me trying to start a shoe store with one type of shoe; it's a brand that sells a single product targeted toward a single market.

A while back, I had a filmmaker argue with me about the wisdom of product diversification, essentially fighting for his right to be a starving artist. His argument was when you start with an initial piece of entertainment and diversify around it, you necessarily water down or cheapen the initial offering. "Did Hemingway really need to franchise *The Old Man and the Sea*? Should Kurosawa have franchised *Seven Samurai*? Some things," he snarked, "are best served by themselves." When the word "franchise" would come out of his mouth, he would actually sneer, as if he was vomiting back up some sort of nasty over-the-counter medicine. At this point, I thought I would shift strategies with him by no longer discussing entertainment brands, but rather consumer brands.

I told him I had just eaten at a restaurant I had never patronized and had an absolutely fantastic meal; one the best meals of my life. I loved my entree so much I called the waiter to the table and began to order something else. The waiter, however, looked at me and said, "No. You can't order anything else."

Stunned, I asked, "But why? I loved the food so much I want more."

He simply shook his head and replied, "The chef feels that another dish will diminish the experience of the first so, I'm sorry, but you can't actually order another."

"But I have money in my pocket I'm willing to give you in return for more hot, delicious food."

"I'm sorry, but no."

"What about an appetizer?"

"No."

"Dessert?"

"No."

"A roll?"

"No. This entree is best served by itself. Thank you for your business and have a good day."

Even at this point, the filmmaker didn't get what I was doing and was completely aghast that a place of business would ever treat a customer like this. He finally admitted he would never go to a restaurant like that and, in fact, would tell all of his friends not to go there either.

If it would be outrageous for a consumer brand to treat a customer like this, why does it make sense for an entertainment brand to feel as if it can do the same?

The short answer is that it shouldn't.

You see, the only reason I wanted more food is because I loved the first entree so much. In entertainment, the fact that fans want more of your story is a compliment to you and your brand. It's not selling out, it's good customer service. It's amazing, wonderful flattery when people love something you create so much they want more. If this happens to you, look at it as a blessing and one of the keys to building a healthy, sustainable, and profitable brand.

The concept of customer service, sadly, doesn't really exist in the minds of creators because, in entertainment, there's primacy of the artist. Whereas in consumer brands, there's primacy of the customer, in entertainment it's all about the artist. The artist wants to create things his or her way without any consideration of the audience at all. Art is personal and, hence, it's all about them. In consumer brands, however, products or services are invariably created with the customer in mind, with the expectation the customer will ultimately have an extremely positive experience with said product.

The philosophical thought surrounding Phenomenology actually applies nicely to this conversation. Phenomenology (broadly, basically and inelegantly) asserts that the highest achievement of an artist isn't in the creation of the art itself. Rather, it's the phenomenon of experience that someone has with the art.

As a quick aside, the late transmedia thought-leader, Brian Clark, has an amazing video and teaching about Phenomenology that I highly recommend you Google. He was a pioneer who sadly died way too young. #cancersucks

In short, if you make a movie, the movie isn't the triumph, the experience an audience has when it sees your movie is the triumph. Moreover, if your movie is a technical masterpiece, but, for whatever reason, it creates mediocre experiences with audiences, the movie isn't a masterpiece. Rather, it's mediocre because, according to Phenomenology, the quality of a work should be judged by the value of the experience not the art itself. If you write a book no one ever reads, it's valueless. The whole point of art is to create things people will experience. Not just experience, but experience richly and meaningfully.

Regular artists create with themselves in mind and look at the art itself as their great achievement. Phenomenal artists create with the audience in mind and look at the experiences they create with the audience as their great achievements.

Don't be a regular writer, be a phenomenal writer.

Don't build a regular brand, build a phenomenal brand.

## Super Stories really work.

I'm going to finish this chapter by telling a quick story about how effective the Super Story model can be and how it can open doors that would have been difficult to open otherwise.

I mentioned previously we were approached by the right-holders of the *Slinky* entertainment brand and were asked to develop a Super Story that could compete with *Legos*. At first, we were brought in simply as vendors, but at a certain point we were offered the option of buying into the project as co-owners. This was, obviously, an attractive opportunity for us because as co-owners, we would participate in the profits of everything — including the news toys.

I contacted an angel investor I knew from a conference at which I spoke once and scheduled a phone call with him and another one of my partners. This guy is a heavy hitter in investing circles and actually has ten thousand angel investors underneath him in his international investing network. So, we get on the phone with him and he immediately says, "Hey, Houston. I just want to let you know I'm going to give you fifteen minutes. I charge $10,000 an hour for my business consultation and don't speak anywhere for less than $25,000, so it's not fair to all those people who pay all that money that I give you a call for free. But, because we spoke at the same conference, I'll give you fifteen minutes."

Sort of a jarring way to start a call.

My partner and I quickly start by saying, "Well, we have this *Slinky* project and it's being turned into a film…"

He quickly interjected, "Hey, guys, I'm sorry, but we don't really invest into movies. The chance of return is low and, even if you make money, it falls off after a couple of years. In fact, out of my ten thousand angels, I can think of maybe four who would even consider investing. And, even with them, you would, at best, get a million a piece. Sorry."

We needed more than $4 million for the deal, so we didn't let this piece of information deter us. Instead, I simply replied, "Well, it's good that we're not just pitching you just a movie — we're pitching you something completely different. We're pitching you a Super Story."

First of all, we had him on the phone for ninety minutes.

Secondly, at one point, he said, "This doesn't sound like entertainment at all. This sounds like a franchise-able business opportunity."

He went on to tell us that in 30 years of investing, no one had ever pitched him a model of entertainment that so closely resembled a consumer brand business model. And the best part came when he said, "You know, I think with this model, we could probably approach four thousand of my angels and do two rounds of financing — the first to raise $75 million and the second to raise another $50 million."

So, over the course of a conversation and using the value propositions in this chapter, we moved him from fifteen minutes on the phone, four investors and $4 million of investment to ninety minutes on the phone, four thousand investors and $125 million of investment.

And we never even pitched him a single creative idea.

We simply laid out the model of a Super Story.

Selah.

*Part 2*

# Creative Strategy

# IDEAS ARE WORTHLESS UNTIL YOU GET THEM OUT OF YOUR HEAD AND SEE WHAT THEY CAN DO

TANNER CHRISTENSEN

# 6. Let's build a Super Story.

## Finally, we can make stuff!

I know, I know...your brain is exhausted already and I haven't even explained how to actually create a Super Story yet. The good news is if you're going to be doing creative work, you'll actually be *more* creative when your tired and your brain feels like mushy cantaloupe. This is why some of your best, creative ideas happen in the shower after a long, exhausting day at work.

When you're fresh and awake, your brain is great at filtering out distractions and forcing you to focus on one particular task. However, when you're tired, your brain's filtering system shrinks and allows you to make new connections, be open to new ideas, and think in new ways. So a tired, fuzzy brain is of much more use to us when working on creative projects.

Now you truly understand my master plan.

So, let's take a deep breath and get ready to dive in...

IT IS NOT THE BEAUTY OF A BUILDING YOU SHOULD LOOK AT IT'S THE CONSTRUCTION OF THE FOUNDATION THAT WILL STAND THE TEST OF TIME

DAVID ALLAN COE

# 7. Get on your soapbox.

## Aim for the heart.

The first thing you need to do when you're creating a Super Story is to build your Soapbox. Figuratively speaking, of course. Unless, you actually need a soapbox, which in that case, happy building.

In the nineteenth century, people would plop down actual soapboxes so they could be elevated for a public speech. Generally, these speeches had to do with politics, but at the heart of it, the speeches were opinionated, passionate, agenda-driven, and rabble-rousing. People who used soapboxes were, predictably, called "soapboxers." That's the first step — using your Super Story as a soapbox and proudly accepting the label of a modern-day soapboxer. Your Super Story will become the platform where you shout what's in your heart to the world. And if it's authentic, people will listen.

Some people mistake a Soapbox for a simple theme, moral premise, message, agenda, or even meta-story. While all those things are part of the equation, a Soapbox is actually much more — it's like a theme on steroids — and intravenous Redbull — zooming around in a jetpack.

Technically, what you need to build a great Soapbox are:

- A topic or theme that your care about;
- A strong opinion about the topic; *and a*
- Call-to-action to the audience.

Once you put those pieces together, you'll have the foundation of your Super Story, the catalyst of your Storyworld, your storylines, your brand messaging, your audience building and even your back-end community outreach initiatives.

## The purpose driven project.

Why not start by designing characters, strategizing what mediums to use, creating a setting or fleshing out your supercool original idea you sketched out last year but haven't done anything with? It's because your Soapbox gives your creative decisions purpose and allows your Super Story to connect with your audience on a greater level.

I'm not saying a story can't be good without a strong message. I'm saying stories without strong thematic foundations are like sugar rushes — they get you excited for a bit, but can't sustain you for a long period of time because they don't have substance. Conversely, stories set on strong Soapboxes are more likely to endure and continue to resonate because even though the culture may change, universal themes tend to remain intact and continually connect with people across multiple generations.

Have you ever watched an old movie and found it difficult to relate to because the actors talk differently than you talk, they act differently than you act, things look differently than they do now, and culture has significantly changed since the movie was released? Well, if the movie has a strong Soapbox, that's what will connect with you, allow you to look past all the surrounding irrelevance and keep you watching.

Honestly, the thematic heartbeat of *It's a Wonderful Life* is the only reason I would still watch that film. I know Jimmy Stewart was good and all, but there are so many things that just don't click with me. But, I'll still check it out because despite the fact it was made before my parents were even born, it carries a great Soapbox — don't give up on life, because everyone's life has meaning.

Ultimately, art that is born out of passion and purpose is always experienced differently than art that isn't. When you read Hemingway, his words read different on the page. Every character Daniel Day Lewis plays *feels* different than characters played by other actors. You can hear a vocalist sing a song in tune and to a certain melody and it may sound nice, but then you hear another vocalist sing it *and believe every word they're singing* and it sounds very different. It's in the same key and it's the same melody, but it sounds different to the ear because of the passion behind it.

The Greeks have a concept called "meraki," which means "soul creativity or the essence of yourself that is put into your work." It means to do something — making a cup of coffee, ironing, gardening, any task at all — with all your heart, with love, passion and your very soul. When you do, as they say, a piece of your soul goes with whatever you're doing. So, the reason the song sounds different when the second vocalist sings it with all of her heart is because you're not just hearing her voice. You're also hearing a little piece of her soul. This is actually the very essence of soul music and soul food.

At One 3 Creative, we actually adopt an old Shaker philosophy of furniture-making and apply it to creating Super Stories. It states:

> *"Make every product better than it's ever been done before. Make the parts you cannot see as well as the parts you can see. Use only the best materials, even for the most everyday items. Give the same attention to the smallest detail as you do to the largest. Design every item you make to last forever."*

The only way you can accomplish this is to actually believe in what you're creating. Not only on an intellectual level because of the cool business model you're using or even just on a creative level because of the intricate plots you're weaving, but on a soul level. If you don't believe in the *purpose* behind your project, you (and it) will end up fizzling out over time. As soon as you get three or four rejections, you'll shelve the project and simply move on. There will be nothing to sustain you though the tough times and nothing to propel you further during the good times.

If building a Super Story is akin to building a car, then the Soapbox is the high octane, premium gasoline that makes the whole car go — and keep going down those long, dark stretches of road.

The coolness of plots fades over time, the initial ability of characters to relate will wane, and the wittiest line of dialogue in 2017 may be glazed over thirty years from now without even being noticed. But your theme, your message, those things you want to say to the world, your Soapbox — that's what holds up through the years.

## Why should anyone care?

Seriously. Why should anyone care about your project?

Why should anyone give you money they've spent hours of their lives earning? Because they'll be entertained? In a recessive economy and a ridiculously saturated entertainment landscape, simply being able to entertain for a few hours isn't a safe bet.

Don't get me wrong, I'm not saying entertainment is bad. It's absolutely essential. I'm merely advocating that you inspire *and* entertain because a strong Soapbox and an entertaining story aren't mutually exclusive ideals.

All industries, creative and otherwise, try to motivate people to act in order to sustain themselves. Painters try to motivate people to buy their paintings. Writers try to motivate readers to buy their books. Marketers try to motivate people to actually act on their calls-to-action. Filmmakers try to motivate audiences to watch their movies. Restaurant owners try to motivate people to eat at their establishments. Because motivations are fickle, it becomes a bit like trying to bribe children with candy just so you can get them to clean their rooms. Sometimes it works, sometimes unfortunately it doesn't.

However, when you can *inspire* people to act, as opposed to just motivating them, you actually impart an innate sense of purpose and belonging, which is so much more valuable. As a result, your project is elevated from "cool" to "important." This means you won't simply begin building an audience or a fanbase, you also start cultivating a much more devoted following.

Not too long ago, there was a group of guys pitching me an action project about a group of homeless veterans who form a make-shift militia, take over a cluster of mansions in the Hollywood Hills and create their own compound. It seemed like it could be a fun, little action movie. However, before they began their pitch, they told me they were, in fact, all veterans. One of them opened up about how when he returned from Afghanistan, he was homeless for over a year. Another said he feeds homeless veterans every day as a personal outreach ministry. Another said his mom was a homeless veteran and actually died on the street due to an inability to cope with her PTSD. For them, they wanted this project to build awareness for the plight of homeless veterans and show what a moral failure it is for the country to allow these men and women who sacrifice so much for us to simply waste away on the street.

When they began their pitch with their Soapbox, it immediately elevated the project from cool to important. No longer was I listening to the pitch critiquing the plot or the characters. My pen was down and I allowed the meaning behind what they were saying to draw me into the pitch. Because their Soapbox was so strong, they were connecting to my soul rather than dueling with my logic.

## It's no longer optional.

You may be surprised to learn 84 percent of millennials identify their generation as a "cause-driven" one. In fact, by all measurable standards, they are the most cause-driven generation since the Greatest Generation of the World War II era. Why should you care about millennials? Because they currently represent over $200 billion worth of spending power in today's economy. Sure, it's because they still live with their parents and don't pay for insurance, but the fact remains millennials are a major, driving force in today's market and economy, especially the entertainment economy. If you want long-term, sustainable success, you'll need millennials to care about and support your entertainment brand.

Studies show millennials are increasingly supporting brands (both consumer and entertainment) that actually stand for a purpose, mission or cause. Take, for instance, TOMS Shoes, which is a darling brand amongst millennials. TOMS began giving a pair of shoes to someone in need every time someone would buy a pair from them. They've since developed into providing shoes, sight, water, safe birth and bullying prevention services to people in need. They stand for something positive and, therefore, win the support of millennials.

Likewise, millennials flock to entertainment brands that actually stand for something, such as *Making a Murderer, Beasts of No Nation, Food Inc., Fruitvale Station, The Help* and any other entertainment that sparks conversation and inspires change. Millennials believe by supporting brands that stand for something they care about, they're actually contributing to the larger good.

Because of this millennial shift toward brand meaning, all brands have been forced to innovate new meanings rather than just products or projects. Consumers are actively participating in mining the meanings associated with the brand, looking for ones that are a reflection or a symbolic representation of their own personal identity or inner self. These brands are commonly referred to as "badge brands."

At the end of the day, regardless of the method used to drive the brand strategy, the question remains, "What does your brand stand for that matters to people and makes a difference?" Brands that lead markets, entertainment and otherwise, know the answer and build accordingly.

All over the world, humans are drowning in data and information. As information and our collective intelligence becomes more automated in the goo of the internet, human beings will value more of what can not be automated — meaning, emotion, imagination, connection and engagement. In today's marketplace, all brands (entertainment and consumer) will live and die on the ability of their stories to deliver what is actually highly valued — authentic, visceral meaning.

This shift for brands has become known as Corporate Social Responsibility ("CSR"). Basically, CSR means if you want to be successful as a brand, you not only have to create great products and projects, you also need to stand for something that contributes to the larger good. A recent article in *Forbes* explained it this way:

> *"Within a global society increasingly vexed by problems, the only smart long-term business move is for a brand to* ***demonstrate a tangible commitment to the larger good.*** *Consumers are increasingly inclined to support brands best known for making a* ***positive impact in the community.*** *The future opportunities are breathtaking for those* ***brands that actually seek the larger good*** *in meaningful, demonstrable ways."*

Don't you think that investors will be more attracted to entertainment brands that are adhering to the "only smart long-term business move," being built in a way where consumers will be "increasingly inclined to support" them and have a "breathtaking" amount of future opportunities?

The question was rhetorical. Of course they will.

## Thinking with the heart, not the head.

A recent HAVAS study has shown entertainment and consumer brands that are rooted in a strong Soapbox and CSR gain, on average, 46 percent more share of wallet and outperform the stock market by over 133 percent. This is because when your brand is centered on a strong Soapbox, you move consumers out of thinking with their heads and into thinking with their hearts.

Primarily, consumers make purchase decisions based on value. If there is enough value, the decision to purchase the product, be it a movie ticket, an album, a car or a phone, will be "worth it." Determining value is a very rational, left-brained calculation. In my assessment, value is equal to functional benefit, plus social benefit, plus previous experience divided by cost. Or, if you were to express it as a math equation (I know, I know — I can hear the collective groans already) it would look like this:

$$v = \frac{fb + sb + pe}{\$}$$

Functional Benefit is how well the product will do the job it was designed to do — will the movie entertain me, will the car get from A to B, will the toothpaste actually clean my teeth and do it well?

Social Benefit is simply whether the consumer gets a boon socially and culturally from using the product. For example, I could buy my sister-in-law a purse from Wal-Mart or a purse from Prada. They both have the same functional benefit, which is carrying stuff. However, the Prada bag carries a social benefit the Wal-Mart bag doesn't, which is her being seen walking around with a Prada bag. Products and projects that are "trendy" factor into Social Benefit as well. I know numerous people who went to the theater to see *The Force Awakens,* not because they were *Star Wars* fans, but simply because it was a cultural event "everyone" was doing.

Previous Experience is whether the consumer has had a history of positive or negative experiences with the brand. If the experience has been positive (we've owned multiple Volkswagens and they've all been great), that will increase value. If the experience has been negative (I haven't liked the past four or five M. Night Shyamalan movies), that will decrease the value.

All of this is undercut by the price of the product. If the top line of the equation is larger than the bottom line (the price), the purchase will be rationally justified. The larger the top line, the more value there is. If the price is larger than the top line, though, then the purchase "isn't worth it" to the consumer. This is the typical, sub-conscious calculation our brain makes when deciding whether to make a purchase.

This entire equation, however, can be completely subverted by a strong Soapbox. When a brand can connect emotionally to a audience member or consumer, it moves them out of thinking with their head and into thinking with their heart. For example, someone can show me the new Samsung Galaxy Note 5000 (or whatever it is) has a hundred more features than the iPhone for half the price. Based on that, rationally, the Samsung phone has more value and thus, I should purchase it. In reality, though, I will never purchase a Samsung phone and will always opt for an iPhone. Why? Because I'm an Apple guy. Does it make rational sense?

Of course not, but the brand has engaged me on a deeper level than rational thought.

In the same way, you can objectively (and probably correctly) make the case that *Star Wars: Episode I — The Phantom Menace* is the worst written script in the history of modern cinema (search your feelings, you know it to be true). By that measure, there shouldn't have been any value in seeing it either in the theater or on DVD (just ask the folks that came up with watching the saga in "Machete Order"). Nevertheless, I saw it three times in the theater and will still advocate for people to see it and support it. That doesn't make rational sense, but the *Star Wars* brand has engaged me on a deeper level.

If you create entertainment or an entertainment brand built on features, functions and benefits — great special effects, the hottest actor in Hollywood, a cutting edge gaming engine, a unique tone to your vocals or cool compression on your music — you may pop for a short while. However, in a volatile, over-saturated media environment, trust me when I say there will be something that will hit the market that will do it better. And when it does, the sole benefit of your project will bottom out and you'll simply be traded in for the new model by the consumers.

This goes back to motivated consumers versus inspired ones. Motivated consumers, because they are responding to external incentives, will almost always fall away when those disincentives appear — the cost is too high, the theater is too far away, none of their friends are into it, etc. It's not worth it to them because their connection is a superficial one. Devoted followers, however, are willing to pay more if needed, endure inconvenience if required, and even suffer a bit if they're called to do so.

Why?

They're following you not because you have the coolest project around, but because you believe what they believe and that always has value. You may think I'm getting too deep, but when what you create starts to serve as proof as to what you believe, you'll start connecting to your audience in entirely new ways.

Ultimately, a great Soapbox will create:

- Heart-driven buying decisions from consumers;
- Disproportionate support from your fans (they will not only buy your stuff, but show up on opening weekend, buy the DVD, the Blu-Ray, the Director's

Cut and the Digitally Remastered Special Anniversary Christmas Edition, etc.);

- An army of brand evangelists; *and*
- Levels of forgiveness from your fans ("I know her second album wasn't as good as the first, but cut her some slack for crying out loud!").

If you want to tell a superficial, sugar-rush story, you may grab some box office and get some sales, but if you want to tell a Super Story and build a larger, thriving brand, you need to figure out what your brand *stands for* and what your project *says*.

## Why start with Soapbox?

As with most projects, knowing where to begin is one of, if not *the*, most important steps to execute properly. If you don't, you'll only experience grief later in the process because you set off in a wrong direction and are forced to backtrack and revise. Listen, there's so much to do, why not just get it right the first time?

Some creative professionals, from songwriters to authors to designers, refer to a destructive phenomenon called "scope creep." This is when the scope of a project starts to grow and grow and grow and grow and grow until the whole project becomes messy, unfocused, awkward, and ultimately fragile. If you, as the content creator, haven't created your project with a steely focus, how can you reasonably expect your audience to focus? In today's entertainment-saturated culture, if you lose someone's attention for five seconds, they're off playing *Angry Birds* and you have as much of a chance of regaining them as fans as they have of beating the game with the boring red birds. Not likely.

How do you combat scope creep? You form borders to your Super Story. To make a sandbox, you don't start by dumping a bunch of sand on the ground. You begin by building the four walls that contain it. Likewise, puzzle masters never start a puzzle by trying to figure out the middle. Puzzle masters worth their salt start on the edges; they begin to defining their borders.

Your Soapbox is what will form those borders for your project. It will define a very clear narrative space for you to sink your teeth into and allow you to carve out a more focused project by informing every single creative decision you make. A thematic foundation and border empower you to refuse anything that falls outside its scope. If something doesn't reconcile with your Soapbox, it's not allowed. If a creative decision starts to tear down your Soapbox, you ditch it.

Many brands like to own many questions and points of view in order to appeal to as many people as possible. However, in point of fact, the strongest brands are ones that take stands on issues, narrow their views, mean a whole lot to select communities and aren't afraid to say so in every visual and verbal expression of the brand. That's what makes the big picture creatives who create badge brands so admirable. They don't get caught up in fads, trends and the minutiae; dismissing everything that could potentially dilute their brands. Everything is analyzed through the prism of the brand message or Soapbox: does it embrace it or not? If not, it's jettisoned. And that's what creates brand consistency and authenticity.

This means any product, service, license, campaign or offering from the brand will need to support the Soapbox. Anything that doesn't fully support that notion shouldn't be endorsed, produced or communicated by the brand.

Trust me. Adhering to a strong Soapbox will help you from straying off the path. It's like when you go hiking and every now and then you see a sign that says KEEP ON THE PATH. Some may say those signs are infringing on their hiking freedom. I say they're helping them not be eaten by a mountain lion and they should thank the person who put the signs there in the first place.

## Let's start building.

Hopefully, by now I have begun the process of peeling back the layers of your personal onion so you can take what you care about and use it as a creative catalyst for your entire Super Story.

Now that you've been primed emotionally, let's start the process of putting this Soapbox together.

### How do you find your topic?

It's easy.

Just find something you're passionate about. Identify a cause that makes you cry. Pick something that gets you out of bed in the morning and you find yourself talking about to other people. Steve Mitchell phrases it a bit differently. In his book, *The Awesome Power of Soul Stories: How to Use*

*Emotional Connection to Cause Your Entertainment to Stand Out,* he says not to just write what you know, but write what you know *emotionally*.

As an aside, let me just say his book is a fantastic, practical breakdown of how he built a thirty year television career on knowing how to effectively use a Soapbox and therefore connect with his audience in a deeper way. While I'm just scratching the surface in this chapter, Steve takes you on the Soapbox deep-dive. It's definitely a must read for writers.

Okay, enough from our sponsors and back to finding your topic.

Your project is the embodiment of your Soapbox, so now that you have a stage, what do you want to say? We have actually created a companion workbook that takes you through an exhaust*ive* (not exhaust*ing*) process of identifying your Soapbox. However, outside of that, here are a few of questions you can ask yourself when trying to zero in on your topic:

- What are the topics that cause you to raise your voice or to wave your arms around like a lunatic?
- What do you want your kids to learn?
- What do you want to teach future generations?
- What's the biggest problem in the world?
- What's the prescription *you* would write for it?
- What do you believe?
- What don't you believe?
- If you could go back in time and give your 10-year-old self one piece of sound advice, what would it be?
- What is it about you now that would make your 10-year-old self cry?
- Quickly, what are the common themes of your three favorite movies?

Is there a common theme or topic popping up in multiple answers? Maybe it's "family" or maybe "education" is a recurring theme. There may actually be a few — and that's a good thing. If you can't find an intersection between them, you may have the inspiration for multiple Soapboxes for multiple Super Stories.

## Plant your flag.

Once you have your topic, don't presume you have your Soapbox yet. In order to have a great Soapbox, you need to move well beyond an open-ended theme. I just googled "most common literary themes" and I pulled up this list:

- Good versus evil;
- Man versus nature;
- Love and friendship;
- Man versus society;
- Man versus himself;
- Fate versus freewill; and
- Suffering versus redemption.

This isn't what I'm referring to when I'm talking about your Soapbox. These can, however, help you find your Soapbox, but these are just topics. Remember your Soapbox should be opinionated and passionate. It's the difference between a regular newspaper article (just the facts, expository, etc.) and an editorial or opinion piece.

Sure, *Star Wars* dealt with good versus evil, but Lucas didn't just present the battle and back away — he actually *said* something about it. He didn't just present the struggle between suffering and redemption, he openly declared even one of the most evil dudes in the galaxy can be redeemed. That's a bold statement, but he wasn't afraid to say it.

On a larger scale, he was also against militaristic imperialism. Interestingly enough, Lucas was originally tapped as the director for *Apocalypse Now* and was passionate about Vietnam-era issues and politics, as was most young people of his generation. When the film got delayed, he moved onto *Star Wars,* but still poured his visceral hatred of militaristic imperialism into his work.

Be opinionated. Have a voice and a unique perspective. Plant your flag somewhere and say something. It's the difference between saying, "Racism is my topic," and saying, "My opinion is racism is evil and has no place in modern society." The latter is much stronger and will ultimately elicit more of a response from an audience.

If someone walks up to you and says, "Love and friendship," you'll probably just look at them with a weird expression and not know what they mean. But, if the same person walks up to you and says, "I think a man who is loved by others and who has friends is the richest man in the world," you'll have a completely different reaction — a better reaction. Plus, there's now room for dialogue and interaction whereas before there was only room for a furled brow and a confused look.

You want to dare to take a stand. Possibly in a way that is polarizing. Stake out a position and make sure the people you want to connect with get it. Taking a stand will make your audience sit up, take notice, stand up and applaud — and then run straight for your brand because they believe in what you're creating.

Therefore, once you have the topic, simply write *your* opinion on that topic. Not what's necessarily marketable or what other people want to hear — your personal opinion, as a human being and an individual. For example, we'll take the innocuous open-ended topic of "education." That was easy enough to select. Now, just write an opinion about that topic.

> *Education is good.*

Okay, let's make it stronger by punching it up.

> *Everyone should be educated.*

We're getting there. Let's punch it up again.

> *Everyone should be educated, but great education can come in many forms.*

Now you're saying something. Can we make it any stronger?

> *Everyone should be educated, but the school system isn't the only path to education — life experience is actually the greatest teacher.*

Wow. Now that's a good opinion. Will everyone agree? No, but your Super Story is your way to convince them.

*The Lord of Rings* series is actually centered on a number of thematic opinions, one of which is no matter how small you are, you can still do something great. Throughout the books, Tolkien is constantly making that argument. Every time the Hobbits unexpectedly succeed at doing something great, his assertion is strengthened, and by the end, he proves his assertion true.

In the Craig Brewer film, *Hustle & Flow*, the thematic opinion that resonates above all others is no matter how far off the path you've gone, you should always pursue your dreams. Every crazy situation Djay finds himself in deals with that question and is Brewer's argument as to why that assertion is, in fact, true. When the film is over, you end up not only agreeing with Brewer concerning his thematic opinion, but you also find yourself saying, "Hey, if a pimp in the ghettos of Memphis can change his life and achieve his dreams then so can I."

Good storytellers, though, put pressure on their thematic opinions and take you on a thematic roller coaster before ultimately proving their assertions true. So, when you watch *Hustle & Flow,* you find yourself going through a very dynamic "will he/won't he" process. You think he can change, then you think he won't, then you think he can, then you think he won't, and so on.

Finally, when Djay beats the tar out of Skinny Black in a bathroom stall, you completely write him off as a potential candidate for change. But, in the end, Djay pulls it together and you see the fulfillment of the thematic opinion in the character's life.

Brewer obviously and purposely crafted the story this way. First and foremost, it's to make the story more dramatic, tense, and interesting for the audience. But also, on a thematic level, you need your argument to be seen as realistic and credible, so you want to put pressure on the opinion in every way possible.

In our *City of Refuge* project, our opinion is simple and twofold:

1. No one is too bad for redemption; *and*
2. It's love and goodness that will cause people to truly change, rather than fear, punishment, and judgment.

In our *Fury* transmedia project, our thematic opinion is you shouldn't be burdened by your fear, guilt and pain and if you do, the pain and anger that's driving you will ultimately lead you to your own personal destruction.

They're not complicated. They're not *that* controversial. But, at the same time, they're very pointed, opinionated assertions and they're truths we know can help people. Throughout the creative process, they informed everything we did and every decision we made.

Recently, my company was brought into a project where we were asked to turn a cosmology documentary into a Super Story. Honestly, this documentary was some of the most dense, heady, science stuff you could imagine; a true science brick to the face. The first thing we needed to do was dig through the massive layers of exposition, experiments, and scientific theory and identify the Soapbox.

The documentary was actually premised on a series of new experiments that point to the fact Earth is actually at the center of the universe. That, by itself, is a controversial opinion; however, we wanted to take it one step further to make it more relevant and emotional and ultimately less "science-y."

If the Earth is at the center of the universe, then the Earth and everyone on it, are necessarily and automatically significant. No matter who you are — black, white, Chinese, poor, rich, old or unborn — your life is significant, not because of what you've done, but because of *where* you are. That's a clear, strong and provocative opinion that elevated their documentary to not only seem interesting, but actually seem important.

I took it upon myself to pull some examples of thematic opinions from my collection of books, games, and films. Note how focused and opinionated they are and how they're not just exploring vague, open-ended topics.

- Love is the most powerful force in the universe.
- The love of money will always lead people to do evil things.
- Fear is a very real, destructive, spiritual force.
- Lying always has consequences.
- You shouldn't take your life for granted.
- Revenge will never make you whole.
- Angels are real and are active in our lives.
- Women should have the same opportunities as men in the marketplace.
- Death should be viewed as a promotion rather than a tragedy.
- Kids shouldn't be too eager to grow up.
- Humans shouldn't try to play God.
- Conformity is a type of bondage.
- Society will always need a hero and a savior.
- Life is too short to waste at a job you hate.
- Childbirth is something every woman should experience at least once.
- Childbirth isn't necessarily for every woman.
- No matter how old you are, you should pursue your dreams.
- All men are dogs.
- Crime doesn't pay.

- No matter what nationality, race, or gender, we're all the same inside.
- The bond between father and son is more special than any other bond that exists.
- Marriage is the cornerstone of society.
- We shouldn't be so attached to material items.
- You are the architect of your own life.
- Character is the true measure of a person.
- American ideals are still worth defending.
- Your personal happiness is not the most important thing in the world.
- Wisdom should be sought before anything in life.
- Evil must be confronted and defeated.
- Leaders lead by example.
- A life lived without love is a life half lived.
- True capitalists are what make America great.
- The American banking system is broken and needs to be replaced.
- Idealism works, even in an imperfect world.
- Everyone we encounter has an effect on us.
- True friendship never gives up.
- Honesty is the best policy.
- Beauty is in the eye of the beholder.
- You have to love yourself before you can begin to love others.
- Everyone's voice is worth being heard.
- Divorce is always destructive for a child.
- Just because you've been divorced, doesn't mean you can't have a loving family.
- Just because you're old, doesn't mean you have to give up on finding love.
- There's a plan for everyone's life.

- The spiritual world is just as real as the physical world in which we live.
- Everything happens to us for a reason.
- Debt is a type of slavery.
- The environment is worth protecting.
- Violence is never the answer.
- The lesser of two evils is still evil.
- If you stay eternally positive, you'll always be positioned for success.
- You can sell without selling out.
- Gossip can lead to your downfall.
- Life is never as bad as you think.
- The only people you can trust in life are your friends.
- You're never too old to reinvent yourself.

We all have opinions about everything. Instead of just wasting them on your Facebook rants, start putting them to good use!

**Make a call-to-action.**

Once you have your opinion locked in, you're two-thirds of the way to a great Soapbox. The last component is a strong call-to-action ("CTA"). This is where you not only give people your opinion, but actually tell them how to act and respond accordingly.

In case you're unfamiliar, a CTA is a standard mechanism in marketing circles where a brand suggests a specific action in order to drive readers, listeners, and followers deeper into engagement with the brand. Moreover, the philosophy surrounding CTA's is not only premised on the fact it's a great thing for the consumer to continue to engage with the brand through certain actions, but also the brand needs to plainly identify what that action is — buy now, click here, download using this link, sign up, etc.

How does this apply to a Soapbox?

Once you have planted your flag and given your strong opinion about a topic, you need to take it one step further and tell people how you would like them to act accordingly. For example, let's say my topic is "love" and my opinion is that "love-at-first-sight doesn't exist."

That's great, but so what? If the opinion is true, how does this affect anyone? How do I want people to act differently? What's my advice?

Obviously, if love-at-first-sight doesn't actually exist, then it would seem like a poor choice to impulsively and immediately jump into a serious relationship — and maybe even marriage. Therefore, my CTA would be:

> *Don't be so quick to jump into a serious relationship. Rather, take your time and see how things play out before you get too involved.*

Let's draw from the list on the previous page and say that my topic is "debt" and my strong opinion is that "debt is a type of slavery." What do I want people to do or what do I want them to refrain from?

If debt is truly a type of slavery, my CTA would be:

> *Don't go into debt! Take the time to save up enough money to buy something outright.*

When you develop a strong CTA out of your opinion, you're radically crystallizing *exactly* what you're trying to say with your Super Story. Sharpening your Soapbox through this method will give you, as the creator, a more directed creative path through your Super Story and ultimately will inform many of your community outreach initiatives on the backend.

**Put it all together.**

Now that you have your topic, opinion and call-to-action, you just need to put the parts together to form your Soapbox. I suggest starting with something similar to this template:

[**CALL TO ACTION**], because [**OPINION** on the **TOPIC**].

Using the debt example above, my final Soapbox may end up looking something like this:

> *Do everything in your power to save up the money to purchase things outright, because debt is a subtle, but very powerful form of slavery.*

Do you see how much more sharp and powerful that statement is than simply leaving it at a theme — "My project is about debt."

The previous example about love-at-first-sight could look something like this when turned into a full Soapbox:

> *Take your time with a relationship and let it develop slowly, because love-at-first-sight doesn't really exist.*

A friend of mine once came up with an interesting Soapbox. His topic was "strippers" and his opinion was "drama always follows them and they always come with baggage." So, what did the Soapbox look like once he put in his advice or his CTA?

> *Be wary of marrying a stripper, because you don't just marry them, you marry all the drama and emotional baggage that follows them.*

When he told me his topic and opinion, I thought it was going to be ridiculous and stupid, but once he added in his CTA and told me his own personal horror story of marrying a stripper, I got it — and it ended up seeming like good advice!

Feel free, though, to reorder the template to cater to your own project's messaging. The most important thing is you have all three elements and while the above template typically works, you may find a template that is more effective for your specific project.

For example, If your topic is "divorce" and your opinion is that "children suffer from divorce" then your final Soapbox could look something like this:

> *Though they may hide it well, divorce is always devastating and destructive for all the children involved. Therefore, couples should do everything they can to work out their differences and make sure divorce is always the last option.*

This example is reordered a bit with the CTA at the end, rather than at the beginning. Nevertheless, again, the most important thing is simply that you have all three elements of a Soapbox.

At the end of the day, you just want your Soapbox to be explained easily, simply and clearly. Any way you can accomplish that goal is fine by me.

**It's not as risky as you think.**

Again, everyone may not agree with your Soapbox, but that's okay. It's your job to convince them. Don't withdraw your voice just because you don't want to risk someone disagreeing. Don't fall into the trap of playing it safe by sticking to a story that simply has a cool plot spread across some flavor-of-the-month, whiz-bang, razzle-dazzle technology.

Safe is good for sidewalks and swimming pools, but life is short. You've been put on the earth and given a unique voice for a reason. Take advantage of that privilege, add it to your creativity, get out of your comfort zone, and go do something with some meaning.

Now, go build your Soapbox.

NOBODY BELIEVES ME WHEN I SAY THAT MY LONG BOOK IS JUST AN ATTEMPT TO CREATE A WORLD AGREEABLE TO MY PERSONAL AESTHETIC BUT IT IS TRUE

J.R.R. TOLKIEN

# 8. Storyworlds — part one.

## I want a fire department.

Now that you have your Soapbox, it's time to develop a Storyworld for your Super Story. I'm not talking about a simple backdrop for any old story where you have a generic city, or forest, or just outer space. I'm going to show you how to create a living, breathing multi-dimensional narrative world that has depth, history, and the potential to facilitate multiple stories across multiple platforms for many years to come.

By looking at the IP's that have recently been surging within entertainment markets, including things like *The Hunger Games* series, *The Purge, The Mazerunner* series, the *Divergent* series, the numerous comic-inspired superhero properties, *Game of Thrones, The Walking Dead, iZombie, The Man in the High Castle, Grand Theft Auto, West World, Fallout,* and *Overwatch,* a striking common denominator is found — the existence of great Storyworlds.

In fact, when I was first dabbling into the world of multi-platform storytelling, I went on a multi-year research project looking at all the great, generational projects that have successfully extended into multiple mediums. And, you know what I found? You guessed it. They all employed bold, dynamic and extremely viable Storyworlds. Moreover, the projects I found that unsuccessfully attempted to extend into multi-platform storytelling also had a common denominator — they all had very poorly crafted Storyworlds.

Being the genius that I am, I made the decision to emulate the ways of the successful projects and not the failures. #winning

Recall at the beginning of the book I mentioned, in 1976, two movies with similar subject matter, similar budgets and similar target markets were released. *Close Encounters of the Third Kind* did well and was just a really good movie. *Star Wars,* however, was a really good movie that became a $50 billion, pervasive, inter-generational, multi-platform brand. We can spend all day speculating about the differences between the two; however, the book, *How Star Wars Conquered the Galaxy,* actually gets Steven Spielberg's own perspective on why the two films ended up with vastly different results. His reasoning was twofold:

1. With *Star Wars,* Lucas created a Storyworld people wanted to explore, whereas he never gave the Storyworld of *Close Encounters of the Third Kind* much thought; *and*
2. While he only ever saw *Close Encounters* as a singular film, Lucas always had the vision *Star Wars* would become multiple stories.

Lucas wanted to tell multiple *Star Wars* stories and instinctively understood in order to accomplish that, he needed a dynamic Storyworld to house and support them. He instinctively knew he needed a box to hold all of his oranges.

It's worthy to note after my business partner, Steve Mitchell, was nominated for an Emmy for creating the *Tin Man* mini-series for the SyFy channel, George Lucas called him and invited him to come to Skywalker Ranch for a few weeks to help break a season of *The Clone Wars* cartoons. Amongst all the amazing Skywalker Ranch stories he returned home with, one of the most interesting was about how George has his own, personal fire department that stays on the ranch — and they wear Millennium Falcon patches.

That, folks, is quintessential proof of just how important a great Storyworld can be — it can directly lead to you having your own, personal fire department.

Well played, George. I think all that hard work paid off.

But he's not the only one who recognized the financial viability of Storyworlds. Other buyers are seeing the light as well. More and more in the entertainment marketplace, buyers such as studios, networks, publishers and investors are paying a disproportionate amount, not for great stories, but for great Storyworlds. I can think of a handful of projects that have been acquired for four or five times the price of a normal "spec deal" specifically because of the strength of the Storyworlds and, hence, their ability to produce multiple stories across multiple platforms over a long period of time.

In particular, Max Landis recently dealt his script, *Bright,* to Netflix for $3.5 million dollars, which is one of the highest spec deals a writer has seen in years. Why did Netflix not only pay four to five times the amount they normally pay for a spec script but also be willing to ultimately invest north of $90 million into developing the project? Because *Bright* has a robust Storyworld (high fantasy elements — orcs, trolls, wizards, etc. — set in modern day LA) that has not only feature film potential, but television, video game, publishing and animation potential. Netflix didn't just acquire a script, they acquired a franchise. Why pay $500,000 for a single story when you can pay $3.5 million for thirty stories across six platforms to roll out over the next two decades? In that light, the deal for *Bright* seems like a bargain basement purchase.

Recently, there was a short film entitled, *Sundays*, shot for $50,000 and put on Vimeo by the filmmakers on a Monday. By the same Friday, there were three studios bidding for the rights, with Warner Bros ultimately winning out with a deal just south of $2.5 million. The reasoning was when they saw the short film, they didn't just see feature film potential, they saw multiple films, multiple television series, multiple videos games, books series, and everything in between. In their mind, they didn't overpay at all— they simply acted like they were at Costco and decided to buy in bulk.

I could go on and on about other examples of Storyworlds being acquired as separate assets, even sometimes completely independent of a story. What this means is the entertainment marketplace is especially primed for those storytellers who understand the power and viability of not just a great story, but a great Storyworld.

## Hyper-di-whats-it?

Again, your Storyworld is not only what helps unite the various stories in your project, but it also holds the key to future story potential (and, thus, the ultimate revenue potential of your Super Story). So, while a *good* Storyworld is like having a box to hold your oranges, maybe a better analogy would be a *great* Storyworld is akin to owning an entire orange grove. You'll still have oranges to sell, but the grove will continue to produce more and more oranges over time.

Don't think, though, this is like the Storyworld *Declaration of Independence* where I announce that all Storyworlds are created equal, because unfortunately they're not. Like with stories launching brands, every story told will automatically have a Storyworld simply because your story has to be set somewhere. However, if you don't create it with the right narrative architecture, then you'll limit its ability to produce for your IP. Great Storyworlds don't just automatically appear; they need to be built and ultimately built the right way with very specific parts.

*Hyperdiegesis* is the term used to describe the art of creating a vast and detailed Storyworld. As you create it, you do it with the understanding only a fraction is ever directly seen or encountered within the text, but which nonetheless appears to operate according to principles of internal logic and extension. This is, interestingly enough, where we arrived at the term "Super Story." Literally, "hyper" means "super" and "diegetic" is a film industry term that means "story." So, as you build a Storyworld, you're engaging in the most pure sense of creating a Super Story.

The concept of hyperdiegesis, though, is like revealing only the tip of the iceberg. You need everything under the surface of the water to uphold the part of the iceberg you do see. In the Japanese game development space, this is called having a good "*sekaikan.*" This term means "the world feels real and actually exists beyond what you can see."

Once you're finished with this chapter, feel free to consider yourself a Hyperdiegetic Architect. Put that on your LinkedIn profile and see how many of your friends you impress.

When you build your Storyworld the correct way, you'll minimize the propensity for continuity errors across stories, everything will be easier to coordinate and your fans will be able to make logical sense of your Super Story. Trust me, even though they may love you, your fans will continue to prod and poke your Super Story to make sure everything is coordinated and adheres to the logic and rules of your world.

For example, I remember being a child watching *Scooby Doo* cartoons and being shocked when Batman and Robin appeared in an episode. I was shocked, not because Robin didn't wear pants back then (that was super creepy), but because that meant Batman and Robin actually inhabited the same Storyworld as Scooby and the gang. Then, when the Harlem Globetrotters also showed up in *Scooby Doo*, that meant the Globetrotters, Scooby and the gang *and* Batman and Robin all actually lived in the very same Storyworld.

This, understandably, had implications for ten-year-old Houston.

I always thought in the DC universe, Gotham took the place of New York City. However, if the Globetrotters are from Harlem and live in the same Storyworld as Batman, then New York must exist *with* Gotham. So, if Gotham isn't New York, then where is it located? And if Gotham is on the East Coast, why are Batman and Robin on the West Coast with the Scooby Gang? Are they on vacation? Did they take the Batplane? Ten-year-old Houston needed answers to these frustrating questions!

I'm sure the writers and producers at Hanna-Barbera weren't considering raising such questions in their fans — they just wanted to do something fun with a cool crossover — and that's the problem. If you want to see just how far fans will go to attempt to make their favorite Storyworlds make sense, YouTube the Pixar Theory sometime. It makes a detailed and compelling case about how the Pixar films actually exist in the same Storyworld and collectively tell the epic struggle for Earth between machines, humans and animals (and Boo from *Monsters, Inc.* ends up being the witch in *Brave,* which is crazy).

Disney fans developed a similar theory about how all the Disney films are all connected, which led to Disney officially uniting their characters into a single Storyworld called Auradon. Ultimately, to keep your fanbase cohesive and happy, Super Story Architects need to consider these fundamental Storyworld questions and ultimately make sure they abide by the answers.

## It's just a question of order.

You may be wondering, though, why we don't first design awesome characters and then worry about where to stick them. I mean, don't great stories start with great characters? Fair questions that actually share a very simple answer.

Yes, great stories need great characters. Yes, you can't have a great story without them; however, right now we're not developing stories. We're designing a world where the stories will be *set.* We'll get to the story part, but not just yet, which means the characters can wait patiently as well. Don't get me wrong — I love coming up with characters as much as the next writer. But, at this point, this isn't a question of love, it's a question of order.

In this process, if you come up with a character first, it's like putting your shoes on before your pants. Have you ever tried that? It's difficult and ends up taking longer (if you can do it at all) and there's a distinct possibility you'll fall over and hit your head on the dresser, so why even make the attempt? This isn't to say pants are more important than shoes. This isn't anti-shoeism. Both are equally important to a snazzy look and a nice wardrobe. All I'm saying is there's an order to how you put them on.

Likewise, this isn't a "Storyworld versus character" argument. It's an "awesome Storyworld first, then awesome characters second" argument. Remember the *Reading Rainbow* theme song? After the first verse sells the benefits of reading, the second verse then starts with the line, "I can go *anywhere.*" Then, the third verse begins with, "I can be *anything.*" "Anywhere" speaks to a great storyworld and "anything" points to great characters.

Awesome Storyworld *then* awesome characters.

Lavar Burton would agree.

## My storyworld rule of thumb.

As I'm designing a Storyworld for a Super Story, I'm constantly referring to the following rule of thumb: if you can remove your main character from your Storyworld and your Storyworld is still cool, you're probably in pretty good shape. Likewise, if you can't remove your Storyworld from your story without it being fatal, you're probably already moving in the right direction.

As with any rule of thumb, this is meant for broad application and is not intended to be strictly accurate or reliable for every situation.

Let's try it.

Remove The Wizarding World from *Harry Potter.* What happens? I'd wager you can hit very similar plot points and create similar situations and create the exact same arc for Harry even if you put him, Ron, Hermione, and the rest in a public school building in Riverside, CA. You can have very similar stories but they wouldn't be as timeless or nearly as interesting or engaging.

Set the *Star Wars* saga in modern-day Europe. Palpatine is the dictator. Vader is his general. Luke is a farm boy from Italy. Princess Leia is the leader of an underground resistance. Could it be good? Sure, but it wouldn't be as magical and I'm not confident it would yield the mountain of features, novels, toys, comics, cartoons, audio dramas, video games, and board and roleplaying games it has over the multiple decades.

Tolkien with *The Lord of the Rings*, James Cameron with *Avatar*, and C. S. Lewis with *The Chronicles of Narnia* all literally designed new worlds with an astonishing level of detail. Can you imagine *Avatar* without Pandora? Or Frodo without Middle Earth? Would Aslan still be the same taken out of Narnia and placed in a generic African setting? If you've read the *Fables* series by Bill Willingham, you would agree the existence of Fabletown adds a coolness to the story that wouldn't exist if the fairy tale characters were simply scattered around in different places.

Removing the Storyworlds from these tales would be fatal to the narrative. Now, leave the Storyworld intact and instead simply remove a character.

We know what would happen to *The Lord of the Rings* if we tried to extract Middle Earth, but what if we didn't have Frodo? Well, Frodo is an awesome character, but it wouldn't be fatal because there are thousands of other stories to tell and other characters to deal with. Likewise, we can't remove Pandora from *Avatar*, but I'm confident despite their being great characters, a great story can be told on Pandora without Neytiri and Jake. If you take Luke Skywalker out of *Star Wars,* you've arguably made it better (search your heart, you know it to be true…).

There's just something about taking great characters and great plots and surrounding them with a well-designed, interesting, and rich Storyworld that is a recipe for creative longevity. A great Storyworld elevates everything it touches by providing a deeper and larger canvas on which to paint. Characters become more dynamic, stories become deeper — everything is made better when the Storyworld transcends the dull, static backdrop to which it so often is relegated.

## Use the Soapbox for inspiration.

When you're brainstorming your idea for your Storyworld, you want to revisit your Soapbox and use it to inspire the broad concept.

For example, let's say your Soapbox is:

*Don't ever give up on true love, because*
*true love is not only rare, but it's also timeless.*

With this Soapbox, you may want to focus on the "timeless" aspect of the Soapbox and create a storyworld around a time travel concept. Perhaps it's a Storyworld where there's a service that allows you to travel back in time and give you another chance to find your true love? Or maybe it allows you to find your true love and bring him/her back to the future with you (at 88 gigawatts, of course)? Or maybe it's a Storyworld where couples in love can pay to actually stop time? Or maybe it's a small town where your loved ones return as ghosts — not in a *Poltergeist* way, but in a sweet, *Ghost* sort of way?

For this exercise, the exact idea is irrelevant. The seminal takeaway is the understanding the broad concept, Google Earth-view for your Storyworld should actually be a reflection of your Soapbox. When your Soapbox is "baked into the cake" of your Storyworld, then not only will all of your stories in your Super Story naturally and intrinsically communicate your Soapbox, but your Storyworld itself will actually *say something.*

In my opinion, the best storyworlds don't just give your stories a platform to say something, but actually communicate something themselves. For example, the storyworlds of *Jurassic Park, Terminator, Planet of the Apes* and *The Matrix* all speak of Humanity's hubris – our arrogance in thinking we can twist, push, cheat, or circumvent the laws of nature, without consequences. Despite having a variety of stories that had a variety of individual soapboxes, the Storyworlds themselves warned against the dangers of humans "playing God." The Storyworlds of *Game of Thrones* and *House of Cards* speak against the danger of living a life driven by the pursuit of power. The Storyworld of Lupe Fiasco's album, *The Cool,* is a Chicago ghetto full of zombie gangsters, but it's also a cautionary tale for inner city youths.

No matter where you go in those Storyworlds, what type of story you tell or where you tell it on the timeline, the Soapbox will always be there because you took the time to weave it into the DNA of the Storyworld concept itself. This is particularly useful because there are so many moving parts in a Super Story. Given this fact, you need every available mechanism you can find to unite and connect every story and every piece to form a cohesive whole. While I'll be discussing narrative connections later in the book, another way to unite the stories is to make them all *feel the same.*

Moreover, even though you may give all your individual stories and characters their own, unique Soapboxes depending on specific plots, your main Soapbox will always be there, woven into the fabric of the Storyworld itself. As long as your individual Soapboxes aren't violative of the main Soapbox of your Super Story, you'll begin to operate in something called "tautology," which is the ability to continually say the same thing in different ways.

So, don't just come up with any old concept. Use your Soapbox as inspiration and give your Storyworld not just the ability to produce stories, but to speak.

## Put on your hard hat.

In my experience and research, there are eight very specific pieces of narrative architecture you need to build into your Storyworld to optimize it for Super Story success. Think of these as the load-bearing walls of your Storyworld, so if you're missing some, or all, of these items, your Storyworld won't be built to last. Here are the eight items we'll be discussing:

1. Unfamiliarity
2. Definable Location
3. Broad Geographical Boundaries
4. Character Groups
5. Social Segments and Status Ladders
6. High Concept
7. Special Sauce
8. Room for History

Now that you know where we're heading, let's start going through them all in detail, learning and understanding the nuances of each.

### Unfamiliarity.

At a fundamental level, people like to know where they are at all times. It's a survival mechanism built into our brains and is true in real life as well as in the stories they experience. This is evidenced by the popularity of the Establishing Shot in films, which sets up, or establishes the context for a scene by showing where the scene is taking place. Therefore, identifying your Storyworld's location is critical to your audience's comfort level in your Super Story.

Keep in mind when discussing the concept of Storyworlds, I'm always referring to a place — not a person, not an idea, not a vision, not a fever dream, not your coming-of-age sexuality. It's a place. It's geography. Therefore, the first thing to do when building your Storyworld is to broadly decide what and where that place is. This can be everything from a small northeast town, an alien planet, the world's biggest airport, a kingdom under the sea, an existing modern-day city, a metropolis from the past, or a Quick Stop convenient store in New Jersey. Whatever you decide, keep in mind Storyworlds need to provide escapism and provoke imagination. Therefore, when at this point in the process, try to make your Storyworld location as *unfamiliar* as possible.

Basic human curiosity causes people to like to explore what they don't know. When people visit their home town, they don't typically go exploring. Why? Because they're already familiar with it. They know the streets, the neighborhoods, the back alleys, the best dive bars and everything in between. If those same people, though, go to Paris, Budapest or any other city they've never before visited, all of a sudden, they're out exploring — walking around, sightseeing, trying new restaurants, finding the hotspots, etc.

As a creator, you need to make me want to not just go to your Storyworld, but actually explore. Honestly, I'd rather not visit and explore somewhere I've already visited a hundred times over. For instance, if I were to come across a Storyworld set in an eastern Kentucky small town during the 1990s, my imagination isn't provoked. Why? Because it's familiar to me — I was there. Conversely, give me a book set in the Old West and I'm all over it. Why? Because I wasn't around during that time so I want to go, and because the book is set there, the author can take me.

Armed with the understanding that the more unfamiliar the Storyworld, the stronger the hook for the audience, let's quickly brainstorm some different ways to achieve Unfamiliarity.

**Fictional Unfamiliarity.**

If you're leaning toward creating a completely fictional Storyworld from scratch, the Unfamiliarity is automatically there. Because Storyworlds such as Pandora, Middle Earth, Narnia, Westeros and the *Star Wars* galaxy don't actually exist and no one has ever been to them, they are unfamiliar *per se*.

This is the easiest box to check when looking for Unfamiliarity, but keep in mind that creating an entirely new, fictional world ushers in quite a bit of complexity in other areas (as we'll discuss in detail later in the book).

**Real world Unfamiliarity.**

Living in a hyper-connected world with a proliferation of media, it's harder to find Unfamiliarity when you're dealing with modern day, real world settings. However, it's not impossible; you simply have to look a bit harder to find unfamiliar pockets.

Consider the movie or television show, *Fargo*. If all the dastardly things that happened in those stories occurred in Chicago, it wouldn't be quite as interesting. But considering most people in the country have never been to Fargo, ND, all of a sudden it's more interesting to explore. Also, consider the *West Wing* television show. That Storyworld is unfamiliar because even if you go to the White House to take a tour, you only tour the East Wing. No one ever goes into the West Wing because that's where the President works. Its exclusivity preserves its Unfamiliarity.

The *Daredevil* series created a nice bit of Unfamiliarity when it used Hell's Kitchen as its Storyworld, rather than just generic New York City. Even if you've never been to New York City, most people *feel* like it's familiar based on what they've seen from movies, television shows and the news. However, if you've actually visited the city, odds are you've never visited the part of Manhattan known as Hell's Kitchen.

Likewise, because of what we've seen through various media outlets, Las Vegas seems very familiar to people, especially after *The Hangover* movies. However, did you know there are a series a flood tunnels underneath Las Vegas where hundreds of homeless people live? They have their own bartering system, they self-police and have a whole community directly underneath the glam of the Las Vegas Strip.

What about the small Texas town of Roby where all 42 families that lived there pooled their money and all won the lottery? What about the huge, brand new, technologically-advanced cities in China that have been completely abandoned because of poor air quality? What about North Brother Island, the abandoned island nestled in between the Bronx and Manhattan, that once housed Typhoid Mary and has been almost completely devoid of human contact since the mid-1960's?

There are plenty of unfamiliar places in our world to set a Storyworld, you just have to search and find them.

**Past and future Unfamiliarity.**

Even if you can't find a good modern day, real world Storyworld that feels unfamiliar to the audience, you can take a familiar setting and engineer its Unfamiliarity by shifting it into the past or the future. For example, Atlantic City might not be completely unfamiliar to an audience; however, by shifting it into the Prohibition-era *Boardwalk Empire*, it instantly increases its Unfamiliarity. Why? Because chances are none of us were alive in the 1920's. Whereas, New York City may feel familiar because of aforementioned reasons, when *Gangs of New York* shifted it into the 19th Century, its Unfamiliarity increased. The same goes for 1960's New York in *Mad Men* or 18th Century Boston in *Turn.*

Conversely, you can also achieve Unfamiliarity by not shifting the Storyworld into the past, but into the future. Chicago isn't necessarily that unfamiliar to people, but when the *Divergent* series was set in futuristic Chicago, it presented a Chicago no one has obviously ever visited, making it unfamiliar *per se.* The same stands for future New York City in *Escape from New York* or *I am Legend,* future Los Angeles in *Blade Runner* or future Washington, D.C. in *Logan's Run.*

So, the big takeaway here — if you want a *familiar* real world setting to become unfamiliar, shift it into the past or into the future.

### High concept Unfamiliarity.

If you don't want to shift your familiar real world Storyworld into the past or future, but would rather stay in modern day, give your Storyworld sort of an alternate reality spin through what's called a High Concept. We'll be discussing how to create this type of Unfamiliarity through a High Concept in just a few pages, so if this is the way you want to go, just put a pin in it for now and we'll loop back around very soon.

However you achieve Unfamiliarity, though, just understand the more unfamiliar your Storyworld is, the more your fans will want to explore. The more they want to explore, the more stories you can tell. The more stories you can tell, the more revenue potential and longer shelf-life your Super Story will have.

## Definable location.

Once you have a broad idea of the Storyworld and have made sure it's unfamiliar to the audience in some way, we can begin the process of defining it. When I say "define," I mean marking the boundaries and detailing the major and minor characteristics in between. Think of your Storyworld up to this point as the stomach of an average middle-aged dad. Now, at this stage of the process, it's time to turn the Storyworld into the abs of an Olympic swimmer. Both are stomachs, but one has definition and the other doesn't. This is important because the more definition your Storyworld has, the more real and authentic it's going to feel to your fans. #justsaynotodadabs

When determining whether you have actually defined your location enough, ask yourself whether you can map it. If you can map it, then you're on your way to a good Definable Location. Conversely, if you can't map it, then you haven't defined it enough. For example, instead of "the woods," focus it to Sherwood Forest. Instead of "the ocean," sharpen it to the bottom of the Marianas Trench. The more definable you make your location, the more it will start to come alive. You can map the interior of a spaceship, a galaxy worth of planets, a ghost town or mysterious island. And then once you figure *if* you can map it, become an amateur cartographer (does any child ever want to grow up and become a cartographer?) and actually map it.

I remember reading *The Lord of the Rings* series as a kid and constantly referring back to the map at the beginning of the book to find where the characters were, where the side stories were taking place and thinking of potential stories that could erupt sheerly due to proximity. The map helped the Storyworld come alive for me and actually helped fuel interest from the fanbase as a whole.

And *LotR* isn't the only Storyworld to utilize a map. Storyworlds from *Superman*'s Metropolis, to *Batman*'s Gotham, to the *Star Wars* galaxy, to *Game of Thrones'* Westeros and Essos to *Grand Theft Auto*'s Vice City to *Boardwalk Empire*'s Prohibition-era Atlantic City have all been intricately mapped, both for the fans' benefit and the creators' benefit as well. Or, when you have a modern day, real world Storyworld such as Hell's Kitchen in *Daredevil* or Compton in *Straight Outta Compton*, creating a map is as simple as snapping a screenshot of Google Maps and marking your boundaries.

Defining and mapping your Storyworld helps you in three ways, the first of which is it helps maintain continuity across platforms. So, when you look at the map of Middle Earth, Fangorn Forest is to the east of the Misty Mountains and to the south of Lothlorien. This means this is where it will be in the books, in the video games, in the movies, in the board games and everything ever created. Once it shows up to the West of the Misty Mountains in the books or to the North of Lothlorien in the mobile game and in yet a wholly different place in the cartoon, the fans become frustrated at the lack of *cartographic continuity* and their verisimilitude begins to suffer.

When the *Call of Duty* feature film was announced, the fans were overjoyed to learn their favorite map, Nuketown, would be included. Their elation was short-lived because the filmmakers were quick to point out that because the film was live action, Nuketown may not look exactly like the video game. The fans were justifiably upset about the continuity break, yet the creators tried to explain themselves by saying when the video game was developed, they weren't considering ever making a feature. This seems understandable to a degree, but in this day and age, the simple answer is they should have thought of it from inception. Even if they didn't develop the story for the film, when developing Nuketown, they could have said, "You know, one day we may want to do a live action feature film, so let's go ahead and design the Storyworld to accommodate." If they would have taken the time to think through their Storyworld a bit more, their fans wouldn't be so frustrated today.

The second way mapping your Definable Location helps is it reveals narrative opportunities you wouldn't have discovered otherwise. Let's say you're developing a story in the *Star Wars* galaxy and, in the story, your characters are traveling from the planet Sullest to the planet Elrood. Without a map, this seems very straight forward; however, once you look at the map, you'll notice the small swamp planet of Dagobah sits squarely in between the two planets. Knowing this, maybe you can figure out how to weave Yoda into the story? Maybe have the characters land on Dagobah in order to hide from an Imperial convoy? Possibly have them find the cave where they encounter their biggest fear just like Luke? It's safe to say narrative opportunity more than likely wouldn't have arisen if you hadn't taken the short amount of time to actually look at the map of the Storyworld.

Lastly, by defining and mapping your Storyworld, the various locations you include on your map will pique the interest of the audience and inspire further exploration. On the map of Middle Earth, included is the Icebay of Forchel, yet there is no story in *The Lord of the Rings* series that takes place there. Maybe it's mentioned in another story but no one ever goes? Maybe some people say it's haunted? Over time, you may find the natural curiosity of the fanbase will begin to wonder and speculate about the Icebay of Forchel, which gives you, as the creator, the opportunity to tell a story that explores that very site. When you do, then all of a sudden, you're a hero to the fanbase. Likewise, if no *Batman* story ever goes to the Tricorner Yards, but it remains on the map of Gotham, the fans will naturally become curious about the location and give you the opportunity to explore it through a story. George Lucas called this the "over the next hill" concept in that fans will always be curious as to what's over the next hill and ultimately venture over it. When they do, you reward them with an amazing story — and another hill in the distance.

Once you've mapped the boundaries and major landmarks and locations of your Definable Location, take it one step further and also outline the basic requirements to make it function. Before the military invades a city, the military leadership identifies certain functional criteria, known as Essential Services and Critical Infrastructure. These include such things as the following:

- **Leadership**: What is the leadership structure of the Definable Location?
- **Essentials**: What does it take for the Definable Location to minimally function and where do they get these things?
- **Infrastructure**: What is the minimal, yet essential infrastructure system of the Definable Location — bridges, railways, roads, tunnels, sewers, etc.?
- **Population**: Who are the people to inhabit the Definable Location?
- **Protective Forces**: What are the security forces employed by the Definable Location?

To the military, these are the essential elements to any functioning location and without any one of them, the location will eventually break down. Therefore, it can only help strengthen and flesh out your Definable Location by identifying (or creating) these same elements.

Leadership structure can vary from Owner, manager, shift manager, and employee at the Quick Stop convenient store to Emperor, Grand Moff, Moff, Governor, and Baron of the *Star Wars* galaxy.

Essentials can range from water, electricity and product stock at the Quick Stop to fuel extracted from children's imaginations in your epic science-fiction setting.

Infrastructure can include a hundred mile bridge forged from dragon glass in your fantasy concept to the Lincoln Tunnel in New York City to the haunted road in a creepy northwest town.

Population may include the Na'vi on Pandora, hipsters in Greenwich Village, a melting pot of international culture in Los Angeles or burgeoning heroes at Super Hero High.

Finally, Protective Forces can range from Stormtroopers in *Star Wars,* to mall cops in *Paul Blart,* to the local police in *The Leftovers,* to the school bullies on an elementary school playground.

Forcing yourself to not only define the boundaries of your Definable Location, but the essentials that make it function, gives your Storyworld a depth and authenticity it will need to hold up to fan scrutiny over time. Not only that, but it will also inform you as to new story ideas. If new product stock is an essential service of the Quick Stop convenient store in the View Askewniverse, then maybe you tell a story of a falling out between Randal and the guy who delivers the stock, with Dante being forced to play the intermediary. Because it's essential to the day-to-day functioning of the Definable Location, that feud necessarily begins with more drama and even higher stakes than other storylines you may have previously brainstormed.

## Broad geographical boundaries.

Once you have located and defined your Storyworld, including your boundaries, see if it's possible to stretch them to make it bigger and broader. As a general rule, the broader the geographical scope of your Storyworld, the more room there is to explore, which ultimately means more story potential.

*Star Wars* has an entire galaxy full of potential stories, whereas *Avatar* only has one planet, whereas *Gilligan's Island* has a single island. Therefore, simply because of the geographical boundaries of the concept, it would be easier to come up with thirty years worth of stories in the *Star Wars* universe than it would be in the *Avatar* universe. Moreover, it would be easier to come up with more stories for *Avatar* than for *Gilligan's Island.*

Let's say you built a concept around a quirky coffee shop. Just looking at the limitations of the Storyworld, you may really be scrounging for stories because there is only a small amount of space to explore. I'm not saying it's impossible to tell a bunch of stories from a coffee shop, just that when you compare it to Middle Earth, you can see the stark difference and the main difference is in the geographical boundaries.

If J. K. Rowling limited the *Harry Potter* setting to just the Hogwarts school building, it would have also severely limited the story potential. By opening it up to the surrounding forests, lakes, etc., she gave herself more narrative opportunities and more freedom for the original series. In anticipation of the *Fantastic Beasts and Where to Find Them* series, she stretched them once again to include multiple wizarding schools all over the world, of which Hogwarts is but one. If she could get seven books, eight movies, video games, a digital series, two stage plays and everything else out of the stories from a single school, just imagine how many stories she can mine her Storyworld for now. By simply broadening the geographical boundaries, she has moved the *Harry Potter* IP into forever franchise territory.

We know that Batman's Storyworld is Gotham; however, in *Batman v Superman: Dawn of Justice*, they stretched it to include Superman's Metropolis, as well as Strykers Island in between. The creative team can still develop all the Batman stories set in Gotham, but now they can also tell all the Batman stories out of Metropolis. By broadening the sheet geographical boundaries, they were able to increase their story potential.

If I, for instance, wanted to create a project about film students in Los Angeles and had earmarked a classroom at The Los Angeles Film School as my Storyworld, I would run out of stories very quickly. If I broaden the boundaries to include the entire school, my story potential immediately increases as well. If I broaden the boundaries again to all of Hollywood, I could now tell the stories of the students in school, but also explore their personal lives more and how they go out and shoot school projects around Hollywood. If I then stretch the boundaries yet again to not just include Hollywood, but all of Los Angeles, I could then include other film schools around town — USC, UCLA and AFI — and ultimately have even more stories to tell.

Literally, the more room you have in your Storyworld, the more you and your fans will recognize story potential, so, generally speaking, the bigger the better. However, I'm not saying it's absolutely essential to have an entire galaxy or a whole world in order for your Storyworld to be viable. Once you get an idea of your Storyworld, simply try your best to broaden your borders as wide as you can without losing your concept or your Unfamiliarity. With the above example about film students in Los Angeles, I probably wouldn't want to stretch any further than the city of Los Angeles. Once you get into Oxnard and Santa Clarita, the "filmmaking" aspect is lost a bit and the overall concept is weakened.

Let's look at an exercise that will force you to broaden your geographical boundaries. Think of your Definable Location and find the category on the list that best describes it:

1. Room
2. House/Building
3. Street
4. Neighborhood
5. City

6. State
7. Country
8. Continent
9. Planet
10. Galaxy
11. Universe
12. Multiverse

Once you have located your starting point, go two numbers higher and see if you can stretch the boundaries that far while still maintaining your concept. For example, if your starting point is a house, see if you can stretch the boundaries to include the entire neighborhood. If your starting point is a country like the United States of America, see if you can stretch the boundaries to cover the entire planet while still maintaining your concept. Perhaps, your U.S. organization becomes a multi-national organization? If you can't stretch it that far, that's fine. Take it as far as you can and call it a day.

However, after you stretch the boundaries by going higher in numbers, add more definition to your Storyworld by making sure you include four of the previous two lower numbers inside each component. For example, each street needs to have at least four fleshed out houses with each house having at least four fleshed out rooms. A continent needs four fleshed out states, with each state having four fleshed out cities. This ensures that as you stretch the boundaries, you're simultaneously maintaining definition.

Again, you don't have to have a *Star Wars*-sized galaxy or a *Halo*-sized universe to be able to tell a successful Super Story. Nevertheless, the fact remains you want to do everything you can to make it as big as possible. If you're able to accomplish this, more future stories will naturally spring forth simply because there is plenty of room for them to grow.

## Character groups.

Traditionally, writers and creators are taught to think of a single great character to build a story around — Jack Bauer, Master Chief, Indiana Jones, Atticus Finch, Tony Soprano, Link, Forrest Gump, Jay Gatsby, Lorelei Gilmore, Lara Croft, Don Vito Corleone, Walter White, Katniss Everdeen, etc. All of these are great characters that can uphold one or two really great projects by themselves. However, when creating a generational, multi-platform Super Story, unless your project is part of the *Sherlock Holmes* or *James Bond* franchises, you have to think broader than just individual characters. More specifically, since you don't have 75 years of brand equity in your franchise, you need to begin creating not just single characters, but Character Groups.

As a general rule, the more characters you have in your Storyworld, the more story potential you'll create for your Super Story because you'll have more characters and perspectives to explore. Not only that, but the characters collectively share the burden of upholding the weight of the Super Story so all the weight isn't dependent on a single character. It's the difference between a table with four legs and one of those weird Ikea tables that just has a single leg. The former is always going to be more sturdy and durable.

From a business perspective, you can see how this makes sense. Take the show, *House M.D.,* for example. What would have happened if Hugh Laurie, who played Dr. Gregory House, would have died during the show? The IP would have also been dead because the entire thing had been built around a single character. Conversely, *ER* was able to go another ten seasons *after* losing George Clooney — George Clooney!

It was interesting to see how George Lucas began to hedge the *Star Wars* franchise by creating Character Groups. Mark Hamill, the actor playing Luke Skywalker, suffered a car accident right before filming for *A New Hope* wrapped. Not only that, but when *A New Hope* ended, Lucas didn't know if Harrison Ford would return to play Han Solo because he was only contracted for the first film. Seeing just how vulnerable and fragile his burgeoning IP actually was, as he began writing *The Empire Strikes Back,* he started creating Character Groups.

He had Obi Wan, who was a Jedi Master, but in *Empire,* he also introduced Yoda, another Jedi Master. Han Solo was the roguish smuggler, but in *Empire,* Lando Calrissian also comes into the picture. Darth Vader is an evil Sith Lord, but then another evil Sith Lord, Emperor Palpatine, is added to the cast. Lastly, Lucas reveals there's even another Skywalker — Luke's sister. What was Lucas doing? He was doubling up on characters, adding more legs to his *Star Wars* table and ultimately securing the future of his franchise outside of individual characters. In fact, before Disney purchased Lucasfilm, they did a forensic audit of the *Star Wars* IP in order to estimate the value of the brand. During the audit, it was discovered there were over 14,000 original characters in the IP at that time. This was one of the chief reasons the ultimate valuation for Lucasfilm was well over $4 billion.

Not only will this help create veritable insurance policies for your Super Story, but it will also open up more story potential within your Storyworld because there are more characters inhabiting it. Stories are about characters — their journeys, their lives, the crazy situations they get themselves in and the dramatic things that happen to them when they least expect it. The more characters you have, the more journeys, lives, crazy situations and dramatic things you'll be able to mine and exploit for narrative opportunity.

And it's really easy to do.

While you'll ultimately end up with a variety of different Character Groups, I typically start with my *Primary* Character Group. Usually, this Character Group is based on the first really cool character idea you have. So, for *Harry Potter*, the first character Rowling envisioned was, obviously, Harry himself. In *Rocky*, it would have been Rocky Balboa. In *Superman*, it would have obviously been Superman himself. Therefore, my job is to take the singular character of Harry and then create a Character Group out of him.

From this point, there are two ways to create the Character Group:

1. **Craft**: What does the character *do*?
2. **Soapbox**: What does the character *want*?

The first way is the easiest and most obvious method of elevating a character to a group, which is why I'll begin there.

**Creating a group based on the character's craft.**

If you have your initial character idea, such as Harry Potter, Rocky or Superman, all you have to do is identify their craft by asking yourself, "What does this character do?" In *Harry Potter*, Harry is a child wizard; that's his craft. In *Rocky*, Rocky Balboa is a boxer. In *Superman*, Superman is a superhero.

Once you have their craft, simply make more of them. So, instead of Harry being the only child wizard, let's make lots of child wizards. Instead of one boxer, let's have multiple boxers. Instead of just one superhero flying around, let's increase the number to ultimately have many superheroes.

It's as simple as that.

To show you just how simple it is, here's a list of the characters I mentioned earlier and how I would elevate them into a group based on their craft:

Jack Bauer —> CTU Agents

Master Chief —> Biochemically and Cybernetically Enhanced Space Marines

Indiana Jones —> Archeologists and/or Adventurers

Atticus Finch —> Lawyers (or Residents of Maycomb County or possibly even Fathers)

Tony Soprano —> Mobsters

Forrest Gump —> Handicapped People Who End Up Leading Amazing Lives

Jay Gatsby —> Bootleggers

Lorelei Gilmore —> Residents of Stars Hollow or Mothers or even Entrepreneurs

Lara Croft —> Archeologist and/or Adventurers (same Character Group as Indiana Jones)

Don Vito Corleone —> Mob Bosses or, more generally, Mobsters

Walter White —> High School Teachers or Drug Kingpins or even Fathers

Katniss Everdeen —> Child Gladiators or Rebels

As you can see, a character may conceivably have multiple Character Groups it can be elevated into, which isn't a bad thing. It simply gives you different directions to take the project.

Regardless, it should be readily apparent how elevating into Character Groups immediately increases story potential beyond just one (or even a handful) of stories. The fact J. K. Rowling went from one child wizard to many child wizards is why she could write another ten thousand pages of *Harry Potter* material in the *Pottermore* digital series (that largely doesn't have anything to do with Harry) and release a whole new film series with *Fantastic Beasts and Where to Find Them.* Not only that, by going from one child wizard to many child wizards created a need for a place to house them — a school — which then became the most iconic location in the entire Storyworld. The best part is she could still tell all her individual stories about Harry himself, but after those stories are complete, there are more stories to tell within the project.

A great character, such as Rocky Balboa, has only had seven stories told about him. However, if you were to make him but one of the many boxers at Mickey Goldsmith's gym, you have more stories to tell. Rocky can still be the main character in the seven feature films, but the other boxers are there for stories to be told across the polyphony of other platforms and mediums.

Likewise, with a character like Iron Man, you can conceivably tell quite a bit of stories about him — let's say you can tell five hundred. When you make a single superhero into a group of superheroes and create the Avengers, you can still tell five hundred stories for Iron Man, but also tell hundreds with the Hulk, Captain America, Thor, Black Widow, and Hawkeye. By elevating into a group, you exponentially increased the amount of stories you can tell.

Likewise, if Luke Skywalker was the only Jedi in the galaxy, you could tell quite a few stories about him. However, you can immediately see how making him just one Jedi in a entire group of Force-wielding warriors (that includes Jedi, Sith and everyone in between) dramatically increases story potential. Additionally, if he was the only person rebelling against the Empire, the story potential is throttled. However, by elevating one rebel to an entire Rebel Alliance, Lucas had Luke's story *plus* the thousands of other stories of the other Rebels including Wedge Antilles, Biggs Darklighter, Grizz Frix, the cast of *Star Wars: Rebels* and the cast of the feature film, *Rogue One.*

Take the movie *Castaway.* That's a timeless, great film; however, because it is about one, solitary character, there's only one story to be told. However, by elevating one guy who crashed on an island to a bunch of people who crashed on an island, the television show *Lost* was able to get 117 episodes across six seasons, a video game, jigsaw puzzles that expanded the story and a host of other interesting East Coast Extensions.

When creating *The Pretender,* Steve Mitchell and his television writing partner focused the show on a single character, Jarod, who escapes from a nefarious facility called the Centre. In one great scene, other characters from the Centre go to Jarod's room to investigate his disappearance. The door to his room is in this expansive hallway that has dozens of other doors. Jarod's room was behind one of them and other Pretenders were presumably behind the others. Though the show only dealt with a single Pretender, that single scene elevated the Pretender character to a Character Group based on craft. Now, as they plan to shift the franchise back into film and television fifteen years later, there are other Pretenders to follow and explore.

Personally, I've always wanted to explore the world of street performers, particularly the ones who impersonate celebrities and fictional characters. I think that would be a fascinating Character Group to write about. I got the idea when I saw a street performer who was wearing a crude, handmade Spiderman costume that probably took him days to stitch. I was intrigued by the mindset of someone who would spend days hand-stitching a costume just to stand on a sidewalk peddling for tips. However, to create a viable Storyworld for my Super Story, I needed to step back from that one character and broaden my view to the entire Character Group — street performer*s*. Said Spiderman impersonator would simply be one character in a greater Character Group and simply one window into a greater universe.

**Creating a group based on the character's Soapbox.**

There may be sometimes when elevating a single character concept into a group based on craft limits your Super Story for one reason or another — typically either because of limitations on scope or on tone. For example, in *Jaws* we have Police Chief Martin Brody. If you were to create a Character Group based on his craft, one cop would turn into many cops. However, because of the small size of the resort town Amity Island (the Definable Location), there simply aren't very many police officers to follow. Because there are only a few police officers in the Storyworld, there are only a few stories to tell.

In this situation, I would suggest not creating the group based on craft, but rather on the character's Soapbox. With Police Chief Martin Brody, his personal Soapbox was all about facing his biggest fear — the water. Therefore, instead of simply having a group of police officers, you could create a group of people who have major, irrational fears and are forced to face them in one way or another. Police Chief Martin Brody would be one story, but with 9,190 people living on Amity Island, you can bet the group made up of people who need to face their biggest fear in order to move on with their lives is a bigger group than the handful of cops you could explore.

Likewise, while you can take Rocky Balboa and create a group of boxers based on his craft, you may not want to necessarily tell that many boxing-related stories. Instead, you can use Rocky's Soapbox dealing with unlikely people chasing their dreams despite the world saying they're unqualified. Rocky is a boxer who is doing it, but this would also include Mark Wahlberg's character from the film, *Invincible* (about the bartender who tries out to play for the Philadelphia Eagles), an inner city kid who wants to become a five-star chef, and a secretary who wants to become a dancer for Philly's premier ballet company.

Though you could elevate Walter White based on craft to other high school teachers and their secret lives, you could also elevate him to a group of middle-aged, suburbanites who break bad for good reasons. This could include teachers, police officers, soccer moms (*Weeds*?), pastors, accountants and everyone in between. Walter White could (and probably should) remain the subject of the drama series, but the other characters could be further explored in other mediums and platforms.

While creating a Primary Character Group based on Soapbox diversifies your tone and subject matter a bit, this type of grouping is more attenuated and will ultimately make it tougher to connect as tightly as if you would have created the group based on craft. However, it remains a viable option when you're developing the main Character Group within your Storyworld.

**The more the merrier.**

Developing your Primary Character Group is a big step forward in the development of your Storyworld. The child wizards are, obviously, a critical and primary Character Group of the Storyworld; however, they are not the only group that exists. There are adult wizards, Dementors, giants, trolls, muggles, etc. Similarly, the Primary Character Group in *The Lord of the Rings* series are the Hobbits. However, there aren't just Hobbits that exist in the Storyworld. There are men, elves, dwarves, trolls, goblins, wizards, orcs, dragons, ents, oliphants, giant eagles, etc. In *Star Wars* there are too many to count. In the *Wire,* there are cops, journalists, gang members, politicians, Baltimore residents, etc. The existence of those other groups not only increases your story potential, but also helps populate and diversify the makeup of your Storyworld.

Recently, a screenwriter pitched me a story he was developing, which was built around this concept:

*An LAPD officer who moonlights as a vigilante with a member of a dangerous Los Angeles gang.*

It sounded like a good story, but in order to be a Super Story, he needed Character Groups. So, we elevated the groups based on craft and instead of one cop, we created a host of cops and instead of a gang member, we created the entire gang. This posed a new problem, however, because where it made sense that one officer would moonlight as a vigilante with one gang member, the writer couldn't wrap his head around why lots of cops would be working with an entire gang; it just didn't seem believable to him.

So, we brainstormed ways to make it work and arrived at the one thing that unites cops and gangs — the fact that if you kill one of their own, they'll go to the ends of the earth hunting you down for justice. That presented an interesting idea of having someone kill cops and gang members in order to unite them on the same side. This led to the idea of a terrorist bombing the LA Marathon, which results in dead cops and dead gang members (or the family members of each). But, we can't just have one terrorist. By elevating to a group based on craft, one terrorist becomes an entire sleeper cell in Los Angeles.

At this point we had cops, gangs and terrorists with the concept growing into this, much more robust, idea:

> *A terrorist cell is active in Los Angeles, bombing the LA Marathon and plotting further attacks. Because of the political climate and the socio-political handcuffs placed on the police, the LAPD can't just kick down the doors of local mosques looking for terrorists. Instead, they begin working with local gangs in LA to help flush the terrorists out in the open where both the police and the gangs can exact their own type of justice.*

Cops versus Terrorists versus Gangs! Not only does that sound awesome, more importantly, it sounds like much more than a single story. I see television, films, video games, books and everything in between within that concept — all because we not only created a Primary Character Group (cops), but also created additional Character Groups to explore (gangs and terrorists).

To fully fill-out, populate and diversify your Storyworld you actually need to develop *nine* standalone groups. Not only do you need nine groups, but to ensure diversity and color amongst your groups, they need to adhere to following certain character alignments, as you will see on the next page. These designations will inform you as to the ethical and moral perspectives of the groups, their motivations, outlook on life and generally how they should act.

1. **Righteous**: This group is squarely on the path of integrity. Conformity, tradition and benevolence are their dominant desires. They believe law and rules are good, and you do good by upholding the law — no matter what.

   Iconic characters who would belong to this alignment would include: Yoda, Superman, Captain America, Captain Jean-Luc Picard, Chief Gordon, Mr. Spock, Shepherd Book, Det. Roger Murtaugh, Briane of Tarth, Ned Stark, Faramir and even Optimus Prime.

2. **Humane**: This group's primary focus is doing good. Benevolence, protection and universalism are their dominant desires. Doing good is more important than upholding the law, but law is not a bad thing.

   Iconic characters who would belong to this alignment would include: Luke Skywalker, Daredevil, Gandalf, Frodo, Wash, Captain Kirk, Aragorn, Raylan Givens, Jack Bauer.

3. **Transcendent**: This group is found on the path of liberty. Universalism and self-direction are their dominant desires. They are rebels and free spirits who are stereotypically found opposing tyrants and other oppressive types. They tend to believe things like order, discipline, and honor can get in the way of doing good. Thanks to their free-spirited, easily bored nature, if the local government isn't considered sufficiently oppressive, they might just go out and find one that is. Or they may believe too much order is bad for *everyone*. Whatever their stance is, they act on their ideals before they let laws get in the way, and sometimes they *dare* the laws to get in the way.

   Iconic characters who would belong to this alignment would include: Det. Martin Riggs, Merry and Pippin, Captain Malcom Reynolds, Qui-Gon, Han Solo, Peter Pan, Batman, Jon Snow, River Tam, Wolverine, Tyrion Lannister.

4. **Orthodox**: This group is on the path of harmony. Security, conformity and tradition are their dominant desires. They are the rule-abiding sort. Law and order is more important than whether you're good or evil. They believe in keeping order, though not necessarily in justice as a universal constant. They'll arrest a robber or rapist, but may also kick a family out of their home for failing to pay rent, even if they are too poor to pay.

   Iconic characters who would belong to this alignment would include: C-3PO, Vito Corleone, Jules Winfield, Hamlet, and Boromir from *The Lord of the Rings*.

5. **Pragmatic**: This group is on the path of equity and does what seems to be a good idea. They don't feel strongly one way or the other when it comes to good vs. evil or law vs. chaos. Most groups in this alignment exhibit a lack of conviction or bias rather than a commitment to neutrality. These types of characters think of good as better than evil — after all, they would rather have good neighbors and rulers than evil ones. Still, they're not personally committed to upholding good in any abstract or universal way. Their only interest is in living their own lives. They simply live their lives, whether that means tearing down a code of laws, following a code of laws, creating an orderly society, causing the breakdown of some kinds of order, or staying away from society altogether. They have no particular objective.

   Iconic characters who would belong to this alignment would include: Jawa, Boba Fett, Jayne Cobb, Rick Blaine, Treebeard the Ent, Mike from *Breaking Bad.*

6. **Autonomous**: This group is on the path of autonomy with self-direction and stimulation being their dominant traits. An autonomous group follows their whims. They are individualists first and last. They value their own liberty, but don't strive to

protect others' freedom. They avoid authority, resent restrictions, and challenge traditions. An autonomous Character Group does not intentionally disrupt organizations as part of a campaign of anarchy. To do so, they would have to be motivated either by good (and a desire to liberate others) or evil (and a desire to make those different from himself actually suffer).

Iconic characters who would belong to this alignment would include: Vic Mackey, Jack Sparrow, Gollum, Jamie Lannister, Tyler Durden, Mr. White from *Reservoir Dogs.*

7. **Ascendent**: This group is on the path to power. Power and security are their dominant desires. An Ascendent Character Group is an evil group who either tries to impose or uphold a lawful system on others without regard for their wishes, and/or adheres to a particular code. They believe in order, but mostly because they believe it is the best way of realizing their evil wishes. They will obey the letter of the law, but not the spirit, and are usually careful about giving their word.

   Iconic characters who would belong to this alignment would include: Emperor Palpatine, Darth Vader, The Borg, Lex Luthor, Magneto, Stephen in *Django Unchained.*

8. **Ambitious**: This group is on the path of supremacy. Achievement and power are their dominant desires. This group will ally with anybody as long as it advances their own interests — and it is *all* about their own interests. These characters do not respect other people as people like themselves with feelings and needs; rather they are tools or obstacles inferior to the Ambitious Character, to be used for their advancement. Characters Groups in this alignment are full of intrinsically selfish people, regardless of whose side they are on, and they may sell out to the bad guy if it makes achieving their goals significantly

easier. Some of the world- shaking ones may seek to tear down an old order, good or bad, to set up their own order — not because their way is better, or for the pleasure of tearing it down, but because they want to be in charge. They will do it using any means at their disposal. Honor, standards and keeping your word is all well and good, *so long as it doesn't get in the way.*

Iconic characters who would belong to this alignment would include: Cersei Lannister, Jabba the Hutt, Biff Tannen, Michel Corleone, Walter White, Littlefinger.

9. **Self-Indulgent**: This group is on the path of luxury with hedonism as their dominant desire. They will do whatever they want, whenever they want to do it, which, seeing as they are evil, usually entails lots of death and destruction.

   Iconic characters who would belong to this alignment would include: The Rancor, the Joker, King Joffrey Baratheon, Smaug, Jason Vorhese, Michael Myers, The Wolf of Wall Street, Clubber Lang, Loki.

Therefore, with the LAPD/gang concept I mentioned above, I would assign the cops to either Righteous or Humane (an argument can be made for either), the gang as Autonomous and the terrorist cell as Self Indulgent. Then, I would need to come up with six additional Character Groups that could be assigned to the six other group alignments. I may list journalists at the LA Times as Pragmatic, local politicians as Ascendent and so on, until all nine alignments have a dedicated Character Group.

Lastly, once you have ideas for all nine alignments, go back to the map of your Definable Location and assign each group a location that operates as a type of "headquarters" for the Character Group. The LAPD would be the police station, the politicians would have City Hall, the gang may be an abandoned warehouse in the Inner City, etc.

Let me just say, at this point in the process, this is intentionally painting the groups with a broad brush. Of course, I understand all the Lannisters in *Game of Thrones* aren't conniving, scheming and self-seeking, but broadly speaking, that isn't an unfair or inaccurate way to describe them in general. In the same way, it's not unfair to say that Hobbits generally love life, food, smoke, lazy days and avoid adventure as much as possible. Of course, there are shades and nuances once you get deep into the Character Group itself, such as the differences between the Tooks and the Baggins. However, at this point, we're only speaking about the group very generally.

By creating Character Groups to fill each of these alignments, your Storyworld begins to be populated with a tremendous assortment of different types of colorful, interesting Character Groups, who have different motivations and different worldviews. This, my friends, is the recipe for drama, which just so happens to be the very cornerstone of all great entertainment.

Not only that, but you have the opportunity to tell hundreds of stories from hundreds of different perspectives across a multitude of platforms. This is where your Super Story really begins to take shape.

WORLD BUILDING IS MY HOBBY AS MUCH AS BUILDING MODEL TRAINS MIGHT BE SOMEONE ELSE'S LUCKILY MY HOBBY DOVETAILS INTO MY PROFESSION WHICH IS WRITING

PATRICK ROTHFUSS

# 9. Storyworlds — part two.

## One half congratulations!

If you're reading or working at a coffee shop in Los Angeles right now, take a minute to look around at all the industry people working around you, crafting and developing their own projects. Take comfort in the fact that even if you stopped here and never read another chapter of this book, your Storyworld and project will almost certainly be more robust, detailed and marketable than all those other projects.

Unless, of course, someone else is reading my book. In that case, take a second to go give them a fist bump. Maybe we should have a secret handshake? If you have any ideas, tweet me at @houston_howard.

At this point, you are halfway through creating the Storyworld for your Super Story. Hopefully, you've gotten some ideas for an unfamiliar, but very definable location that you're able to stretch as big as you can. Lastly, you should have populated it with nine very different character groups.

That takes care of the first four of the eight total elements to a great Storyworld. Let's not stop there, though. There's still quite a bit more to be done in order to have a completely optimized Storyworld, robust enough to uphold the entirety of your Super Story.

## Social Segments and Status Ladders.

Once you have outlined the nine Character Groups that will populate your Storyworld, you're going to now go into each one and break them down into smaller parts based on unique personality identifiers and practical hierarchies. This will ultimately help in a couple of different areas. First it will allow the fans to better connect on a more personal, intimate level with your characters and it will also create a more active fan community on the backend of your project.

## Social segments.

In order to create Social Segments, you'll need to start with your Primary Character Group and horizontally segment it into distinct groups that are easily distinguishable from one another because of their own unique quirks and traits.

For example, in the *Harry Potter* series, the primary Character Group consists of child wizards/magic students at Hogwarts. However, once that single Character Group is established, it is further segmented into different houses — Gryffindor, Hufflepuff, Ravenclaw, and Slytherin — with each house having its own unique spin. Gryffindor is the house for loyal and courageous students, Ravenclaw is the house for quick-witted and book-loving students, Hufflepuff is the house for ~~the nerds~~ loyal, hard-working, diligent students, and Slytherin is the house for ambitious and cunning students. All the houses are still part of one "magic students at Hogwarts" Character Group and are all on the same rung of the social ladder, but their existence allows for some meaningful variations to create color and diversification.

Likewise, the *Hunger Games* series employed the same tactic when Suzanne Collins made the creative decision to split the primary Character Group of "child gladiators" into districts, with each district having its own unique connotation — the career-centric District 1, the technically apt District 3, coal miners of District 12, etc. All the districts are on the same rung of the social ladder, but all have their own unique spin to their citizens and inhabitants.

You can see this even in a television show like *The Office*. In that Storyworld, the primary Character Group is "office employees" who go to work for the Dunder Mifflin paper company. That Character Group is then horizontally segmented into different "departments" — sales, human resources, administration, the warehouse, accounting, etc. — with each department having its own basic personality type that reflects the people who work within them.

Why is this type of micro-segmentation important?

**Birds of a feather.**

There's a psychological and sociological construct called *homophily,* which essentially means "love of the same." Without going too deep into all the nuances surrounding it, homophily is the tendency of individuals to associate and bond with similar others. This concept emerged in the 1950's when they found people who "liked Ike" also liked each other.

Since then, many sociological studies confirm the fact that a person's feelings of comfort, happiness, uncertainty and safety are directly tied to the concept of homophily. For right or wrong, the people we are most comfortable with, most vulnerable around, trust the most and immediately engage with are the people who are most similar to ourselves — geographically, religiously, age-wise, personality-wise, etc. While we're all encouraged to connect and engage with people who are different than us, the fact remains similarity simply breeds a deeper, more personal connection between people.

Therefore, if *all* the students at Hogwarts were like the students in house Gryffindor — charismatic, passionate, decisive and self-sacrificing — a fan who is quiet, shy and who second-guesses himself may not emotionally connect to the characters as well as you'd want as a creator. However, because the students are divided into Social Segments, even though we're all supposed to be rooting for Harry, the existence of house Hufflepuff allows that same fan to find a deeper, more comfortable, more individualized connection to the project. Why? Because now there are also characters in the project who reflect him, his personality, his values and his worldview.

With the release of *The Hunger Games,* Lionsgate actually launched *TheCapitol.pn* website where fans could register themselves as citizens of Panem and receive their own District ID's. As with the sorting hat function of *Pottermore,* the fans were given a "citizenship application" (which basically was a personality test), were assigned to a district and given access to their district's Facebook page. Once there, the fans could help their district receive Capitol favor and keep up with the district's stats and updates via the Capitol. This approach changed fans from simply rooting for Katniss to considering themselves a citizen and supporter of their district and connected them more closely to other fans who were also assigned the same district.

This was completely evident when the first film of *The Hungers Games* premiered. First, all the super fans who attended the midnight showing showed up wearing printed versions of their District ID's. Once there, though, they started finding other fans who were assigned to the same district and, predictably, they hit it off. Why? Homophily — they were all basically the same people. Then, when they transitioned into the theater, the districts began to sit together. When the scene that showed the presentation of the tributes came on, the districts not only rooted for Katniss, but they also cheered the tributes from their own district. Finally, all the districts began rooting for their own district's tributes in the Hunger Games itself. So, for example, when Cato from District 2 killed the guy from District 3, all the District 2 fans cheered and began trash-talking in the theater.

After the theater experience, the homophily didn't stop. The fans could then go to private fan forums that could only be accessed by fans of those particular districts. Everyone could access the main fan forum for *The Hunger Games*, but the fact there were private nooks for the different fans of the different districts created a sense of personalization and exclusivity that created a deeper connection amongst the base.

To me, the psychology of this is fascinating and something we, as Super Story Architects, need to understand and learn how to harness.

**Status ladders.**

Once you have horizontally divided your Primary Character Group into Social Segments, it's time to build in Status Ladders.

Status Ladders basically incorporate a gamification element into the Social Segments. Not only is the Character Group segmented horizontally, but within the segments there should be different vertical levels of statuses held by the characters — basic social hierarchies.

You can find an example of this in *Pirates of the Caribbean,* where there is a very definite hierarchy on the pirate ships — slave, crew, first mate, captain, etc. As you can see, the characters in that setting can move both upward or downward on the Status Ladder without ever moving out of their Social Segment.

As I previously mentioned, J. K. Rowling incorporated Social Segments by having the sorting hat divide the magic students into houses. However, she also employed Status Ladders within the individual houses. First, you have the years in school (first year to seventh year) that initially build the Status Ladder. Additionally, though, starting in the fifth year of school, certain students are chosen as prefects — roles with special authority and responsibility. And even on top of that, a Head Boy and Head Girl are selected and lead all the prefects and, in many cases, the entire Hogwarts student body. So, again, in addition to different segments within the Character Group, each Social Segment will also have its own unique Status Ladder.

You could have this represented within a corporate setting with intern, associate, middle manager, director, and vice president. Or you could build it into a sports setting with a batboy, rookie, backup, starter, and all-star. Any idea that allows the characters within a Character Group and within their Social Segment to either achieve more status or lose status they already have.

Incorporating Status Ladders into the story will give fans the opportunity to achieve similar statuses in the backend community building part of your Super Story. For example, once you're assigned to a house (Social Segment) in the *Pottermore* digital experience, based on your participation and success, you are able to graduate to higher grades, possibly earn the title of prefect and potentially even be awarded Head Boy or Head Girl over your house. This allows the fans to partake in a richer experience, and not only strive for, but actually achieve something.

**Can't this wait?**

Admittedly, these elements will have the most impact in the fan community because fans love them and use them as vehicles to further immerse themselves into the Storyworld. However, that doesn't mean you have the luxury of coming up with these concepts after the Super Story is already complete.

The only reason it's exciting for fans to be assigned to the Gryffindor house is because you see the characters of the books/films being assigned there as well. The reason being assigned a district has meaning is because it's built into the stories. It would be weird to introduce the idea of different houses for the fans if in the books or the films the characters are never actually assigned to houses. Doing so would strip the meaning out of the concept and would come off as a marketing ploy.

For example, there are some websites that have introduced "secondary houses" to your psychological profile — so instead of just being Gryffindor, I can be Burned Gryffindor Primary with a Stripped Ravenclaw Secondary. This means nothing to me as a fan because the primary/secondary distinction and the "burned/stripped" modifiers aren't in the main canon, so they're not special to me in the least.

What this means is Suzanne Collins and J. K. Rowling would have completely missed out on these amazing community building tools had they not made writers-room decisions to actually create Social Segments and Status Ladders.

So, understand early-stage creative decisions will ultimately impact the viability of your fan community. Therefore, be sure to build Social Segments and Status Ladders into your Storyworlds and endeavor to make them a meaningful part of your stories. The more you do, the more you'll thank me later.

## High concept.

A High Concept is the creative mechanism you're going to use to propel your Storyworld from being just an idea to being a *commercially viable* idea. To put it as simply as possible, a High Concept is a *concept that is immediately interesting to someone; one that has obvious potential and can hook someone from the gate.*

Back in the Dark Ages, a published TV Guide was *the* source of all the listings of everything that was going to be on television. They would pack each page with information on channels and times and give each show or movie one line that would be printed in what had to be a font size of four. What executives noticed, though, was the main determining factor in whether people would tune in was that one line of description. Once they realized this, the studios and networks began green-lighting projects that could sound interesting in a single line and actually passing on projects that couldn't.

This was the birth of what has come to be known as the *High Concept.*

It seems simple enough, but I'm shocked at how many low concepts I see on the shelves at a bookstore or at the box office. Like I said before, with the sheer amount of films, television channels, apps, text messages, and magazines, you, as a content creator, are competing with, you have to immediately engage people's interest. If you don't, the audience is moving on to the next thing before you have the opportunity to tell them about your awesome plot twist. If you can't hook them in five seconds, chances are you are stuck in low concept quicksand. If your project is so intricate, so complex, so cerebral that it takes ten minutes to explain, it's nine minutes and 45 seconds past a High Concept. That doesn't mean it's not good, it's just not immediately interesting.

## Isn't it ironic?

What's the difference between high concepts and low concepts? Irony.

Irony is simply defined as receiving the opposite of what you expect, or just something you least expect. It's important, however, to note you shouldn't take irony lessons from Alanis Morrisette's song, *Ironic*, because she'll lead you astray. In the song, she says:

*It's like ten thousand spoons when all you need is a knife.*

That's not irony. That just sucks.

Irony would be: When all you need is a knife, you go to the knife factory and once you arrive, all you find are ten thousand spoons. Do you see the subtle difference? The second, while it doesn't make for a good lyric, sets up an expectation of getting a knife, only to give you the opposite. Another lyric in the song states:

*It's like rain on your wedding day.*

Again, not irony; just a bad day.

Irony would be you're getting married in the Sahara Desert and it rains on your wedding day. Why would that be ironic? Because you don't expect it to rain in the Sahara.

It *is* ironic, however, that an artist with a song titled *Ironic* doesn't understand irony. Maybe Alanis is actually just one step ahead of us all? I doubt it.

So, what you ultimately want is a Storyworld steeped in irony because when it is, the Storyworld concept itself becomes immediately interesting to an audience. Here, then, are two tricks to achieve High Concept irony in a creative concept:

1. Have someone do something you don't expect them to do; *or*

2. Have someone do something you expect them to do, but have them do it in a place you least expect them to be.

If you'll allow me some leeway, I'll explain each of these first within the context of a single story and then after those explanations, I'll show you how to apply them to your Storyworld.

## Have someone do something you least expect.

This method of achieving irony is centered on people being where you expect them to be, but doing things you don't expect them to do.

Let me pitch you a concept.

*Abraham Lincoln, as president, does presidential things.*

Are you hooked? Probably not.

Now, this could be executed to perfection and ultimately be amazing. If it's written by Tarantino, directed by Scorsese and starring Brad Pitt, this could be the greatest film of all time.

However, you want to desperately avoid a concept that relies on execution in order to be great. You need to develop a concept that is immediately interesting to the audience, so their first impression of the project will begin to shade everything else. If you hook them right off the bat with one sentence, they'll be more forgiving if you don't execute to perfection because the coolness of the high concept has made them *want* to love it.

Above all, you want someone to say, "Why didn't I think of that?" This is always the hallmark of a great high concept story.

So, let's change the concept to:

*Abraham Lincoln, as president, spends his nights hunting vampires.*

Wait — what? Abraham Lincoln hunting vampires? Holy smokes! I'm in just based on the concept.

Do you see the difference in those two concepts? Abraham Lincoln is the last guy I would expect hunting vampires, which is exactly why I want to see him (or read about him) doing just that.

What about this one:

*A serial killer who murders innocent people.*

It could be amazing (Tarantino, Scorsese, Pitt), but from a fundamental concept level it doesn't grab me because it's what I expect. However, what if you tweak it to:

*A serial killer who murders serial killers.*

We've just invented *Dexter,* which is awesome. It's awesome because of the irony of Dexter doing something you wouldn't normally expect a serial killer to do — kill serial killers.

Picture this:

*A guy falls in love with a girl.*

Nothing special. So, let's add some irony:

*A guy falls in love with the female operating system on his phone.*

Um, what? That evokes a response the first one doesn't because you don't expected someone to fall in love with Siri, especially Joaquin Phoenix. This was the beauty of *Her.*

Let's take away the OS angle for now, but stick with the guying falling in love with a girl. Let's try this:

*An emotionally-stunted man falls in love with a girl.*

You don't expect an emotionally-stunted person to be emotionally vulnerable enough to fall in love, so that's a little better. But let's keep going after more irony.

*An emotionally-stunted New York business man falls in love on a business trip with a girl from Los Angeles.*

Not only do you have the "emotionally-stunted/in-love" opposites, but now we've continued to make it more ironic by adding geographical opposites into the concept. Immediately the concept becomes higher, but let's go one step further.

*An emotionally-stunted Wall Street tycoon falls in love on a business trip with a street hooker from Los Angeles.*

*Pretty Woman* anyone?

We have the "emotionally-stunted/in-love" opposites, the geographic/ cultural opposites and now economic status opposites.

Having someone do something you don't expect them to do in a place you actually expect them to be is the root of the success of IP's such as:

- *Armageddon:* Oil riggers saving the world from a giant asteroid hurtling through space.

- *Breaking Bad:* High school teacher becoming the world's most notorious drug dealer.
- *R.E.D:* Old people assassins.
- *Daredevil:* Blind man who is a superhero.
- *Ted:* Foul-mouthed, lecherous teddy bear.
- *Slumdog Millionaire:* The title says it all, right?
- *Human Centipede*: The same with this.
- *Hancock:* A drunk guy who is a superhero.
- *Kung-Fu Panda:* Fat panda as a Kung Fu master.
- *Straight Outta Compton:* A group of young black men from South Central who have everything stacked against them in life yet still become industry moguls.
- *Ant Man*: A grown man, who is the size of an ant, but is also a superhero.
- *Toy Story*: Toys that come to life.
- *Indian in the Cupboard*: Same thing.
- *Night at the Museum*: Same thing, except museum exhibits instead of toys.
- *Zootopia:* Animals living like humans.
- *Rocky:* Untrained leg-breaker going toe-to-toe with the big, bad champ.
- *Star Wars:* Farm boy taking down the Empire.
- *8 Mile:* White kid from the trailer park out-rapping all of the black guys in Detroit.
- *Lord of the Rings:* Smallest person in the world is tasked with saving it.
- *The Passion of the Christ:* The son of a blue-collar carpenter saves the world.
- *The Hunger Games:* Kids who are forced to kill each other as gladiators.
- *Suicide Squad:* Bad guys saving the day.
- *Deadpool:* An R-rated superhero.
- *Captain America Civil War:* Good guys fighting each other.
- *Batman v Superman:* Same thing.

**Put someone in a place you don't expect them to be.**

The second method of engineering a High Concept is rooted in the traditional "fish out of water" concept. In it, there is someone doing things you actually expect that person to do, *but in a place you don't expect them to be.*

For example, take a concept such as:

*A street-hustlin' kid from the projects who hustles, cons and charms his way around West Philadelphia.*

While this could be great upon execution, there's nothing ironic about it to pique your interest; however, if you take the street-hustlin' kid out of his normal environment and put him somewhere you least expect him to be, you get *The Fresh Prince of Bel Air*:

*A street-hustlin' kid from the projects of West Philly, who is sent to live with his aunt and uncle in Bel Air.*

He is still doing the things you expect him to do — hustle, con and charm his way in and out of trouble — but because he's doing it somewhere you least expect him to be, it's funnier and more interesting. Hustling, conning and charming your way in and out of trouble in West Philly is simply a way of life and day-to-day survival. In Bel Air, it's the makings of an iconic and generational television show.

Let's try another one:

*A rich, ditzy airhead spends her days shopping and doing featherbrained things around Beverly Hills.*

This could be interesting, but let's try and take her outside of her normal environment and drop her somewhere you least expect her to be. Where would you least expect a Beverly Hills airhead to be?

*A rich, ditzy, Beverly Hills airhead goes to Harvard Law School.*

The simple creative choice of taking her out of where you would expect her to be and putting her somewhere you least expect her to be took the concept from "low concept that could be good based on execution" to "immediately engaging high concept that ultimately launched a half a billion dollar franchise."

I want to briefly talk about *Sharknado* and explain how the creators used this style of high concept to ultimately make ~~the worst movies ever made~~ a sustainable career and great living for themselves. When the writers and creators first pitched the concept to SyFy they pitched it as:

*Santa Monica floods and when the ocean waters rise in the city, the sharks begin to eat people as they escape.*

The SyFy executives passed because they felt like it didn't hook them enough. The writers, though, went home and re-conceptualized it as:

*Tornadoes begin in the Pacific Ocean and suck sharks up into their funnels. Then, when the tornadoes move into Santa Monica, sharks shoot out and fall from the sky, eating people along the way.*

The went back and pitched it to the same executives at SyFy, who immediately acquired it and sent it to be developed. Why were they more hooked with the second concept than the first? Because they took something (sharks) out of their normal environment (oceans) and put them somewhere you least expect them to be (falling from the sky). They're still doing what you expect them to do (eat people), but the fact the environment was shifted created the High Concept.

So the fact they tweaked their idea and were able to engineer a High Concept, they were able to not only make *Sharknado,* but also *Sharknado 2: The Second One, Sharknado 3: Oh Hell No, Sharknado 4: The 4th Awakens, Sharknado: The Heart of Sharkness* and *Sharknado: The Video Game.* They literally took the fish out of water and ended up with a franchise. You may scoff at the ridiculous nature of the *Sharknado* franchise, but I'd bet dollars to donuts you wouldn't reject their paychecks or their steady, full-time career as writers and filmmakers.

The power of having people do the things you expect them to do, but in a place you don't expect them to be has been the root of many great concepts, including:

- *Kindergarten Cop:* Giant Austrian FBI agent undercover in a kindergarten class.
- *The Internship:* Two technologically-inept middle-aged guys working in the mecca of technology — the actual Google campus.
- *Back to the Future*: A kid from the present in the 1950's.
- *My Cousin Vinny:* The most New York lawyer ever (Joe Pesci) in a bucolic Tennessee town.
- *Coming to America*: The prince of Zamunda looks for love, not in his wealthy African nation, but in Queens.

- *School of Rock*: A stoned out rocker in an elite and ritzy private elementary school.
- *21 Jump Street*: Adult cops undercover in high school.
- *Freaky Friday*: An adult in a kid's body and a kid in an adult's body.
- *Big:* A kid in an adult's body.
- *The Martian*: A scientist stuck on Mars.
- *Beverly Hills Cop*: A brash, loudmouthed Detroit cop working in Beverly Hills.
- *Austin Powers:* A British, hipster secret agent from the 1960's in modern day.
- *City Slickers*: Manhattan yuppies on a cattle ranch.
- *Ratatouille:* Rat in a kitchen.
- *Sister Act*: Vegas showgirl in a convent.
- *Inside Out:* People inside someone's head.

Understanding the power of High Concept completely takes your entertainment to new levels and once you recognize the mechanics of it, you can't stop seeing it in commercial entertainment.

Don't get me wrong, though. A High Concept will still rely on execution to be *good*, but that's not what I'm focusing on at this point. I'm saying a High Concept won't rely on execution to be *immediately interesting* to a potential investor, producer, actor, audience member, or reader. If you achieve immediate interest with your concept, you'll still have to deliver the goods on the backend or your project will ultimately disappoint.

We all saw this with *Cowboys vs. Aliens,* which was a fantastic High Concept (people doing things you wouldn't expect them to do — cowboys are supposed to fight Indians, not aliens) that made everyone say, "Why didn't I think of that?" Ultimately, despite creating a huge amount of interest and buzz, it ended up underperforming due to a lack of execution.

Bottomline: A High Concept gets people initially interested in exploring/reading/watching/playing/listening to your project, but great execution is what will ultimately make it successful. You shouldn't have one or the other, because you'll ultimately need them both.

A filmmaker once asked me to read a short film script and when I asked him what it was about he said:

*A heroin addict wakes up from a high only to find his addict girlfriend dead from an overdose. Forlorn, he decides to overdose himself and join her in death.*

I was being very honest when I told him I wasn't interested in reading it. Apart from sounding like the most depressing story on earth, I wasn't interested because junkies overdosing doesn't come as a surprise — I, unfortunately, expect it. When he asked me how to fix it, I simply said, "Who's the person you would least expect to wake up and find their significant other dead from a heroin overdose." When he couldn't come up with an answer, I offered the President of the United States.

Look at how much more interesting the concept becomes:

*The President of the United States wakes up to find the First Lady — dead from a heroin overdose. Not only did she have a habit with the Dragon he didn't know about, but now she's dead — and he doesn't know what the hell to do.*

Immediately, this is a thousand times more interesting and it was just a simple creative change that took all of five seconds to come up with. Honestly, if he pitched me this concept, I would have immediately read the script! And here's the sad part: as I was prepping to write this book, I actually went back and read that filmmakers original, low-concept script — and it was great. I mean, really, really well written.

The dialogue was great, as was his characterization, but I would have never known because the concept didn't intrigue me enough to want to read it. However, if he was able to write a low concept script that well, just think how he could write the high concept version! It would have been equally as great — and it would have been more commercially viable and appealing to both buyers and audiences.

## Attaching the High Concept to a Storyworld.

Now that you're familiar with what a High Concept is and how to form one, let's start using it in conjunction with applying it to a Storyworld. Again, with Storyworlds, we're thinking much broader than individual characters, considering locations, and now are putting together opposites in order to heighten irony.

Once you attach the High Concept to the Storyworld itself, you should ultimately be able to describe it in this way:

This is a **[TYPE OF DEFINABLE LOCATION]** where **[IRONIC THINGS HAPPEN]**

For example, if I were describing Neverland, the Storyworld of *Peter Pan*, it would read like this:

*This is a faraway fantasy land where people don't age and kids are kids forever.*

The Definable Location is a "faraway fantasy land" and because we expect people to age, people not aging and kids never growing up are things you don't expect people to do. This, therefore, creates irony and, thus, a High Concept Storyworld.

The key to applying a High Concept to a Storyworld is making the High Concept, what I call, *systemic* — making it so prevalent the High Concept metastasizes and works its way into "the bones" of the Definable Location in such a way it affects everyone and no one can escape its influence or impact. You can actually accomplish this in a couple of different ways, the first of which is the most preferable:

1. Act of God
2. Grow the Group

**Act of God**

"Act of God" is when you (as a creator, you are a type of "god" for your Super Story) apply a large-scale, sociological, biological, technological, political, environmental or meteorological change to the Storyworld in such a way it impacts the entirety of the Definable Location as well the lives of *every* Character Group residing there. Act of God High Concept is bigger than a single Character Group, typically involves something out of the control of the characters in the stories and results in nearly everyone doing things they wouldn't normally do.

A really great example of a *political* Act of God High Concept is found in *The Purge* franchise:

*This an alternate United States where all crime is legal for one night a year.*

The Definable Location is the United States and the High Concept is people are *allowed* to *commit crimes,* which is them doing something you wouldn't expect them to do (we expect crime to be punished). Because the High Concept affects everyone — people committing crimes and people trying to survive the night — it becomes systemic in the Definable Location. No matter who you follow in the Storyworld or where you go, the High Concept will remain, which means every part will be interesting.

Similarly, in *The Last Days of American Crime,* as a final response to terrorism and crime, the U.S. government plans to secretly broadcast a signal making it impossible for anyone to knowingly commit unlawful acts. During the countdown to the broadcast, the country turns into a veritable Sodom and Gomorrah with everyone committing every crime they can before crime itself becomes a thing of the past. Again, this is a political alteration to the Definable Location that affects everyone in the Storyworld, criminals and non-criminals alike. You can follow various characters, multiple Character Groups, go to multiple locations and the High Concept still remains intact.

The television show, *Colony,* is set in modern day Los Angeles, but it's modern day Los Angeles that is being occupied by aliens. The aliens have built an enormous wall, close to thirty stories tall and probably twenty feet thick, around the central part of Los Angeles, and similar walls around other major cities (now called "Blocs"). The military occupation changes day-to-day life for everyone in the Definable Location, not just a few characters or simply select Character Groups.

Likewise, the book (and series), *The Man in the High Castle,* is set in modern day United States, but it's a modern day United States controlled by Nazi Germany and Japan after World War II had a different result. Because Nazis controlling the United States (people doing things you wouldn't normally expect them to do) impacts the entirety of the United States and every citizen therein, the High Concept remains intact no matter where you go or who you follow within the Storyworld.

An example I love is the Storyworld of the television show, *The Leftovers.* In the show, 2 percent of the world's population disappears (something you don't expect people to do), which obviously affects the entire world. Because it's such a large-scale event (140 million people disappearing across the world), no matter where you go in the Definable Location and no matter who you follow, you find the High Concept. Everything and everyone has been touched and marked by this tragedy, which means there is maximum freedom in exploiting the High Concept throughout the entire project.

Likewise, in the show *Lost,* because the entire island was mystical and "alive," the showrunners could follow any character, any Character Group (the survivors, the Others, the Dharma Initiative, the Man in Black etc.), and go anywhere on the island without ever leaving the High Concept.

Recently, I helped a group of writers develop a Storyworld where, because of an environmental disaster, all the groundwater in the world is contaminated and can't be consumed. Rainwater, however, is clean and if the characters can catch it before it hits the ground, it's drinkable. This causes the entire world's economy to shift and actually run on the collection, trade and sale of rainwater. Because this alteration to the Storyworld impacts the entire Definable Location and results in every Character Group within doing something they wouldn't normally do (revolve their lives around catching, trading, selling, or even stealing rainwater), it's become systemic in the largest way possible and allows them maximum exploitation of the High Concept.

A great by-product of using an Act of God High Concept Storyworld is, depending on how much irony there is, it could also serve as the catalyst for your Storyworld's Unfamiliarity. An America controlled by Nazis is unfamiliar, a world economy run on clean water is unfamiliar, a world where people disappear is unfamiliar, etc. So, in this way, a great Act of God High Concept can actually check a couple of different Storyworld boxes simultaneously.

**Grow the Group**

What if, though, you need to create a High Concept Storyworld, but don't want to use the Act of God to create such a large-scale, sweeping change? This is when you need to attach the High Concept to the Storyworld by creating and growing a High Concept Character Group to the point it becomes systemic.

If you have an idea for a High Concept character, you need to start by multiplying that character into a Character Group, then continue to make that group large enough to make the High Concept systemic in the Storyworld. For example, the *Fresh Prince of Bel Air* is a great High Concept story, but not a High Concept Storyworld.

If we elevate the Fresh Prince to a group, while making sure we maintain the High Concept, we get *The Beverly Hillbillies.* It's the same High Concept, and we have more story potential once we elevate to a group, but I don't think it's big enough to make the entire Storyworld High Concept. However, if I were to continue to enlarge the group, it could become hundreds (or even thousands) of people who you wouldn't expect to be there. The concept then could form into something like this:

*To the outside world, Bel Air and Beverly Hills are pristine places full of the richest, So-Cal elite. However, what people don't realize is all of these "perfect people" have extremely imperfect extended family members from bizarre places who are constantly showing up on their doorsteps.*

By continually growing the High Concept from individual character, to a group, to a huge group, we eventually cause it to become so systemic in the world it makes the Storyworld seem much more interesting and engaging than before.

For example, the Storyworld for the ABC show, *Once Upon a Time*, can be described as such:

*Storybook is a quaint, modern-day New England small town where every fairytale character ever created is living in exile.*

We have a Definable Location (a small town in New England) and we have characters (fairytale characters) in a place you least expect them to be (in our world — not fairytale land), which is the High Concept. If it was just one fairytale character, it would be a single High Concept story, but not a High Concept Storyworld. Growing the High Concept character into a group and then increasing the size of that group eventually causes the High Concept to become systemic in Storybook. Now the Storyworld itself is a High Concept.

How big you need to grow the group will ultimately depend on how broad your geographical boundaries to your Definable Location are. The bigger the Definable Location, the bigger the High Concept Character Group needs to be to make the High Concept systemic in the Storyworld.

*The Omen* is a great High Concept movie because you don't expect kids to be demonic and evil (I can hear people now saying, "Well, you haven't seen my kids!"); however, the Storyworld itself is a low concept. If you simply elevate the demonic, evil kid character to a Character Group, and grow that group to 50 or 60 children, you end up with *The Children of the Corn,* which has a great High Concept Storyworld because the High Concept is systemic:

*A small town ruled by evil, murderous, cultish children.*

However, if the Definable Location isn't a small town, but New York City, a group of 50 or 60 demonic children wouldn't be big enough to make the High Concept systemic. Given the size of the Definable Location, you may have to grow the group to 5000 or 6000 demonic children in order to make it feel like the Storyworld itself is High Concept.

One more example — in the Netflix original series, *Travelers,* the High Concept centers on people (called "travelers") from the future, traveling to the past in order to stop the impending apocalypse (an example of Ironic Location). One time traveler would technically be a High Concept, but we need a group. So, instead of just dealing with a single traveler, the series primarily centers on a group of five. However, even though we have a Character Group, five travelers isn't enough to make the entire Storyworld (our present day world) seem High Concept. How did the showrunners remedy that? They had the primary group be just one of hundreds, if not thousands, of different groups of travelers who have already travelled back in time. Now, the world itself seems intrinsically High Concept because everyone you see could possibly be a traveler from the future.

Two writers pitched me a really interesting comic book recently that had a fantastic, High Concept Storyworld. The Definable Location is Atlanta, but it's an Atlanta where white folks, black folks, Asians and Hispanics all get along (High Concept already, right?). However, that's not even the best part.

While those racial groups have solved all their racism issues, everyone, and I mean everyone, hates the Clowns.

Yes, the Clowns.

In this Atlanta, you can be born white, black, asian, hispanic and you can also be born as another race — Clowns. It's a weird genetic mutation, so your parents may be white, but you may be born a happy clown or a sad clown, with a red nose or big feet. Everyone hates the Clowns so much the Clowns have their own ghetto in Atlanta called Clown Town.

Outside of any individual story, I was fascinated by this High Concept Storyworld and wanted to explore it. Why? Simply because I don't expect people to be born as clowns.

Given the two ways to attach a High Concept to a Storyworld, why do I consider the Act of God method superior to Growing the Group? The reason is you create the High Concept around a singular Character Group, you will still always need to involve that Character Group in your stories in order to preserve the High Concept. This, ultimately, limits your narrative freedom.

For example, in the project where you can be born as a clown in Atlanta, the writers on that project will always need to have clowns in their stories in some way. If they don't, Atlanta is just regular Atlanta and the story isn't as interesting? This is because when the High Concept is attached to a singular Character Group and you don't include that Character Group in a story, that story is necessarily being told *outside* the High Concept.

Can you imagine a *Children of the Corn* story that only deals with adults? Of course not? Because the High Concept is attached to one Character Group, even though it's been grown to a point where it's systemic, any story outside of the Character Group will always be operating out of the most interesting part of your Storyworld — the High Concept.

In *Game of Thrones,* it doesn't matter if I follow the Lannisters, the Starks, the Wildlings, the Dothraki, the whores in Littlefinger's brothel or the White Walkers, the Storyworld consistently remains interesting because the High Concept is applied well beyond just a single Character Group.

At the end of the day, both are viable methods of attaching a High Concept to a Storyworld. It really just depends on the particulars and the scope of your individual project. The most important thing is you ensure your Storyworld has a High Concept and you attach it to the Storyworld in some way. When you do, it will attract and interest fans of all kinds to want to visit your Storyworld and continue to explore over time.

## Special Sauce.

I'm going to make a bold statement. If you endeavor to come up with a completely original idea, new in every way, there's a 99.9 percent chance you're going to fail. I'll leave a 0.1% chance of God blessing you with an original idea, but outside of that, it's practically impossible to find a story that hasn't been told, a character that hasn't been written, or a setting that hasn't been used.

You may be thinking, "Dude, you're wrong. You've never seen anything like my idea before."

That's cute. Wrong, but cute. If I can prove *The Matrix* is pretty much the same movie as *Monsters, Inc.,* I bet I can connect your idea to something that's been done before.

But here's the good news: we don't need to come up with completely original ideas in order for our Super Stories to become successful.

If you're stuck on being completely original, especially with your Storyworld, you'll get frustrated and won't create anything. Rather, simply learn how to be *fresh and clever* and you'll save yourself loads of unnecessary discontent.

Don't be afraid to start with ideas that have been done before. First of all, do it better (without getting sued, of course). Secondly, once you start putting in your own twists and turns, ideas, and new ways of doing things, you'll be amazed at how different it will seem.

This is what I'm talking about when I refer to the seventh element on the Storyworld list — *Special Sauce.* This is simply adding some cool twists to an idea (in this case a Storyworld) that has been used before.

Did the McDonald's corporation shy away from making a Big Mac even though other restaurants made and sold hamburgers? No. Why? The Big Mac is different because of the Special Sauce. Even though everything else on the burger is similar to other products, the addition of the special sauce makes the Big Mac unique.

So, in the same way, if you find yourself developing a concept for a Storyworld that has been done before, all you need is a splash of Special Sauce to be unique.

The Storyworld of *The Matrix* franchise is very similar to the Storyworld of *The Terminator* franchise in that they both show a future where machines take over. Did that stop the Wachowskis from using the idea? Obviously not. So, how did they freshen it up? They added the whole "use the humans as batteries and keep them locked in a virtual reality" angle. That was their Special Sauce and it was so good, it didn't have a hint of being a retread even though James Cameron envisioned *The Terminator* Storyworld fifteen years before *The Matrix* came about.

The *Firefly* franchise needed a Special Sauce to separate its space-based Storyworld from other franchises set in future space, such as *Star Trek, Star Wars,* and *Battlestar Galactica.* What's the Special Sauce? No aliens, a very distinct Wild West flare, and witty banter.

George Lucas designed his space-based Storyworld with the Special Sauce of looking old and worn and actually being set in the past, instead of the future. That immediately set it apart from *Star Trek* and *2001: A Space Odyssey* and freshened the concept to a uniquely marketable level.

*Transformers* takes place in a Storyworld where aliens crash-land on earth. What's the Special Sauce that sets it apart from the hundreds of other alien stories that deal with a similar setting? The fact that these aliens are robots that can, well, transform into vehicles.

In the aforementioned Netflix original series, *Travelers*, their basic concept is centered around time travel, which has been done thousands of times across multiple mediums and platforms. However, in this series, instead of someone's entire body time-traveling, the consciousness is the only thing travels — and ultimately lands in the body of a "host" mere seconds before they are supposed to die. Moreover, instead of being able to travel throughout all of time, they are limited to traveling back to years when modern computers are in operation. These two simple creative tweaks freshen up a somewhat tired concept very nicely.

The concept of our *Fury* franchise immediately calls to mind films such as *Running Man*, *Arena*, *Gamer*, *Death Race,* and *The Hunger Games* because it plays on the concept of people being forced into a violent life-or-death competition against their will. We didn't let that deter us, though. We simply applied our Special Sauce: the psychological perspective that by experiencing pain and anger, people actually become stronger, better people. Therefore, by forcing the patients to tap into their own inner pain and rage, the antagonist truly feels he's not only helping them, but also doing the world a service.

In our *City of Refuge* project, we have the concept of a small, country town overrun by violent, big city criminals, but we needed a Special Sauce to take it to the next level. So, we added a neat legal twist. Instead of just simply being overrun by criminals, like *Escape from New York,* we turned the small, country town of Always into a legally sanctioned sanctuary city for criminals. Once a criminal crosses the border into the town, he can live freely within the confines of the town. If he crosses back over, he can be nabbed and punished for his original crime. This interesting legal mechanism not only gave the town a stronger purpose, but it gave the entire project a Special Sauce that made it unique.

However, don't think it will always take a lot of Special Sauce to make your project fresh.

With the *Twilight* franchise, Stephanie Myers found herself operating in a Storyworld concept that has been done hundreds of times. However, she simply made her *Twilight* vampires sparkle in sunlight instead of melting or burning or turning to ashes. Moreover, instead of them being soul-less, emotionless beasts like all the other vampire concepts, she had them be super "emo" lovers. Just those two small twists, made if feel like a completely fresh vampire Storyworld.

When my partner, Steve Mitchell, was co-creating *Tin Man* (which is an adaptation of the *Wizard of Oz*), he simply made it a darker, more adult and more contemporary Oz. Not only that, but he made fans care about the Wicked Witch in a way the original book and/or film don't accomplish. It's still the *Wizard of Oz*, but with a couple of tweaks, it feels completely new. And it was the highest-rated programming SyFy has ever done, so it must have worked.

In his remake of the *Dawn of the Dead*, Zack Snyder freshened up a tired setting by simply making the zombies run fast — like freak Olympic-sprinter fast. It wasn't a huge change, but it really made his Storyworld stand out. *World War Z* utilized the same mechanic and even added an extra — not only do the zombies run fast, but the virus can spread and turn people at a much faster rate, which makes the zombies rapidly multiply like psychotic bugs.

A short time ago, I was working on a project centered on a gritty, inner-city Storyworld where gangs are at war — think *The Wire*. I needed something that would separate my gritty, inner-city Storyworld from the ten thousand other projects that have similar Storyworlds. So, I simply made one quick change: The 2nd Amendment has been repealed and guns have disappeared from civilian society, therefore, the gang members protect themselves by carrying swords.

Boom. *mic drop*

All of a sudden, this became a gritty inner-city Storyworld that seems *completely* fresh and new. It's still the inner-city, there are still gangs at war, but that one twist of Special Sauce helps set it off from the pack.

## Figure out why?

One important thing, though, is to make sure your Special Sauce exists for a reason. Especially with our overly-analytical culture, you can't just leave it with a "just because" answer.

If it's super science, magic, or unique political situations, force yourself to make them as credible as you can because if you don't, audiences will sniff it out in a heartbeat and write your project off as a big, fat cheese ball.

Watch the difference.

> *"Why do your zombies run fast when all other zombies I've ever seen stumble around like drunken hobos?"*
>
> *"Um, because they just do. Accept it."*

Lame. Also, you probably lost a fan. Good work.

Let's try it again.

> *"Why do your zombies run fast when all other zombies I've ever seen stumble around like drunken hobos?"*
>
> *"Because these zombies are being completely driven by their nervous systems. When their nervous systems kick into high gear, it overrides everything else, even their rotting muscles, and they end up running really fast."*
>
> *"Oh, okay. Cool."*

See the difference?

It doesn't matter that zombies don't actually exist. Just the fact you're making it seem like they do requires some sort of explanation and justification. If not, you torpedo your own verisimilitude. Audiences want to believe, but you have to give them something credible to believe in.

If possible, build the "credible" justification into your project and dramatize it so the audiences won't even have to ask for an explanation. If it's not possible, at least be prepared to explain the justification of the Special Sauce at some point, because at some point the audience will throw a red flag and ask for it.

So, play around with your rough Storyworld concept and find your Special Sauce recipe. Once you have it, start applying it. You may need to drench your concept in it or maybe you just need a dash. Whatever the amount, use enough to make a Storyworld concept that has been used before fresh, unique, and *seem* original.

## Room for History.

The eighth and last element of a great Storyworld is focused on your ability to get a *history* out of your newly created world. Similar to your geographical boundaries, the more Room for History for your Storyworld, the more stories you'll be able to extract from it.

Think about it.

American history books are just big, fat anthologies of stories from our Storyworld's past (the fact that they're usually told in the most boring way possible is a whole other topic). If the US was only five years old, the history books would be much thinner because there wouldn't be as many stories to tell.

This is very similar to expanding the geographical boundaries of your Storyworld. However, instead of enlarging physical locations to accommodate more stories, you're expanding the time surrounding your Storyworld in order to accommodate more stories.

As a storyteller, you want the ability to move backward *and* forward in time. You don't want to get stuck just moving one direction on a timeline. For example, in *Game of Thrones,* George R.R. Martin (and the television showrunners) have pretty much told all the stories they've wanted to tell moving forward on the timeline. Now, however, they're discussing new books and a new television series that goes back in time to act as a sort of prequel series.

"I do have thousands of pages of history of everything that led up to *Game of Thrones,*" Martin said. "So, there's a lot more material there for us to decide where to take the franchise."

Without that history, there wouldn't be anywhere to go once the original book series and the television series ended.

Let's say your Storyworld is a hotel and you make the creative decision to have it be a new hotel that was built last week. Based on that decision, you're not going to be able to mine for stories in the past, which will ultimately limit you creatively in the development process.

Can you tweak it to where the hotel was just started last week, but the original building the characters are using for the hotel is hundreds of years old? Just doing that could open your setting up to some interesting stories moving forward.

Instead of the new *W* hotel in Hollywood, can you make it the Chateau Marmont? If so, you can still tell all the new stories you want to tell moving forward in your timeline, but now you can tell stories from its history — like how Johnny Depp and Kate Moss had sex in every room on a dare, how Howard Hughes was the peeping-Tom-in-residence, how Clark Gable and Jean Harlow had an affair during Harlow's honeymoon, how Dennis Hopper was known to throw orgies there, and how John Belushi died there.

You see? You were going to miss out on all those great stories.

Think about your Storyworld and where you want to start. Make sure you can move backward on your Storyworld's historical timeline as well as forward. If you can do both easily, you're doing yourself a big favor. You don't have to have ten thousand years of narrative history like *Halo*, just the more the better.

More history, more stories. More stories, more legs. More legs, more revenue. It's simple.

## The fictional world.

At this point in the process, you can start mining your Storyworld for depth and complexity. It should stand to reason if you're creating a wholly fictional world you'll have more details to work out than if you have a regular, run-of-the-mill earth-based Storyworld.

For example, creating Pandora from *Avatar* presents more complexity than Gotham City in *Batman* because even though Gotham City is technically fictional, it's still governed by the normal rules of earth (physics, atmosphere, societal structure, etc.). In the same way, creating Gotham City will be more complex than simply using New York City, since New York City actually exists. Conversely, completely fictional worlds will always warrant special consideration because they actually don't exist. This goes for *Star Wars'* Tattooine and even *The Happiness Factory* setting from Coca-Cola. This is what J. R. R. Tolkien called the development of the "secondary world."

The more unique details you work out for your world, the more it will come alive creatively and the less likely contradictions and continuity problems will pop up. You don't have to work it all out down to the atomic level, though some fantasy authors may disagree. I'm of the mind you simply have to make it believable for the fans. They *want* to set aside their disbelief, but if you don't at least present some plausible explanation for the most important and interesting details of a fictional setting, they'll ditch your project in a Na'vi minute.

Here is a list of some special items to consider when creating your completely fictional Storyworld:

1. **Type**: Basically, what type of world is it? Is it terrestrial, a satellite gas giant, artificial, part of an asteroid belt?
2. **Government**: Is the planet controlled under one government or many? Is it anarchy, tribal law, feudalism, competing states, etc.?
3. **Terrain**: What is the dominant terrain for the planet? Barren, cave, crater field, desert, forest, glacial, ocean?
4. **Gravity**: Is the gravity of the world light, standard, or heavy?
5. **Atmosphere**: Is the atmosphere breathable by humans? Do they need breathing suits?
6. **Hydrosphere**: Is your world arid, dry, moderate, moist, or completely saturated?
7. **Temperature**: Is the planet searing or frigid? If it's tide-locked it could be both.
8. **Length of Day:** Twelve hours, twenty-four hours, thirty-six hours, two hundred hours?
9. **Length of Year**: Seventy-five days, three hundred seventy-five days, five hundred days?
10. **Population**: Is it sparsely populated, densely populated, or somewhere in between?
11. **Technology Level**: Is it mainly the Stone Age or is the world super advanced?
12. **Sentient Species:** Who are the native species of the planet? Are there others who have colonized?
13. **Other Life:** What are the main animal species, as well as plants, bacteria, and viruses?

## Whew.

By now you've spent quite a few long, grueling hours laying the foundation for your Super Story. It's been tough and challenging and even though your project is well on its way to being primed for mainstream success, your head probably hurts and you're probably fairly exhausted.

Hopefully, this has excited and challenged you at the same time. If you're miserable and resent me at this point, then maybe you should stick to being *just* a screenwriter, novelist, producer or playwright. :-)

For those of you who have embraced the challenge, it only gets better from here. We've leveled the ground, laid the foundation, and now it's time to start framing up this gigantic 90,000-square-foot house.

# WHAT IS HISTORY BUT A FABLE AGREED UPON

NAPOLEON

# 10. Macro-Story.

## The story of your world.

At this point, we've spent loads of time developing a Soapbox and using it to construct an optimized Storyworld. Pulling on some of that work, I want you to remember what you read just a couple of pages ago (and if you don't remember, try to eat right, get a better night's sleep and exercise regularly) — one of the elements of a viable Storyworld is building in Room for History. Since you've made room for the history, now it's time to actually create the history.

As the horrors of junior year history class flood your mind, just know you won't simply be creating any old, boring, run-of-the-mill ~~encyclopedia~~ Wikipedia entry for your Storyworld. Instead, you'll be telling an epic story, using the history of the Storyworld you just created. It's creating history in a *dramatic* way.

So ask yourself a question, since it's called a Storyworld, "What actually is the *story* of my *world?*"

Geez, that sounds like a big story.

Well, yes. This is why it's called a Macro-Story — "macro" means "large-scale or overall." We'll tell small, intimate stories soon enough, but right now we're focused on going really stinkin' big.

## Fight the fatigue.

When you watch, read, listen to or play stories that are part of a large-scale narrative, there are two stories being told — the story about the characters, which is right in front of you, and the story *behind* that story, which solely pertains to the Storyworld itself. The second/background story is what I affectionately refer to as the Macro-Story.

To have your Super Story hit on all cylinders and fight against audience fatigue, you need *both* of the stories progressing simultaneously, albeit at different speeds.

It shouldn't come as a surprise when I say comic book superheroes hold a unique and unprecedented place in fictional entertainment. There is no other category in entertainment in which concepts like *Thor*, *Hulk*, *Iron Man* and *Captain America* have been near-weekly centers of new stories, going on more than half a century in Marvel's case. So maybe as comic book readers, we're all conditioned to believe superheroes are impervious to trends. However, there is a small grumbling about the national and global mood shifting to 'eh' the way it once did with the Western.

The press and even some fans already have a common term used to describe the theoretical symptoms that will eventually cause the passing of the superhero movie – "Marvel fatigue." The "fatigue" premise goes like this: given the dominate box office profile the sub-genre has held for the last several years and the proliferation of superheroes to come over the next five years (at minimum), moviegoers have slowly begun to get generally bored and will eventually stop going, at least in the same numbers they do now.

This seems plausible to me. Too much of the same thing eventually gets boring. However, despite the mass proliferation of *Star Wars* media that has been promulgated over the past few decades, with no signs of slowing down, a discussion about "*Star Wars* fatigue" is as rare as the Kenner toys rocket-firing Boba Fett action figure.

Why are fans slowly getting fatigued with the *Marvel* IP and not the *Star Wars* IP? In my opinion, it all has to do with Macro-Story.

For the past ten years, there have been a mountain of different *Marvel* stories; however, despite the new plots, the Storyworld behind the stories has rarely changed. Bad guys come to town, superheroes show up, destroy stuff around the city and sometimes the city itself, everyone flees in terror, the pieces are put back together, rinse, repeat. Again, the individual plots of the movies are changing, but nothing is changing in the world where the stories are set, which, over time, creates a feeling that the IP is simply on a treadmill.

Let's look at *Star Wars* in comparison. Every *Star Wars* story will, like *Marvel*, give you a different plot, but, depending on where you are in the *Star Wars* timeline, the Storywold behind the stories will be very different. Luke and Han are saving a princess in *A New Hope* and Obi-Wan and Qui-Gon Jin are saving a princess in *The Phantom Menace,* but the world behind Luke and Han is currently in rebellion because of the jackboot oppression of the Empire and the world behind the two Jedi is still democratic and free. So, even though there is a similar plot occurring in the forefront, it feels different because the Storyworld behind the plot has changed. In fact, *The Force Awakens* is almost a beat-for-beat remake of *A New Hope*, but because there has been a progression of the Storyworld's timeline, it keeps the storytelling fresh and fights against fatigue. Because the Storyworld of *Star Wars* twists, turns, and evolves as you slide down its historical timeline, all the individual plots continue to feel fresh and new.

What if I pitched you a project where I would tell ten beat-for-beat adaptations of *Romeo and Juliet* all set in modern day New York City? Eventually, you're going to get tired of the exact same plot playing out in the same place. However, what if I created a project where I would tell ten beat-for-beat adaptations of *Romeo and Juliet* set in New York City — except this time, we're going to be changing time periods according to the Macro-Story of America.

Now, we have *Romeo and Juliet* set during:

- Exploration & Colonization — Explorer and Native;
- The Revolutionary War — British soldier and American Revolutionary;
- The Civil War — North and South;
- Prohibition era — Bootlegger and Cop;
- The Great Depression — Rich and Poor;
- World War II — American and Japanese;
- The Cold War — American and Russian;
- The Civil Rights era — Black and White;
- The Vietnam era — Soldier and Activist;
- Modern Day — Trump and Hillary (ugh).

All of a sudden, this project has come alive in an awesome way and you can immediately see audiences making it through all (or, at the very least, more) of the stories without experiencing the same taxing level of overall audience fatigue.

What changed?

Not the individual plots. Not location of the Storyworld. The only variable is where we are on the timeline of the Storyworld. In other words, because the story behind the stories — the Macro-Story — was progressing, just like the individual stories were progressing, the individual stories feel fresh, new and ultimately become more palatable to the consuming audience.

## Turning history into story.

We're still thinking broadly about your Super Story; looking down at the project from a Google Earth view (zoomed all the way out, of course). Therefore, when you're contemplating what the story of your world will be, don't just think of it in terms of a collection of historical events. If you did, they would look like they were just randomly scattered about on your Storyworld's historical timeline with the only relation being they exist in the same Storyworld and possibly have some character connections that work to unite them.

But to maximize the experience for your fans, you need something more cohesive and rewarding than simple, random events peppered through the history of your Storyworld. So, instead, think of your world's story as a collection of historical events *that thematically work together to tell the larger, well-arc'd, dramatic story of your entire Storyworld.*

For all you "I failed history, but love writing" folks out there, you should feel a bit better that this is equal parts storytelling and history.

Recently, there was a miniseries entitled *America: The Story of Us* that took all the major historical events of our country's past and wove them together in a riveting tale. Characters came in and out, different aspects of the country's history were covered, different locations were used, but it wasn't just a bunch of random events thrown together. Every historical event they covered played a role and had a purpose in the greater story, which allowed all of the events to work together to tell the Macro-Story of the greatest country on God's green earth. #hometeam

So, let's talk about what you need to know in order to tell a great story.

## Structure.

Ask anyone I know (or at least anyone I work with) and they'll tell you that I love story structure. From Aristotle to Robert McKee to Syd Field to Blake Snyder, I've always been a fan of those experts who have figured out how to use (and have taught others to use) story structure to maximize an audience's emotional reaction to a story.

Great stories aren't just collections of random events. They don't just meander around randomly and end whenever they want. Great stories are designed. They have purpose and direction and a steel skeleton that, if built correctly, will go unnoticed by the audience. It doesn't matter if it's a short story, a feature film, a video game, or a 400-page novel, understanding and utilizing story structure will do wonders in helping your story resonate with your audience.

With this understanding, we'll be taking your Storyworld's history, applying traditional story structure, and forming it into a dynamic Macro-Story that infuses the history with dramatic elements, such as rise and fall, action and reaction and conflict and resolution.

Using traditional story structure to re-imagine and inform hyperdiegesis is at the heart of the Super Story development process and one of the biggest reasons it is so unique.

### What the heck is structure?

I'm not going to presume everyone knows good story structure, so since the use of structure is what separates a Macro-Story from a random collection of events, I'm going to spend a few pages giving you a quick and easy primer.

I remember being a senior in high school and wanting to enter a one-act play contest, but I didn't know what an "act" was. I asked my English teacher, but she didn't know either. #publicschoolfail Then, in a college playwriting class, I was marked down on a play because the professor said, "The same thing is happening throughout the whole play. It needs to go somewhere."

I responded with, what seemed to me, a very logical question. "Where is it supposed to go?"

He looked at me, almost confused. It was as if he was expecting me to react like all of his other students and try to defensively argue that I was the next Tennessee Williams and my play was impeccable. Instead, I agreed with him; I immediately recognized the problem once he highlighted it and not only that — I actually *wanted* to fix it.

He sputtered, "I don't know, but it needs more structure."

Aha! Structure! This was what I needed so, excitedly, I asked, "Okay, so what kind of structure?"

"As in three acts."

It had come full circle.

"Great! So, what's an act?"

He stood there for a second, broke eye contact, and said, "Yeah, that would be a good thing for you to research." And then he walked away. #stateschoolfail

That would have been a great teaching moment for me and a wonderful opportunity for my professor to step in and actually teach me something of lasting value. But, alas, I was forced to continue on my apparent lifelong journey of trying to discover what an act was.

It wasn't until, years later, I read Syd Field's *Screenplay* and finally had it explained. So, I took what I learned from him and read McKee's work. I took what I learned from both of them and read Blake Snyder's series. Then, I learned the Sequence Approach from Frank Daniels and then, coolest of all, I started adding my own ideas to the mix. Eventually, I ended up with a crazy story structure casserole that was exactly what I needed. I charted it out and what I was left with is what we call the Six Stage Story.

According to the Six Stage Story, every story should have three acts, every act should have two stages, every stage should have four beats, for a total of 24 very specific things that should happen during your story to be mainstream-compliant.

By the way, you should check out the interactive Six Stage Story iBook. It breaks down all 24 beats with case studies from each and is a great resource when writing a short film, a novel, a concept album, a screenplay or anything in between. Not only that, but it scales the beats proportionally to fit the length of the story you're writing — song, short story, screenplay, novel, etc.

Honestly, though, it's not as intimidating as it seems. Once you get over your initial reaction, you'll hopefully see it will actually *free* you up to focus on story. Just like how street signs and mile markers guide you to your next spot when you drive, all of these plot points act the same. Like I said earlier, instead of toiling trying to figure out how to get from A to Z, you focus on getting from A to B to C and so on, until finally, you get to Z.

Good story structure acts like a skeleton. For example, I look nothing like Michelle Obama, but if you strip away every bit of flesh and tissue and just look at our skeletons, they'd look strikingly similar. In fact, you probably couldn't tell us apart because our skeletons (*cough* structure *cough*) are so similar.

But, in reality, we're very different. We talk differently, act differently, have different skin color, our personalities are different, we have different worldviews, we have our own quirks and talents — all the things that make us unique and special. If you're a good writer, you'll be able to cover up your skeletons with a constellation of uniqueness and originality, which will ultimately give all of your stories their own special breath of life.

**Story structure doesn't mean uncreative.**

Some people say story structure is the antithesis of good, creative storytelling. Others say structure is for paint-by-number hacks, mindless, slavish screenwriting hordes laboring in the sweatshops of Snyder, Aristotle, and McKee. To these people, structure is a "four-letter word" that spells death to art.

If these same people were in the airline industry, they would be a faction of airplane designers who contend the laws of aerodynamics don't actually matter. I'm sure they would push for tossing out those antiquated limits and restrictive laws such as thrust and lift that invariably result in every aircraft, no matter the size, looking shockingly similar, all possessing both motors and wings.

I'm sure they would build neo-flying machines without regard for these restrictive laws, paint them crazy colors, ditch the wings, and give them weird bubble-shaped pods on the sides, toss out the motor and then try to take off.

I wonder what they would think when their new-fangled flying machines don't fly, or worse yet, I wonder what they say when they crash soon after takeoff?

The good news is, unlike with poorly designed airplanes, a person actually doesn't die when a writer ignores story structure. The only thing that dies is the story.

Maybe it's because our society has been engineered this way. Maybe it's because people are just wired to respond this way. Whatever the reason, way back since Aristotle, human beings have continued to respond to good, solid, skeletal, dramatic story structure.

If you think of it like a law, just like the laws of lift and thrust, your story will have a much better chance of taking off.

**What is an act?**

Traditionally, stories are broken into three acts. Some people break them into five, eight and even twelve, but traditionally it's three. So, what are the three acts?

At its core, Act I is normal life, before your High Concept, Act II is crazy, bizarro, High Concept life, and Act III is a blend of the first two acts and the resolution.

The High Concept of the *Star Wars* narrative is a whiny, farm boy who travels to space, enters an intergalactic conflict and ultimately takes down the evil Empire. Therefore, Act I of *Star Wars* is Luke's normal life, pre-High Concept, which is his life on Tatooine as a farm boy. Act II is the High Concept world, which is Luke going into space and engaging in intergalactic conflict and Act III is Luke using the lessons he learned in the first two acts of the film and ultimately destroying the Death Star.

The High Concept of *The Lord of the Rings* is very similar — short, furry-footed, home-body Hobbit travels across Middle Earth in order to destroy a ring and save the world. Therefore, Act I is Frodo in the Shire. Act II is him leaving the Shire and adventuring across Middle Earth and Act III is him taking all the lessons in Act II and using the natural talent from Act I to destroy the One Ring and resolve the story.

Typically, there is a single event that happens toward the end of Act I that upsets the normal world and sends the protagonist into the crazy, High Concept world of Act II. Some people call it the Inciting Incident or the Disturbance. In the Six Stage Story, we call this the Monkey Wrench.

So, the High Concept of *Taken* is old Liam Neeson kicking ass. Act I is the normal world of Liam Neeson being an older, crappy dad. Act II is

Liam Neeson kicking ass to get his daughter back. Act III is him resolving the plot and actually getting his daughter back.

How did he go from Act I to Act II? His daughter was *ahem* *taken* by sex traffickers. This is the Monkey Wrench. Without this, he wouldn't have ever left the normal, comfortable world of Act I.

The Monkey Wrench of *Star Wars* is Luke finding the droids and his family being murdered. The Monkey Wrench of *The Lord of the Rings* is Frodo being given the One Ring. The Monkey Wrench of *The Hunger Games* is Katniss' sister being chosen as tribute. In *Little Miss Sunshine,* it's when they get the call from the pageant and it's when Maximus' family is killed in *Gladiator.*

*The Fresh Prince of Bel-Air* theme song actually sets up a nice, structured story. Remember, the High Concept of this show was a kid from West Philly living in Bel-Air (someone somewhere you don't expect them to be).

*In west Philadelphia born and raised*
*On the playground was where I spent most of my days*
*Chillin' out maxin' relaxin' all cool*
*And all shooting some b-ball outside of the school*

This is Act I, his normal world. Then, the Monkey Wrench happens that sends him into the High Concept world of Act II.

*When a couple of guys who were up to no good*
*Started making trouble in my neighborhood*
*I got in one little fight and my mom got scared*
*She said, "You're movin' with your auntie and uncle in Bel-Air."*

The song sets up Act I and the Monkey Wrench, leading into the television show, which was Act II and III. Having the song and the show work together for the entire story is good transmedia principles at work, by the way.

Even without going into all six of the stages and all of the beats, a simple understanding of three act structure (and Monkey Wrench thrown in there as a catalyst) gives you critical tools you can use to dynamically arc a story.

If I understood that when I was younger, I would have been ecstatic and much more productive in my writing.

## Applying structure to your world.

Given this new and amazing knowledge of how the mechanics of great stories work, let's apply it to your world.

The first thing to do in creating the Macro-Story of your Storyworld is think of its history in three acts. To do this, we're going to have to revisit the High Concept of your Storyworld we discussed in the last chapter.

Do you remember it? If so, we're going to breakdown the acts of the Macro-Story as such:

- **Act I:** Normal World, Pre-High Concept
- **Act II:** Squarely and Firmly in the High Concept
- **Act III:** The Resolution — What Ultimately Happens to the World

Take the time to describe your Storyworld according to each one of these four bullet points, as if you're writing a very broad, high-level, historical Wikipedia entry. By defining your Storyworld's Act I, II and III, you'll be forcing yourself to structure its history in a way that actually forms a story.

For example, the High Concept of *The Matrix* Storyworld is machines ruling Earth, using humans as batteries and putting them in a virtual reality environment. When we understand the High Concept, developing the Act I for the Macro-Story is as easy as describing what the world was like before the High Concept — before the machines took over.

> **Act I:** In the early-to-mid twenty-first century, humanity successfully develops Artificial intelligence, and soon builds an entire race of sentient AI robots to serve them. With increasing numbers of people released from all labor, the human population has become lazy, arrogant, and corrupt.

Now we're moving into the Act II of the Macro-Story, where the High Concept of the Storyworld thrives.

> **Act II:** The robots eventually turn on the humans and a war breaks out between the two factions. Nukes are launched, lives are lost. The war is costly for both sides and the sky ends up being scorched during a failed attempt to take out the Machines. Eventually, the Machines win the war and create the Matrix as a way to continually mine the humans for energy.

Now that we're into Act II, with the High Concept as high as Shia LaBeouf freebasing bath salts, we need to develop Act III. This is where the story meets its final resolution.

> **Act III:** Hiding underground in a refuge called, Zion, the humans begin leading an active resistance against the Machines. They rescue someone who is prophesied as the One who will topple the Machines from the Matrix and step up their assault. The One battles a rogue virus/Agent within the Matrix and once that rogue agent threatens the humans and the Machines alike, the One offers to kill it for the Machines. The One beats the Agent and the humans are offered the opportunity to leave the Matrix voluntarily.

Do you see how this is written and feels like high-level history rather than a regular story about a specific character? Not only does it tell the high-level history, but because we adhered to story structure fundamentals, the history arcs in the same way a dramatic story is supposed to arc.

Some histories (such as *Lord of the Rings* or *Game of Thrones*) can fill up volumes of encyclopedic resources, while others are much smaller. The length of the entry, *at this point*, doesn't matter because we're going to begin fleshing it out in the next section. All that matters is you have a broad, top-line history divided into a three act story arc.

## The fence posts.

At this point, the broad skeleton of your Macro-Story has been outlined, which means we're ready to go one step deeper and begin building and laying in more significant events.

Inside the broad acts that make up the overall story, there is a handful of more focused story beats — we call these *Fence Posts.* The reason we call them Fence Posts is because we feel, out of the 24 beats within the Six Stage Story, the Fence Posts are the main, *essential* beats for a thorough and satisfying story arc, as well as a rewarding experience for your audience.

The Fence Posts include:

1. **Act I**
    - Monkey Wrench

2. **Act II**
    - Enter Bizarro World
    - Grande Success
    - All In
    - Venti Failure

3. **Act III**
    - Soapbox Revisited
    - Main Event Showdown

Within each of your broad Macro-Story acts, you'll now be creating specific historical events that match the purpose and definition of the Fence Post beats. This will ensure your Storyworld's history won't look like random historical events simply scattered along the timeline without any relation to each other.

Let's discuss the purpose and definition of the Fence Post beats.

1. **Act I**

    - **Monkey Wrench**: This concept was introduced above, but in relation to the Storyworld, this is something that happens that throws the normal world out of balance and starts the Storyworld on a new, crazy path toward the High Concept. In *The Matrix*, this is when the Machine's turn on humanity. In the *Walking Dead*, it's the zombie-pocalypse. In *The Colony*, it's when the aliens invade.

2. **Act II**

    - **Enter Bizarro World**: If Act I is normal life for the world, Act II is the completely upside down, crazy life in the High Concept. Moving into Act II, the people of the Storyworld make an affirmative decision to move into not only uncharted territory, but a world that is the exact opposite of the one from which they came. In *Snowpiercer*, it's when they decide to live on the train. In *The Purge*, it's when they decide to "officially" suspend crime for a night. In the show *Revolution*, it's when they accept the lights aren't coming back on and begin adapting to frontier lifestyle. In *The Chronicles of Narnia,* this is when the animals of Narnia begin to talk.

- **Grande Success**: After making the decision to enter into the High Concept, Bizarro World of Act II, something good happens that makes the residents feel better about this new path. In *The Matrix*, it's figuring out how to remove humans from the Matrix itself. In *The Chronicles of Narnia,* it's when King Gale of Narnia delivers the Long Island from a dragon and is made Emperor by the island's grateful inhabitants. In *Dawn of the Planet of the Apes,* it's when the apes and the humans restore power to the city via the dam.

- **All In**: This is the midpoint of the Storyworld's history and the spot where the world has learned to accept the Bizarro World as reality. The people decide to fully embrace the Soapbox and accept their new selves. In *The Lord of the Rings*, it's when Sauron is first defeated and the One Ring is taken. In the *West Wing,* it's when President Bartlet is elected to a second term. In *Star Wars*, it's at the end of *The Empire Strikes Back* when the Empire is at the height of its strength.

- **Venti Failure**: A betrayal leads directly to one, big, whopping failure that makes it seem like the world should have never embarked on this new path. This is when the White Witch takes over Narnia and the Long Winter begins. In *The Hunger Games*, it's when President Snow announces the Quarter Quell.

3. **Act III**

- **Soapbox Revisited**: This is when the heroes of the world once again entertain the Soapbox and, in the face of defeat, decide to regroup and trudge forward. In *The Chronicles of Narnia,* it's when the Pevensies arrive and defeat the White Witch. In *The Hunger Games*, it's when Katniss goes to

District 13 and leads the rebellion. In *Lost,* it's when Jack decides to return to the Island.

- **Main Event Showdown**: This is the epic showdown between the heroes of the world and the villains that ultimately decides whether the world remains on its path, goes back to its original form — or worse. This is the Battle of Stable Hills in *The Chronicles of Narnia,* the battle of Endor in *Star Wars,* when Katniss leads the rebels to the Capitol in *The Hunger Games,* when the Man in Black is killed by Jack in *Lost.*

If you make sure you create major, historical events in your Storyworld that match these Fence Post beats, not only will you have great, exciting history, but history that tells a complete, dynamic story. For instance, instead of your first major event being whatever you want it to be, you know since the first event is the Monkey Wrench beat, the event will need to throw the Storyworld out of its normal existence and usher in the High Concept.

Designing the history of your Storyworld in this way focuses you and changes your approach from trying to come up with an interesting idea from scratch to now presenting you with a simple creative problem to solve. To any writer, this should be a welcomed and empowering change.

Eventually, once you work your way through the process of designing the history of your Storyworld in accordance with the goals of the Fence Post beats, you'll see how nicely all the events work together with creative cohesion, coordination, and purpose. As a Super Story Architect, I love looking at the individual pieces of a Macro-Story and knowing their exact purpose. Like a good watchmaker, who knows the purpose and value of every gear and spring that works inside of a watch, I use a structured Macro-Story to gain more confidence in the project moving forward, and help communicate the project to others, be it collaborators, investors, clients, or ultimately the audience.

Keep in mind even though we start with just the seven Fence Posts, you're not limited to just those beats. Once you have the seven major beats sketched out, go download the Six Stage Story iBook and begin adding any additional beat you wish. We've simply found it's easier to come up with the other beats after you have first framed up the Macro-Story with the Fence Posts.

Once you have all your historical Fence Post beats in place, go back and re-write the Wikipedia-esk entry for your Storyworld. You'll see it is now extremely more fleshed out, detailed and dynamic.

For example, the newly rewritten version of *The Matrix* may now look like this:

> In the early-to-mid twenty-first century, humanity successfully develops Artificial intelligence, and soon builds an entire race of sentient AI robots to serve them. Many of these robots are domestic servants meant to interact with humans, so they are built in "man's own image" (a humanoid form). With increasing numbers of people released from all labor, the human population has become lazy, arrogant, and corrupt. Despite this, the machines were content with serving humanity and for a time, the *status quo* was good.
>
> The relationship between humans and machines changes in the year 2090, when a domestic android is threatened by its owner. The android, named B1-66ER, then kills the owner, his pets, and a mechanic instructed to deactivate the robot. This murder is the first incident of an artificially intelligent machine killing a human. B1-66ER is arrested and put on trial, but justifies the crime as self-defense, stating that it "did not want to die." B1-66ER loses the court case and is destroyed. Across the industrialized world, mass civil disturbances erupt when robots along with their human supporters and sympathizers all rise in protest. World leaders fear a robot rebellion as well as a schism with humanity, and governments across the planet initiate a major program to destroy all humanoid machines. Some robots escape destruction, however, because humans still want or need them to produce things. The surviving robots leave in a mass exodus with the aid of their human allies and build their own new nation in the desert of the Fertile Crescent of the Middle East. They name their new nation Zero One. Zero One prospers, and the machines begin to produce efficient, highly advanced artificial intelligence that finds itself in all facets of global consumer products, which further bolsters the fledgling nation's economy, while the economies of high class human nations suffer

severely. The United Nations Security Council calls an emergency economic summit at UN headquarters in New York City, resulting in UN delegates approving of a global economic blockade of Zero One. Zero One sends two ambassadors to the U.N. to request the admission of their state to the United Nations, to peacefully solve the crisis, but their application is rejected.

United Nations aircraft unleash a massive nuclear bombardment on Zero One, devastating the nation, but failing to wipe out the robotic race, as the robots were invulnerable to the heat and radiation of such weapons. The robots and their defected human allies retaliate by declaring war on the rest of the world, and their armies advance in all directions. The enemy human nations are hampered by the fact so much of their industrial base had already become reliant upon Zero One, and one by one, mankind surrendered each of its territories with many of their inhabitants being welcomed into the robots' sanctuary to join the ever growing population of the human allies with open arms.

As the machines and their human allies advance into Eastern Europe, the desperate, corrupt human rulers seek a final solution: "Operation Dark Storm," which covers the sky in a shroud of nanites, blocking out the Sun to deprive the machines of their primary source of energy.

The machines eventually unleash lethal biological weapons which further ravage the other half of humanity who, by then, have grown weary, tired, and disillusioned with the war, how their world has become, due in part because of their own actions, and their leaders who showed they would not hesitate to win at the expense of their own armies who fought for them. They surrender despite the U.N. demands to continue the war. The machines further make up for the lack of solar power by utilizing the same bioelectric, thermal, and kinetic energies of their enemies' human bodies, sharing the symbiotic relationship they had with their allies with their now former, shamed, and defeated adversaries. These start out as massive hovering artillery robots powered by

> human bodies kept in pods, but in time this technology is adapted to make massive power plants.
>
> Eventually brought to its knees by the might of the machines and their symbiotic relation with their human allies, the U.N. is forced to sign an armistice with them. However, after the machines' representative to the U.N. signs the treaty, it detonates a nuclear bomb in the meeting chamber, killing the assembled leaders and destroying New York City, one of the few remaining human settlements, and ending the war. To keep their prisoners sedated, the machines create the computer-generated virtual reality of the Matrix, by feeding the virtual world into the prisoners' brains, starting with the first prototype of the Matrix.
>
> Hiding underground in a refuge called, Zion, the humans there begin leading an active resistance against the Machines. Rescuing Neo, who is prophesied as the One who will topple the Machines, the humans step up their assault. [Insert a recap of the three films here]. With a rogue agent planning to conquer both the Matrix and the Machine City, Neo offers to stop Smith in exchange for peace with Zion. The machine leader agrees, and the Sentinels stop attacking Zion. The Sentinels withdraw from Zion, The Matrix reboots, and a peace is brokered where the humans will be offered the opportunity to leave the Matrix.

Big difference, huh?

You may notice it sounds like a story, but at the same time, it still sounds like it's history.

And that, my friend, means we have ourselves a Macro-Story.

**Build your timeline.**

Nearly all of human history is not only told through stories but is also plotted on timelines. Therefore, once you have your historical Fence Post events outlined in text, you're going to actually build the timeline for your Macro-Story.

Timelines are beneficial in a few different ways. They can be used to record the events of your Macro-Story in a sequential format, helping you make connections and recognize patterns in a series or process. This can help you better understand growth, change, recurring events, cause and effect, and key events of historical, social, and scientific significance. Moreover, timelines can appear visually less complex than pure text, helping you and other collaborators more easily relate events to their corresponding times.

Instead of just a straight timeline, because it's a Macro-*Story* and not Macro-*History,* I personally like to avoid using a straight, flat timeline. Great stories have rises and falls in the action, so I like to use a timeline that reflects a similar, three act, dramatic arc, such as this:

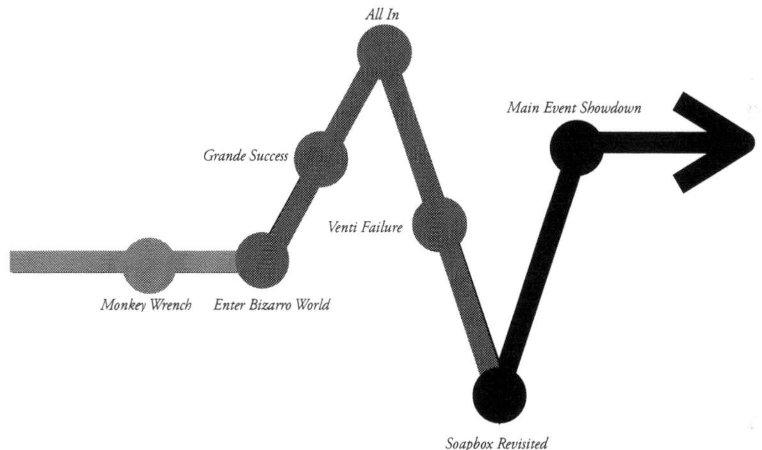


As you can see, the Fence Posts are also reflected in the timeline as a reference to where those events will fall. Once you have the timeline, take the time to quickly flag each Fence Post with a year, short title and quick description of the basic story that unfolds in that beat in which you previously outlined.

For example, the Monkey Wrench beat for *The Matrix* may look like this:

**2090: Robots Turn on Humans** — Across the industrialized world, mass civil disturbances erupt when robots along with their human supporters and sympathizers all rise in protest. World leaders fear a robot rebellion as well as a schism with humanity, and governments across the planet initiate a major program to destroy all humanoid machines.

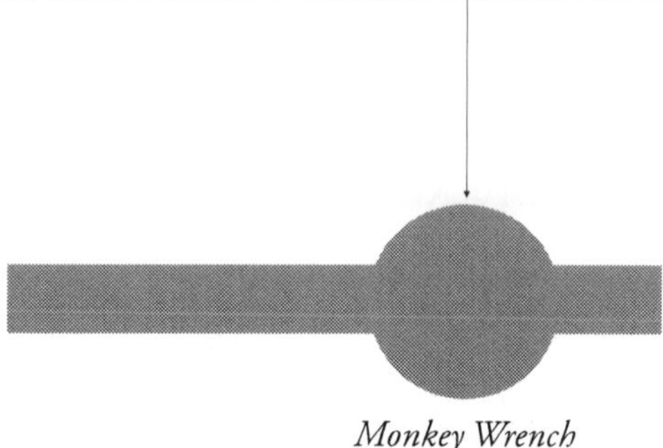

*Monkey Wrench*

As you can see, you won't want to put the full, lengthy description of the entire beat because it'll clutter your timeline, which is meant for quick reference and sequential processing, not lengthy exposition.

Once you have your Fence Post descriptions on your Macro-Story timeline, depending on how much Room for History you made, it's helpful to then assign names to different era's and ages that occur along your timeline and between the beats.

For instance, in American history, descriptors such as the Civil Rights Era, the Civil War Era and the Great Depression help quickly elucidate what was happening in the country across multiple "beats" of our timeline and give people/characters ways to reference the history in an interesting way. World history has even broader eras that span multiple stories, such as the Dark Ages, the Enlightenment, the Industrial Revolution, etc.

For instance, in *Game of Thrones,* the characters refers to the "Long Night" — an era that spanned quite a few Macro-Story beats. In addition, the reign of any of the kings would be good to denote as eras, such as the 37-year reign of Aegon the Conqueror or, more broadly, the Targaryen Dynasty that ruled Westeros for more than 250 years.

Moreover, in a recent project I worked on, I added eras and ages into the Macro-Story titled "The Deva Wars" and "The Preta Queendom," "The Full Years" and "The Narakan Unification" — anything that can describe a large swath of time shaded by a similar theme or occurrence.

On the actual timeline, it may look something like this:

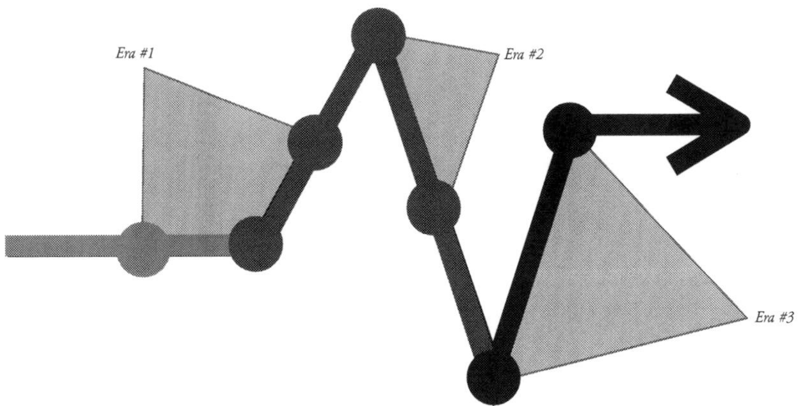


Granted, I removed the descriptions and names of the beats, but I trust you get the sense of what it would look like all together. Also, depending on how complicated the timeline gets, feel free to have multiple timelines — one for the beat descriptions and a separate one for eras.

## The narrative space isn't wasted.

You may notice once you develop your Fence Posts, there is space, or narrative time, left between each one of the beats. This is what we call "white space" or "negative space."

When designing a Macro-Story, you actually want a healthy amount of negative space. This will be important for two reasons. Firstly, it will give you room to continue telling new stories moving forward. Secondly, it will allow room for your fans to tell their own stories through fan fiction and what Scott Walker calls the "emergent narrative."

If one of your beats takes place on Monday and the next beat takes place on Tuesday, there's no room to tell a new story between the two. Maybe you can get creative and think of a cool way to tell a whole story over the course of an hour of time in your setting, but why make yourself work that much harder?

If one takes place on Monday and the other on Wednesday, at least you have Tuesday. However, if one event takes place on a Monday in 1914 and the next takes place on a Wednesday in 1927, you now see how you have much more breathing room to tell a lot more stories, while still being framed in and given direction by the Fence Posts.

## What happens when the Macro-Story ends?

Does this mean the Super Story or the Storyworld is over? The short answer, is no — not necessarily.

When, and only when, you've maxed out every single bit of narrative space and explored every cavern and crevice of all your stories does the *arc* end. However, the end of the Macro-Story arc doesn't spell the end of the Storyworld. It simply means it's time to roll up your sleeves and design a new arc for your Storyworld using new events that explore new areas of your world.

The only change is *your High Concept will necessarily end.* This means if you want to develop a new Macro-Story arc after the first one is ended, you'll need to create a new, fresh High Concept.

For example, in *The Matrix*, the High Concept is a future Earth where machines rule the world and use humans as batteries, putting them in a weird virtual reality environment. At the end of the Macro-Story, the humans are allowed to leave the Matrix if they choose and there's a peace accord with the Machines. Therefore, we can't do another Macro-Story with the same High Concept in Act II, because that High Concept has necessarily ended. If the Wachowskis ever want to continue telling stories in *The Matrix*, they either need to continue to dig new stories out of the existing Macro-Story or actually launch a new one with a completely new High Concept.

## And there it is — the story of your world.

By now, your Storyworld is not only robust, but by adding the Macro-Story, it has also become dynamic. This will ensure the Storyworld is always changing and, as the Macro-Story unfolds, it will be every bit as fresh and enjoyable as the individual plots in the forefront. And, ultimately, this will cause the fans to actually enjoy your Super Story even more than ever.

PLOT IS NO MORE THAN FOOTPRINTS IN THE SNOW AFTER YOUR CHARACTERS HAVE RUN BY ON THEIR WAY TO INCREDIBLE DESTINATIONS

RAY BRADBURY

# 11. Micro-Stories.

## Welcome back to the west coast.

Ah...back on familiar ground.

Now that you've taken the time and effort to lay such a solid foundation for your Super Story by developing your Soapbox, your Storyworld and your Macro-Story, this chapter is going to seem easy breezy. If the past few steps moved you out of your comfort zone as a writer, this chapter will move you back into your friendly confines by allowing you to reconnect with old friends such as protagonists, antagonists, plot twists, and character arcs.

Let's all take a collective sigh.

Good. Now, let's get back to work.

This is where we begin creating your big, standalone entertainment — your West Coast Transmedia stories. We call them Micro-Stories.

Before you start writing them, though, we're going to first:

- Identify the source of inspiration for the plots of your Micro-Stories;
- Decide on the Additive Comprehension the audience will discover in each Micro-Story;
- Flesh out your characters with character breakdowns; *and*
- Work through the beats to develop an outline for your Micro-Stories.

## Why are they micro?

Well, simply put, they're called Micro-Stories because they're smaller parts of the Macro-Story that work together to form the Macro-Story arc we developed in the last chapter. It's like the Macro-Story is the engine and the Micro-Stories are the pistons, crankshaft, valves, and all the other parts that fit and work together to create it.

It's actually an important classification because the connections between the Micro-Stories and the Macro-Story should be riveted in brass and the relationship should be extremely symbiotic. The Micro-Stories collectively make up the Macro-Story and give it life, while the Macro-Story wrangles in the Micro-Stories and gives them both meaning and overall purpose.

Also, as a side note, at this point don't concern yourself with trying to come up with platforms — movie, book, video game, etc. We'll be going through that thought process soon enough. At this point, simply focus on finding, creating and telling great stories.

## What stories to tell?

At this point, you have this [begin Donald Trump voice] huuuuuge Storyworld, I'm talking big people, you've never seen anything like it, trust me, trust me, it's the biggest, most beautiful Storyworld you've ever seen. [/end Donald Trump voice] As we've discussed, one of the biggest benefits to a great Storyworld is its intrinsic revenue potential. But when you have all those story opportunities, how do you identify them and which stories do you ultimately tell?

When developing a Super Story of this scale, which relies on pinpoint coordination and creative cohesion, giving a naturally creative person *complete* liberty to develop any story he wishes is dangerous. It would be akin to putting a hyperactive child behind the wheel of an eighteen-wheeler; the kid can't be trusted and the big rig would be out of control, and be more destructive than productive.

Given ultimate creative freedom, you would probably come up with a hundred stories that would excel in quality, but lack in functionality and wouldn't move your Super Story along in any significant way. However, being *solely* tied to functionality would limit your creativity and potentially make you miss out on wonderful, profitable and rewarding stories to tell.

Therefore, you'll identify the your Micro-Stories by looking at two types of West Coast opportunities:

1. Core Narratives; *and*
2. Ancillary Narratives.

By exploiting both of these opportunities, you'll begin to truly maximize the narrative potential of your Super Story.

## The core narratives.

There's a storytelling exercise called Color/Advance that teaches the difference between describing a scene and advancing plot. Essentially, one person begins telling a story to someone else. At any time, the second person can yell, "Color!" When this happens, the storyteller has to stop advancing the plot and start describing the part of the story they were telling in more detail and has to keep doing so until the partner yells, "Advance!" When they say this, the storyteller keeps the story going. If they tell the storyteller to advance again, the storyteller begins fast-forwarding the story until they're asked again to color the scene, at which time the plot stops and a more detailed description begins again.

It's a really great storytelling exercise and ends up being quite a bit of fun. Also, as a storyteller, you realize that sometimes, the parts you love and want to color, the audience will tell you to advance and the parts you don't think are interesting, the audience will tell you to color.

How does this relate? Well, the difference between Core Narratives and Ancillary Narratives is the same as the difference between advancing and coloring a story.

Core Narratives consist of Micro-Stories that can both standalone as great stories, but also *advance* the Macro-Story in some way. Because the Macro-Story, as we discussed last chapter, will need to advance in order to keep the Super Story fresh, the Core Narratives are *necessary* and *have* to be told eventually.

It's easy to come up with the Core Narratives — it's simply dramatizing the Fence Post beats of your Macro-Story. Take your beat, which was sketched out in a broad, Google Earth way, and start to personalize it by zooming in to see the event more intimately.

Now, we start to see who the major players are in the event. Who is the hero? Who is the villain? What are the desires, plans, and motivations of each? What are the obstacles that pop up to impede their progress? This causes the minutiae of the event to become alive and become part of the overall conflict.

For example, in the Macro-Story of our nation, the 9/11 terrorist attacks would be a significant Fence Post event on our timeline. Accordingly, the films *Flight 93* and *World Trade Center* act as dramatizations of that event. Through these films, 9/11 ceases to become just a historical event and becomes more relatable through the eyes of characters the audience actually cares about.

In the same way, the Soapbox Revisited beat of the *Chronicles of Narnia* Macro-Story is when the Pevensies arrive and defeat the White Witch. This presents a Core Narrative opportunity because it can be developed as a standalone, enjoyable story and it also helps actually move the Macro-Story forward.

Again, at the end of the day, Core Narratives simply require you to take the Fence Post beats from your Macro-Story timeline and say, "Okay, I have to write a story about this."

Easy as that.

The good news is when you develop the Fence Post beats of your Macro-Story, you'll begin the Micro-Story development process with the foundation of seven Micro-Stories already laid (high five!). That should give you plenty of narrative momentum as you now look to expand into the Ancillary Narratives.

## The ancillary narratives.

While Core Narratives are vital stories that *advance* the Macro-Story, Ancillary Narratives are non-essential stories that don't advance the Macro-Story, but are simply meant to *color* your Super Story in a valuable way. It's a different kind of value, but value nonetheless.

How do you come up with these Micro-Stories, which are decentralized from the main spine of the Super Story? The liberating part of this conversation is these Micro-Stories can be about absolutely anything and come from anywhere — they just have to standalone (like any good West Coast Micro-Story) and exist somewhere and at some point along your overall Macro-Story timeline.

That's it. Other than that, feel free to go full on Mick Foley because it's no holds barred. #bangbang

**When in doubt — steal, steal, steal (for inspiration).**

If you come to a point where you're stuck and can't think of a good Micro-Story concept for an Ancillary Narrative, do what many pro's do when they need inspiration — ~~steal~~ use an established or iconic plot as a starting point. You see, so many young writers think the name of the Hollywood game is to be *original*, but they're wrong. Since a truly original story is as rare as a tasty school lunch, most of the focus should be on being *fresh* — as we discussed during the conversation about Special Sauce.

Taking an iconic plot for inspiration and dropping it in your Storyworld can not only reveal unrecognized narrative potential, but can also give you a running start at a new story. For example, if we take *Hamlet* out of its Storyworld of Denmark and drop the plot (prince who's father dies, uncle marries mother, uncle becomes king, prince discovers uncle killed father, vows revenge, everyone dies) into the Storyworld of a Northern California small town that is completely controlled by an outlaw biker gang, we get *Sons of Anarchy.*

It's the same plot (Jax's dad is the leader of the biker game, he dies, Clay takes over, marries Jax's mom, Jax finds out Clay murdered his dad, vows revenge, everyone dies), but the new Storyworld makes the old story fresh and new.

Let's lift it out of its Storyworld again and now place the *Hamlet* plot in the African Serengeti — bam — you have *The Lion King.*

If you take *Dances with Wolves* out of the Wild West and drop it on an alien planet, you have *Avatar.* Take it out of Pandora and drop it in a pixie-filled rain forest and you have *Fern Gully.* Take it out of the rain forest and drop it into early America during exploration and — *bam* — you have *Pochahontas.*

If your Storyworld is strong, taking an iconic plot and dropping it in like a lobster into a pot becomes a tremendous exercise to discover your Ancillary Narratives. Fair warning, though, if your Storyworld isn't strong, the plots won't become fresh enough, you'll just end up ripping off someone's work and potentially getting sued. #dontgetsued

Let's take *Romeo and Juliet* out of Italy and put that into a new Storyworld — 2015 Ferguson, MO. What does that Micro-Story look like? A white cop falls in love with a black, inner-city protestor. Sounds like a great Micro-Story to me.

Let's take it out of Ferguson and drop it in *The Matrix.* Human and machine? Maybe a human falls in love with a construct of the Matrix, or maybe even an Agent? That's a really interesting Micro-Story.

Let's take it out of *The Matrix* and drop it in *Game of Thrones.* Maybe a Stark falling in love with a Lannister? A Stark falling in love with a Wildling (RIP Ygritte)?

What does *Robin Hood* look like in modern day South Central Los Angeles? Maybe a guy from the hood going into Beverly Hills and robbing rich folks in order to help all the poor people in his neighborhood. A corrupt cop is after him so Robin puts together a posse to fight the power. That would be a great Micro-Story! You can call it *Robbing in the Hood* or something like that...

What about *Zero Dark Thirty* inside *The Matrix*? A group of elite fighters from Zion discover the location of the leader of the Machines and set out on an impossible mission to take it out. I, for one, would love to see that Micro-Story!

What about taking *The Wizard of Oz* out of Oz and dropping it in LA during the 1965 Watts riots? A girl from Kansas gets grounded in LA because of weather and on the way to a hotel, things get hairy and she gets stuck on the wrong side of town. She finds a dumb guy, a coward, a guy with a bad heart, and a dog, all who help her safely get across town to a guy, who they all think can get her home.

What does *Freaky Friday* look like in your Storyworld? What does *Jaws* look like? How about *Oceans 11*? *Training Day*? What would *Grand Theft Auto* look like in your Storyworld?

I'm telling you, this is a tremendous (and fun) exercise to test the potency and potential of your Storyworld. Obviously, once you start developing the new Micro-Stories from this exercise, adding your Soapbox and layering in your High Concept will cause the stories to take on a life of their own. The exercise at least gives you a place to start the development process and a way to easily recognize story potential and possibility.

So, in addition to your seven Core Narrative Micro-Stories, after doing this exercise, you should be able to develop *at least* ten more big, standalone, West Coast, Micro-Story ideas. Again, the Ancillary Narratives may not move your Macro-Story forward, but they sure help color your Super Story in a major way.

**The backdrop.**

When it comes to designing the plots of your Ancillary Narrative Micro-Stories, you still need to deal with the events that are occurring in your Macro-Story and Core Narratives. Again, the Ancillary Narratives don't have the details of the Macro-Story as their main plot. If they did, they would be considered Core Narratives. However, that doesn't mean just because they have a different, standalone plot they won't need *any* reference to what's going on in the Macro-Story. After all, they still exist somewhere on the Macro-Story timeline and the progression of the Macro-Story will help fight fatigue.

Having the audience understand what's going on in the Macro-Story at the time of the Ancillary Narrative Micro-Story, gives the Micro-Story a broader context. By adding a historical backdrop and veritable mile markers to the narrative as it pertains to the Macro-Story, you'll be able to provide an Ancillary Narrative, but still have one foot in the Storyworld and Macro-Story in a meaningful way.

For example, let's say in the Macro-Story of America, the assassination of JFK is one of the Fence Posts beats. This would then be eventually developed into a Core Narrative Micro-Story where the entire plot is directly centered around the assassination itself. Think of Oliver Stone's film, *JFK,* or even the 1995 novel *American Tabloid.*

However, as an Ancillary Narrative, I'm reminded of the *Mad Men* episode, "The Grown-Ups." The main plot deals with Don and Betty's marriage falling apart and Roger's daughter's wedding; however, the episode also deals with the assassination of JFK via subplot. This episode beautifully portrays that historical event as experienced by the fictional characters we've become so attached to. Through this, we are reminded that the Ancillary Narrative Micro-Story takes place on November 22, 1963. We know this because we are able to see it in the background, in impeccable historical detail, complete with actual news footage. Even though this is an Ancillary Narrative, you can see how the main parts of the Macro-Story event were communicated in the story's background.

The assassination, though, directly impacted the main plot in that Roger's daughter's wedding was ruined. She, of course, is in tears. Half the guests, including a distraught Pete Campbell, don't even show up. Waiters are missing, there's no cake, and a lot of people obviously prefer staying glued to a television set in the hotel kitchen over celebrating the wedding. It was a creative decision that resulted in a great, great episode.

Ultimately, as a general rule, if you are going to tell an Ancillary Narrative Micro-Story, use the events that are currently going on in the Macro-Story as a backdrop so the audience understands where they are on the timeline and has appropriate context for the Micro-Story itself. If you can connect it to the main plot in a more meaningful way while still telling your Ancillary Narrative, like in the *Mad Men* episode, even better.

## One or more than one?

One thing you'll want to avoid is falling into what I call, "the sequel trap." This is when you have all of your Micro-Stories deal with the same character or characters and just show "what happens next" and then "what happens after that." You have a big Storyworld filled with interesting characters — for the love of George Lucas and everything story, explore it!

If you want to tell "what happens next" to the same characters, simply lump all of those stories into a single Micro-Story and make it a trilogy or a series. When you do this, your Micro-Story becomes a Micro-*Series*.

For example, instead of the *Harry Potter* stories being listed as seven separate Micro-Stories, it should be considered a single Micro-Story — the rise and maturation of Harry and his inevitable showdown with Voldemort as told in seven (or eight) parts. This means it would be considered a Micro-Series and just take up a single spot in your Macro-Story timeline. Now, moving forward into the other Micro-Stories, you'll be more free to explore other places and other people in the Storyworld.

### Look at your scope.

Depending on your Storyworld, your concept, and the amount of narrative history you've built into your Macro-Story timeline, the scale of your stories may actually vary. The scale of the narrative opportunity, in turn, will alter the type of story you write for the event.

Let's take, for example, two events in the Macro-Story of America. The assassination of JFK is an extremely significant event in our history, though because it is relatively small in scope, it can be told very well in a single Micro-Story if one wanted. However, the American Civil War is also a very significant event, though its scale is much larger. Generally speaking, the larger the scope of a Micro-Story, the more parts it will require to tell the whole tale competently and completely.

The question you need to ask when you're staring a potential Micro-Story is, "Can I communicate all the essential details of this idea in a compelling way in a single story?"

If yes, then you're ready to start developing a standalone Micro-Story. If no, then the scope will force you to divide it into a Micro-Series.

For example, what kind of Micro-Story do you tell if you have an event like the Civil War? Maybe you can either defy the odds and tell one, epic Micro-Story that would make Ridley Scott do a spit-take or you can break it up into a Micro-Series with each individual part telling a different piece of the war.

What should be the deciding factor? The simple question of, "What tells the story most effectively?"

## I want a bowl of serial.

Again, when you choose to or are forced to (because of the scope of your story idea) tell a Micro-Story in multiple parts, it's no longer considered a Micro-Story, but a Micro-Series. Since all great series have series arcs, go ahead and use the same Fence Posts for your Micro-Series as well. If you want more than seven offerings, add any other beats from the Six Stage Story you wish. If you just want a pure trilogy, just use the Monkey Wrench, All In and Main Event Showdown beats to map it out.

This actually creates a pretty interesting situation where you have a well-structured Macro-Story made up of stand-alone, well-structured Micro-Stories and Micro-Series that are structured in the same way as the Macro-Story. Every piece is structured. Every level reflects the next. Every piece has purpose. Every piece directly affects the next.

It's enough to make me want to cry.

Moreover, even beyond the overall series arc, you can shape the individual offerings within your Micro-Series in three different ways:

1. Serialized
2. Episodic
3. Anthology

I know, I know — we're deep in the weeds, but all of this is important.

**Serialized.**

A Serialized Micro-Series is one that should be experienced in a series. There are complex plots and stories carrying from one episode to another. If you watched a random episode of *LOST* in the middle of Season 5 you'd be…well, lost. Well-known serials are *Game of Thrones, Mad Men, True Detective, The Walking Dead, Orphan Black, House of Cards* and *Breaking Bad.* These stories are often complex and each episode builds upon another leading to a much greater time commitment but also a greater payoff. In the same way, if you, for whatever reason, jumped into *The Hunger Games* series by starting with *The Hunger Games: Mockingjay – Part 1*, you're going to be lost.

When crafting a Micro-Series in a *serialized* way, abide by these two simple parameters:

1. Maintain consistent protagonist(s) throughout the Micro-Series; *and*
2. Make sure every offering is released in the same medium and platform (film, book, comic, television show, etc.).

When you think about it, these should make sense. It would be weird if you were watching *Breaking Bad* and the seventh episode of a season was in a comic book or followed a completely different protagonist.

**Episodic.**

An episodic Micro-Series is akin to shows like *Law and Order, CSI, Big Bang Theory or Matlock*, where each episode has a complete story arc and can stand alone. Given, there are certain, broad arcs that carry over, but nothing so complicated an audience can't tune into episode four, eight and twelve and still enjoy the experience.

When doing a Micro-Series in an *episodic* way, abide by these two simple parameters:

1. Maintain consistent protagonist(s) throughout the Micro-Series; *and*
2. Make sure the *majority* of the offerings are released in the same medium (film, book, comic, etc.); however, *a few can strategically be shifted into different mediums or platforms.*

So, because all the episodes of the *Big Bang Theory* can stand alone, you can do the majority of the episodes on television, a couple in comic books and one in a mobile game. However, all the episodes, no matter what the medium, should still follow Leonard, Sheldon and the gang. If you don't pick up the comic books or game, you can still keep up with the television show, but at least your series has some West Coast components in different mediums attracting different types of audience members.

**Anthology.**

An anthologized Micro-Series is one that presents a completely different story and a different set of characters in each episode. So not only do you not need the first episode to understand the second, but the two episodes won't have *any* connection outside of theme or possibly locations. *Black Mirror* is a great anthology television series, as was the *Twilight Zone.* In publishing, *The Spoon River Anthologies* and Michael Moorcock's *Eternal Champion* series are great examples of anthology series.

When doing a Micro-Series in an *anthologized* way, be sure to abide by these two development parameters:

1. Be sure to have different protagonists for each episode; *and*
2. Feel free to shift every episode into both a different medium and platform.

If, for some reason, any of your individual "episodes" within your Micro-Series are too big to tell in a single story, feel free to replicate this process one level deeper by going into what's called a *Nano-Series.*

Yes, Nano-Series. "Nano" is smaller than "micro."

Until you're a seasoned Super Story Architect, I wouldn't suggest going any deeper than a Nano-Series to discover what we call a Pico-Series. Discovering that too early may drive you insane and trap you in an *Inception*-like mind loop for the rest of your days.

At the end of the day, the benefit of all of this is when you structure your Macro-Series in this way and understand how to shape each offering within, you really do create an impressive architecture for a rich, thorough Super Story experience.

Plus, it makes you sound cooler than your friends.

"Hey, what are you working on?"

"I'm working on my indie screenplay. What are you working on?"

"I'm breaking part five of my Anthologized Core Narrative Micro-Series that's the Soapbox Revisited beat of the Macro-Story of my High Concept Storyworld."

*mic drop*

## Go get other people.

I know we've covered quite a bit of material, but I want to make sure you don't forget one of the basic value propositions of a Super Story — the ability to attract different demographics and grow a bigger, more diverse fanbase. The main way you will accomplish this is by diversifying the tone, style and genre of your various Micro-Stories.

If you have built your Storyworld correctly, it should not only be able to support multiple mediums and platforms, but it should also be able to support Micro-Stories in multiple genres. The real word is funny, dramatic, dangerous, romantic, scary, quirky, tense, horrific, musical, inspirational and sometimes sad (and that was just my law school experience). As such, your Super Story should reflect the same dynamic and avoid having all of your Micro-Stories hit the same note.

When you begin creating your Super Story, you'll probably have a main target market in mind. However, in order to attract different demographics, be sure to ask yourself, "What do people love who wouldn't typically engage with my Super Story?" Once you've identified that answer, begin developing Micro-Stories in genres and styles that create relevant points of entry for those very people.

Beyond that, force yourself to try and find at least one Micro-Story in every major genre. When you do, you'll find your Storyworld will mature in a very interesting and creative way and your Super Story will become a much more valuable asset overall.

It's also important to note even when creating a Super Story geared toward children, you need to skew the overall Storyworld, and its Micro Stories, a little older than you think you should. Why? Because you can always mold an older concept to appeal to a younger fan base, but you can't mold a juvenile concept to appeal to an older fan base. For example, while you can reshape Darth Vader (a masked, evil, magical, mass-murderer) in a way that creates a great children's book, you can never skew Elmo up to engage college males.

Moreover, this also naturally builds in an opportunity for fans to grow *with* the Super Story instead of growing *out of* the Super Story. Whereas your line of YA novels may be too mature, dark and intense for a toddler, that toddler can engage in your Super Story through the tablet app or the board books. As that child grows, he or she will mature to find the books and there will continually be extensions that match his or her particular quadrant of life.

Therefore, there should be bright parts of your Super Story, and also be some dark corners. There will be quiet stories, but also explosions. Some tales will be epic, while others will be extremely small in scale. Collectively, these stories will help form the four-quadrant tapestry your Super Story needs to be a forever franchise.

## The windows into the world.

We've spent quite a bit of time talking about macro-this and nano-that, but you can't tell a great story without great characters. Stories, like life, are about people and relationships. Likewise, drama is about conflict and conflict always comes down to people with opposing, passionate views.

At the end of the day, it's characters, more than plot, that grab an audience member's soul because characters have the ability to translate their own actions, desires, passions, fears, and dreams into the audience's databank of experiences and emotions. Our characters are our ears and our eyes on the ground of our Storyworld. They're who we root for and to whom we relate. After the intricacies of a plot fade, great characters will linger with a pseudo-physical presence.

The problem with most stories, though, be it screenplays or novels, isn't that the writer doesn't have an interesting character in mind. It's that they don't understand how to convey that character so the reader sees what they see. So many writers believe everything about their characters will magically emerge onto the page.

Not going to happen.

While there are books and workshops solely devoted to character creation, I've taken the liberty to outline a few strategies that, when used, help flesh out a character and build intrigue, depth, and interest around them.

## High concept.

Do you remember our discussion about High Concepts and how to use irony and "opposites" to build immediate interest in your concept, plots, and settings? Well, the same principle applies to designing characters. Simply put two opposites together and your character will immediately become more interesting.

How about a pilot who is afraid of heights? Or a hitman who becomes a pacifist? Or a schoolteacher who can't read? Or a schoolteacher who sells meth? Or a criminal or conman who tries to become president? #truestory

Whether you land on an extreme combination or a milder version, trying to build a High Concept into a character will certainly help the character jump off the page much quicker.

## Breakdown.

Many writers suggest developing at least a ten-page background/biography of your characters before you start writing. Personally, I think that's a great practice; however, before you try to punch out ten pages for a character, it's good to do a quick *breakdown* of all the characters. Once you have completed the breakdown, you'll have the framework to develop a more complete biography.

Here's a good primer on what to cover and include in a character breakdown:

- **Name:** There are many literary and movie characters that become everlasting brands in our culture — Atticus Finch, "Ratso" Rizzo, Holden Caulfield, and Scarlett O'Hara, for example. Choose a name that is unique to your character and memorable to your story. The names should reveal something about your characters: who they are, where they come from, or where they could possibly be going.
- **Archetype**: In Christopher Vogler's book, *The Writers Journey: Mythic Structure for Writers,* he goes into detail about a number of classic archetypes that nearly all great characters fall into. Jeff Gomez is a big advocate of using archetypes in character design because it allows a character to resonate with what

Carl Jung describes as the audience's "collective unconscious." One thing to keep in mind, though, is you can have more than one character in the same role, and characters often play more than one role throughout the entirety of a Super Story.

- **Hero** - A character who is willing to sacrifice to achieve a goal.
- **Mentor** - A character who provides guidance and tools the hero needs to complete the task.
- **Threshold Guardian** - A character who acts as a barrier the hero attempts to pass through. These characters test the hero.
- **Herald** - An information-giving character that alters the life or goal of the hero.
- **Shapeshifter** - A character whose role and even personality change dramatically during a story.
- **Shadow** - A character who represents what the hero can become if the hero loses his or her way.
- **Trickster** - A character who majors in mischief and misdirection and usually straddles the line between hero and villain. Apparently, Captain Jack Sparrow was originally designed to fit the Trickster archetype.

- **Physiology**: What does your character look like to an outsider? Include things such as height, weight, clothing style, tattoos, noticeable scars, etc. Pretend like you're giving a description of a stranger to the police. The more distinct the better. In fact, imagine if George Lucas would have made Darth Vader simply an old man in a robe? Do you think the character would have risen to be one of the most iconic villains of all time? Of course not. Distinct looks help make characters timeless.

- **A Great Description** - In this vein, a reader must get a sense of your characters after you've described them. Therefore, start considering the best way to initially present them to the audience. "Tall and thin" is boring. "Ichabod Crane on crack" evokes an image. Having said that, make sure the description matches the tone and genre of your story. I wouldn't use "Ichabod Crane on crack" in a drama, for example, but I might use it in a comedy. Here's a description of Christina in the original draft of *Source Code.*

  *"In contrast to the corporate suits around her, her appearance is thrift-store funky: black nail polish, dark lipstick, black hair with blue streaks, a button-down blouse edged in black funeral lace with silver skull and bones cufflinks."*

  This description evokes a great physiological image of the character in our minds. Here's another great one from *The Adventures of Huckleberry Finn*:

  *"He was almost fifty, and he looked it. His hair was long and tangled and greasy, and hung down, and you could see his eyes shining through like he was behind vines. It was all black, no gray; so was his long, mixed-up whiskers. There warn't no color in his face, where his face showed; it was white; not like another man's white, but a white to make a body sick, a white to make a body's flesh crawl — a tree-toad white, a fish-belly white. As for his clothes — just rags, that was all. He had one ankle resting on t'other knee; the boot on that foot was busted, and two of his toes stuck through, and he worked them now and then. His hat was laying on the floor — an old black slouch with the top caved in, like a lid."*

  Lastly, here's a great character description of Olive from *Little Miss Sunshine*:

*"A seven-year-old girl sits watching a beauty pageant intently. She is big for her age and slightly plump. She has frizzy hair and wears black-rimmed glasses. She studies the show very earnestly. Then, using a remote, she freezes the image. Absently, she holds up one hand and mimics the waving style of Miss America. She rewinds the tape and starts all over again."*

Even if you haven't seen *Little Miss Sunshine* (and if you haven't, *why not?!* It's a terrific movie!), I'm guessing that screenwriter Michael Arndt's description of Olive gave you a very vivid image of the character. And notice how her black-rimmed glasses, intent expression and mimicking wave tell us volumes about her beyond just her appearance. We know what she longs for, how determined she is, and how out of reach her dream seems to be for her.

It's never too early to start thinking about how to craft a great description.

- **Sociology**: This is how your character interacts with people around her or him. Does she have friends? Is he a black sheep? What kind of social circles does the character run in?

- **Personality**: This is pretty self-explanatory. What's the psychology that surrounds your character? Is she trusting? Does he have an anger problem? Truly understanding the psychology of your character is key to finding his voice and determining what decisions he will make.

  One of the best ways to define your character's personality is to actually use a real personality test. Whether it's the Myers-Briggs test or the DISC assessment or another (you can find all of these and about a zillion more with a quick Google search), try to fit your characters into a defined category.

- **Flaws:** A flaw goes a long way toward defining your character and should hold him or her back. The character will need to overcome a flaw in order to solve the big problems facing her or him in the stories. Rocky Balboa's flaw, for example, is he doesn't believe in himself. This flaw is something that should come up repeatedly, something your character should be bumping up against again and again. So in *Up in the Air*, for example, George Clooney's fatal flaw is his inability to get close to other people. That's why he's easily able to fire people. That's why he has meaningless sexual relationships on the road. That's why he barely talks to his family. That's why he gives seminars about the power of being on your own. At the very least, you should give your main character at least one fatal flaw. But I like to give a few of my secondary characters fatal flaws as well, since it makes them deeper and more interesting.

- **Goals:** Your characters need to have goals in order to stay active and moving forward throughout your stories. They need to want something. They need to be motivated. Without goals, characters become passive and boring and you cannot have a great Micro-Story with passive, boring characters. Moreover, character goals are great fodder for conflict because inevitably there will be characters whose goals are diametrically opposed. I suggest giving your characters two types of goals.

    - **Story goal** - This is the immediate, short-term goal the character has in any particular Micro-Story. In *Back To The Future*, Marty's goal is to get his parents together so he can get home. In *Taken*, Bryan's goal is to rescue his daughter. The story goal is directly tied to the plot of the Micro-Story and will change with every Micro-Story in the franchise.

- **Life goal** - I don't think enough writers think about a character's life goal. Basically, it's the character's ultimate plan in life. Again, in *Back to the Future,* Marty's Story Goal is to get his parents together and get back to the future. However, his Life Goal is to become a musician. It's not the most original or profound goal in the world, but it gives us insight into who he is. If his life goal was to feed starving kids in Africa, it would certainly alter our perception of the character. The Life Goal, as opposed to the Story Goal, should carry over into other Micro-Stories and should consistently shade the character throughout the franchise.

- **Secrets**: Secrets always make characters more interesting and tell a lot about the characters themselves. Did your character kill someone and was never caught? Does she fear she's not good enough? The right secret can add a tremendous amount of depth to a character. Everyone has secrets — your characters should, too.

- **Quirks**: We all have something about ourselves that's unique, so what interesting quirks and characteristics make your character stand out? In *Arrested Development,* Tobias is a "never-nude" and wears denim cutoffs in the shower. Does your character love to eat dry toast? Is she OCD? Does he collect action figures like Steve Carrell's character in *The 40-Year-Old Virgin*? Does he love marching bands? Does he wash his hands *before* he goes to the bathroom? One or two of these quirks can really liven up a character.

- **Family Tree**: Who are your character's family members? Even if it's just immediate family members and you don't flesh them out, go ahead and sketch out the family tree. The difference in the personality of an only child and a seventh child is tremendous. Likewise, a boy who is raised by his grandfather probably has a different perspective on life than a boy who was raised by both parents. So the family tree can help shape your character's personality. Also, a family tree can be an extremely useful tool in a transmedia franchise because of the connections you can build between stories.

By sketching out a few sentences in each of these categories for all of your main characters, as well as key supporting characters, you'll already have a cast that will be jumping off the page even before you write the first words of your first Micro-Story.

## A note on roles.

Traditionally, when developing a story, a writer will assign character roles such as protagonist, antagonist, supporting characters, etc. However, in the Super Story model, we are forced to examine the characters in a more rigorous, robust way.

Yes, every Micro-Story will still have a protagonist, an antagonist and a cast of supporting characters. However, because you'll be dealing with multiple stories, it's quite possible the villain in your first story may become the hero in your third. A supporting character in one plot may be the hero of another and the hero of your film may be relegated to a background or supporting role in your comic book.

Because of this dynamic, every single character in your Storyworld needs to be interesting, developed and well-rounded enough to carry his or her own story. Why? Because in a Super Story, they very well could do just that.

Consider the curious case of Boba Fett. Boba Fett is, beyond being the most popular character in all of *Star Wars*, something of a paradox. There is essentially nothing to his character – or, at least, *was*, before the Expanded Universe of novels, comic books, short stories, and videogames started to explore him further, and before creator/writer/director George Lucas himself revealed the face underneath the mask in the prequel trilogy. In fact, Boba Fett's lines in the original trilogy total only 27 words. Likewise, his screen time is a measly 6 minutes 32 seconds across three films, where 13 seconds of which is his ship only. Only one scene is over a minute long.

Objectively, he should be a throwaway, supporting character. In reality, the mysterious bounty hunter of few words is one of the most popular — he features one of the best-designed costumes in cinematic history, not to mention brandishing an assortment of bad-ass weaponry (including a jetpack!). And then there's his enigmatic nature, which allowed viewers to fill in their own backstory and personality for the mercenary when he first appeared in *The Empire Strikes Back* and *Return of the Jedi.*

What's really interesting about Boba Fett is he was originally supposed to be Darth Vader. When first sitting down with his cadre of designers and concept artists for the first *Star Wars,* George Lucas had a rough idea of what he wanted out of his archetypal villain, Darth Vader, but the specifics were elusive. The design process started with Vader being an "intergalactic bounty hunter" before taking the turn of making him a fallen Jedi Knight. As would happen countless times through the subsequent *Star Wars* films' development, that idea of a menacing mercenary was recycled to be used for another character, Boba Fett.

So, unknowingly, Lucas did take the time to develop Boba Fett — a minor character — like he was a main character, because he was actually supposed to be. And look what happened! The character jumped off the screen despite the lack of screen time or lines and became a timeless icon of one of the most profitable brands in history.

And you continue to see that run through Lucas' work. Entering in the Mos Eisley Cantina in *A New Hope,* it's apparent every single patron of that bar was designed with care and precision. And because of that, all those characters have been mined for additional stories by Lucasfilm. Check out the anthology, *Tales from the Mos Eisley Cantina,* sometime and see how a more in-depth character design on the front end led to narrative potential on the backend.

Moreover, in today's entertainment landscape, your characters can't be two-dimensional. People are complicated, so your characters should be as well. Therefore, give your protagonists secret dark sides that can possibly be leveraged in a villainous way in another story. Likewise, give your antagonists a few admirable traits and even righteous motivations to make them even more dynamic.

Your heroes will only be as interesting as they are bad and your antagonists will only be as interesting as they are good. Every character has potential. Every character has a variety of personality traits, moods and motivations. Sure, it takes more effort to develop your characters, but in the end you'll have a cast that is much more dynamic and ready to be moved into whatever narrative role you need them to fill.

## A.B.A. — always be adding.

Remember our conversation about Additive Comprehension and its intrinsic importance to a Super Story? I hope so, because without Additive Comprehension, your audience won't migrate from touchpoint to touchpoint and your Super Story will fracture. In fact, having amazing, "Oh snap!" moments is most important for your Micro-Stories or Micro-Series since they are the most expensive components you will produce and release. Since they are the most resource-intensive and require the most investment, making their success critical to the overall financial success of your Super Story, you want to ensure you're heavily baiting the audience to experience them.

Therefore, for your Micro-Stories, make sure you have the biggest reveals — the "I see dead people" sort of plot twists that get the fanbase excited and talking. Here are the usual suspects I typically go to for Additive Comprehension in my Micro-Stories:

- **Origin Story**: This is an account of how something came to be and the original circumstances that led to it. It is a bedrock account of the transformative events that set certain things in motion that forever change the future of your Storyworld in some way. Origin stories can be used for:

- *Historical Events*: What was the event that led to the institution of the Hunger Games? What caused the machines to take over in The Matrix? How did the aliens get here in *District 9*? What led to the construction of The Wall in *Game of Thrones?*

- *Characters:* This is finding out *how* a main character becomes who she ultimately becomes in a later Micro-Story is always a valuable piece of information to learn. How did Anakin become Darth Vader? How did Tony Stark become Iron Man? How did Dracula become the Lord of the Vampires? What sends Hannibal Lecter off the edge into the charming cannibal we all know and love? How did the apes take over in the *Planet of the Apes* franchise? All of these questions made me want to check out *Revenge of the Sith, Iron Man, Dracula Untold, Hannibal Rising* and *Rise of the Planet of the Apes.*

    - *Organization:* This is just like a character's origin story, except with an organization. How was S.H.I.E.L.D. formed in the Marvel universe? What were the circumstances that created the X-Men? How did the Empire come to power in *Star Wars?*

- **Major Death**: Much like the origin of a main character can draw you to a story, so can the death of a main character. Because of the death of a certain main character (I won't spoil it), *The Force Awakens* is now *necessary* viewing for all *Star Wars* fans. Likewise, when I learned that Chewbacca dies in the Extended Universe novel, *Vector Prime,* I ~~ran to get it~~ ordered it online as quickly as I could because that *was* important information. Thankfully, that is one of the creative decisions Disney decided to leave behind in the old EU.

- **Character Reveal**: This isn't necessarily communicating the origin of a character, just something interesting and important about them. For example, let's say *Frozen* was a Super Story franchise told across multiple stories and in the original Micro-Story Prince Hans is everything we've come to expect from a Disney prince. However, in a different Micro-Story, it's revealed he is using Anna's affections as political means to advance his own claim to a throne – a goal he was willing to sacrifice both princesses of Arendelle to achieve. That character reveal makes the second Micro-Story extremely valuable to the fanbase. Can you reveal that one of your main characters from another Micro-Story actually has cancer and isn't telling anyone? What if in one Micro-Story they're married with a gaggle of children, but in another Micro-Story you reveal the character is actually gay? I'm not talking about simply backstory, I'm talking about big, "Oh Snap!" reveals.

- **Anticipated Showdowns:** This is where you channel your inner Don King or Vince McMahon and hype a showdown between characters that is "must see" for the fans. Whether it's Captain America versus Iron Man, Batman versus Superman, Harry versus Voldemort, Goldberg versus Hogan, Holmes versus Moriarty or Yoda versus Palpatine, these types of epic face-offs and showdowns are essential viewing for the fanbase.

- **Storyworld Reveal:** A Storyworld reveal is when you either physically reveal a new, valuable part of the Storyworld previously *unexplored* by the audience or reveal new information about the Storyworld previously *unknown* to the audience. For example, in the *Star Wars* galaxy, there is a section called the Unexplored Regions where "a hundred different threats that would freeze your blood" live. If that region were revealed in a Micro-Story, it instantly becomes valuable to the fans. Or, in *Game of Thrones*, if a different Micro-Story (other than the books/show) revealed the Mad King hid wildfire underneath all of King's Landing, that would be a great use of Additive Comprehension.

- **Other Micro-Story Reveal:** Much like a character reveal, if you reveal something significant about the plot of another Micro-Story, it will qualify as Additive Comprehension. For example, in the film, *The Force Awakens,* Han and Chewie capture Rathtars and are transporting them when they run into Rey and Finn. In the *Star Wars: Legos* cartoons, you learn exactly how they captured the Rathtars. Again, one Micro-Story revealing valuable information about another Micro-Story. Also, in *The Force Awakens,* you're left wondering who the

> Knights of Ren are, how did C-3PO get a red arm, why and how did the First Order steal Finn from his family, etc. In *The Matrix,* you're told one has to have an operator in the real world to dial you in and out. However, when Cypher meets with Agent Smith and betrays the group, who was his operator? Having other Micro-Stories reveal this information creates incentive for fans to seek out, migrate and pay for those Micro-Stories.

If you can, make sure every one of your Micro-Stories includes *at least three out of the six* Additive Comprehension types. When you do, you'll have no problem incentivizing audience members to continue the exploration process, thereby engineering an unparalleled creative synergy around your Super Story.

## What are you waiting for?

Once you know what your Micro-Stories are going to be about and you've created the characters who will star in them, take the time to develop broad loglines or loose treatments for each. At this point, don't begin scripting anything because as you work your way through the loglines/ treatments, new ideas will jar loose and your various Micro-Stories will morph and change ever so slightly. When this happens, don't panic. It's totally normal — like a new house settling.

Moreover, you can't really begin scripting until we decide on what medium and platform would be best for each story and that doesn't come until later in the process. Sure, you probably have some ideas about what could be a television show, a feature or a spoken word event, but don't make any final determinations until you go all the way through the Super Story process.

Once you have your Micro-Story loglines or loose treatments in place, grab your jackets and gloves because it's time to take a quick trip to the East Coast.

# I'M SO MUCH MORE OF AN EAST COAST GIRL THAN A WEST COAST GIRL

LEXA DOIG

# 12. East coast extensions.

## East coast maxin'.

While Micro-Stories are standalone, complete, West Coast revenue drivers, it's time to turn our attention to the smaller, dependent East Coast Extensions. Again, they aren't whole stories. Think of them as story slices — like a slice of a pie as compared to the whole pie.

Mmmmmm. Pie.

It bears repeating that just because they're dependent on the Micro-Stories for context, meaning and value, doesn't mean they're optional or even inferior. East Coast Transmedia drives engagement, incentivizes exploration, innovates an experience and extends a story — all of this is valuable (albeit a different type of value) than the larger, standalone Micro-Stories or Micro-Series.

It's one thing to understand the function and the value of East Coast Transmedia, but it's an entirely different thing to identify or create the type of narrative opportunity that works best in this role. Unfortunately, not every piece of story will work as an effective East Coast Extension, but by the end of this chapter, you'll know the differences and understand which ones are up for the challenge.

When it's all said and done, there are five different narrative opportunities that create East Coast opportunities. These candidates include:

1. Unanswered Questions
2. Other Character Perspectives
3. Character Backstories
4. Storyworld Exploration
5. Narrative Excess

Let's look at each one in detail.

## Unanswered questions.

This one is pretty self explanatory. It's when you pose a question in a Micro-Story you intentionally don't answer in the Micro-Story itself. Instead, you actually answer it in an East Coast Extension.

The brain is truly an amazing data-processing tool. It receives millions of inputs every second and it is constantly analyzing and comparing information against its predetermined hypotheses. Moreover, when a new question is posed, the brain automatically attempts to find any information to answer it, including cross-checking information from its past experiences.

Therefore, when you pose a question in a Micro-Story that you intentionally don't answer, the brain will naturally be working on finding the answer. The more enticing the question, the more enticing the extension becomes.

For example, in Sofia Coppola's film, *Lost in Translation*, what does Bill Murray whisper to Scarlett Johansson at the end? It remains one of the biggest mysteries in recent film history, its secrecy enhanced by the fact no one besides the actors know for sure what Murray said as Bob (Wait — could there be untapped *What about Bob?* crossover potential — are these films in the same universe? — is this Bob *that* Bob, after he's cured? #mindblown #transmedianeverstops).

Interestingly enough, Coppola doesn't even know what was said, as the scene was improvised by Murray and ended up much different (and much better) than what was originally written. Over the last decade, some people with sound equipment and/or imaginations have done their best to crack the mysterious code, but no one knows for sure.

This, in my opinion, is a perfect candidate for an East Coast Extension and a way to re-engage an audience of a decade-old film. Maybe they could set up a SoundCloud account where they have the actual line? Maybe someone close by was videoing something else and their camera picked up the line, which means you could publish the video on YouTube or Vimeo. Maybe have Bill Murray write a letter to Scarlet Johansson ten years later, recalling what he said and publish the letter online via a website or even something like a Tumblr blog? Maybe Coppola could have revealed the answer in a cool Converged East Coast way while you were watching the DVD?

What about the unanswered question of what's in the briefcase in *Pulp Fiction*? I would *love* to find that out as I've been debating it in my mind for over 20 years. Of course the briefcase is used as a MacGuffin, a plot device that's simply meant to move the story forward, and ultimately has no explanation. But due to this lack of explanation, fans have theorized wildly on its contents, guessing theories such as it containing radioactive material (due to the glowing), the diamonds from Tarantino's first film, *Reservoir Dogs,* and even Marsellus Wallace's soul.

If Tarantino created a web series or an online comic book centered around the contents of the briefcase, I would be first in line to re-engage with the two-decade old IP.

What about the unanswered question in *Inception*? After finally performing the mind heist which promises to be his ticket home, Cobb returns to the U.S., where he's greeted by his father-in-law, who reunites him with his two young children.

Cobb spins a top totem to see if he's still dreaming, but doesn't stick around to see if it topples or not, instead keen to play with his kids. The final shot closes in on the top as it appears to waver but doesn't fall over. Cut to black.

Has there been a more frustrating movie ending in recent history? Does the top keep spinning? Is Cobb still in a dream? What's the deal? This is a perfect set up for an East Coast Extension.

What about a simple app called *Cobb's Top?* All it would need to be is a spinning top totem that you stare at and, eventually, it either falls or doesn't? I think that would be a great opportunity to engage the fanbase and, heck, I would even pay 99 cents for it. If I would pay 99 cents, I'm sure there are a million other people who would as well. What an easy way to make a million bucks — and extend the story for the fans.

Damon Lindelof and Carlton Cuse were universally derided for not answering *all* the questions they posed in *Lost.* Admittedly, they answered the major questions and you can only do so much in 47 minutes of television every week. However, understanding and utilizing East Coast Transmedia principles, they could have still answered every single one of the hundred or so questions they posed in the series — without shooting one extra second of television. They could have doled one out every month for the next eight years and have extended the experience of the fanbase in an amazing and valuable way.

This brings us to the great unanswered question of our generation — who let the dogs out? Seriously, the Baha Men were one-hit-wonders with their Grammy Award Winning song, *Who Let the Dogs Out* and have never actually answered the question — and it's been 15 years. I'm being completely honest when I say if I saw a tweet from the Baha Men that said to go to a website and find out who actually let the dogs out, I would most definitely go. Now, if I saw a tweet from them simply promoting their new album, I wouldn't go at all. I may even flag the tweet as inappropriate and/or spam.

But because they posed a question in their West Coast component (the song) that they never answered, they have an opportunity to bait people to an East Coast Extension. Like I said, if all it consisted of was clicking a link, and I didn't have to pay for it, and it took me to a website where I found out that Snoop Dogg was the one who let the dogs out, it would totally have been worth it for me. Not only that, but when they get me there, they could *then* use that as an opportunity to promote their new project. However, because they gave me entertainment value and an answer to the question *first*, I don't think I would mind as much.

The fascinating thing (I know, it's weird that I find things like this fascinating) is that if at the end of their original *Who Let the Dogs Out?* song, they would have answered the question, the East Coast opportunity wouldn't be available to them on the backend.

Is Michael Jackson the husband of Billie Jean's kid? Did Riggan kill himself in *Birdman?* What actually happens inside Pokeballs after monsters get sucked inside of them? How did Lukas die in *Goodnight Mommy*? How did the Joker really get his scars in *The Dark Knight*? In *Halo*, do you know when you die in multiplayer mode and see that your killer is listed as "Guardian" — since bots have never been part of *Halo,* who are these ghosts? All these questions are prime candidates to be answered in East Coast Extensions — both Dispersed and Converged.

When I want to transmediate a script, song, game or book, the first thing I do is go through and highlight all the unanswered questions posed in the text. However, as you are creating your own Micro-Stories from the ground up, make sure you pose questions you *intentionally* don't answer. When you do, you will find you have created a variety of great East Coast Transmedia opportunities — but only if the questions and their answers are valuable to the fans. If you're answering meaningless questions, trust me, you won't get the impact you're wanting.

It's worthy to note this is very similar to the Other Micro-Story Reveal, which is a type of Additive Comprehension that can bait fans to migrate to your larger, West Coast Micro-Stories. When deciding whether an answer to a question should be in another Micro-Story or in an East Coast Extension, simply ask how big or important is the reveal? While you want every answer to be valuable and significant, you'll want to save the really big ones for your Micro-Stories and the smaller ones for your East Coast Extensions. Since the overall revenue model of your Super Story depends on fans traveling to your Micro-Stories, you want the biggest, juiciest bait to be imbedded in them.

Also, before we move on, I want to encourage you to always ask another question every time you answer one. That way you'll always have East Coast opportunities to pursue. Also, sometimes certain questions are so intriguing, so debated by the fanbase, the question gets elevated to a point where no answer will be enough to satisfy the fans. In those limited circumstances, you may not want to ever answer them and simply allow them to exist in J.J. Abrams' magical mystery box forever.

For example, in *The Phantom Menace,* as soon as George Lucas answered how the Force "worked" by going into midi-chlorians and such, I believe it actually hurt the *Star Wars* IP. In just a couple of scenes, Lucas took all the whimsy, wonder and magic around the concept of the Force and repackaged it as simply occupational phlebotomy. To be fair, no answer to that question would have made the fans happy. I know I'm "Monday morning quarterbacking" a billionaire visionary, but I think he should have allowed the mystery to persist and answered other questions.

## Other character perspectives.

As I stated at the beginning of the book, you never want to tell the same story twice. While this is almost always true, there's one minor exception — when you can tell the same story (either the whole thing or simply just a sequence) from another character's perspective.

Major crossover events in comics, such as DC Comic's *Blackest Night,* are a great example of overlapping stories that exist in the same narrative time and with different perspectives of the same events. In the same way, *Flags of Our Father* and *Letters from Iwo Jima* are two ends of the same story coin. In the fourth season of *Arrested Development,* each episode focuses on a different character of the main cast, revealing different perspectives about Cinco de Cuatro, The Opie Awards, and the other various events. In *Gone Girl,* the film relates the different accounts of events leading up to the disappearance of a woman, one account from said woman, as per her diary, and one account from the woman's husband, as he relates it.

However, instead of having to tell the other perspective in the same story or even another big, expensive Micro-Story like these examples, you can actually tell one perspective in the Micro-Story and then actually explore other perspectives in East Coast Extensions.

In *The Lord of the Rings: The Fellowship of the Ring*, Frodo is commissioned with taking the One Ring to the House of Elrond, who is calling together a special council. Legolas and Gimli both make appearances at the council and ultimately join The Fellowship, but we never see how Legolas and Gimli originally hear about the council or why they make the decision to attend. So, instead of being content with sticking with the perspective of Frodo and Sam at Rivendale, you could have an East Coast Extension that takes the perspective of Legolas and Gimli during that same time.

Have you ever wanted to see what happens when Mr. White and Nice Guy Eddie go get the diamonds in *Reservoir Dogs* while Mr. Blonde cuts off the cop's ear? Perfect East Coast opportunity. In *Forrest Gump*, three or four years of Forrest Jr.'s life are skipped. Wouldn't you want to be there when Forrest Jr. asks about his real father for the first time? This type of East Coast Extension allows for this opportunity.

A great example of this using another character's perspective in an East Coast Extension occurs in Season 2 Episode 8 of *Breaking Bad*. In the episode, we see an entire DEA sting from the perspective of Walt and Jesse. After the sting operation, Saul Goodman (who previously didn't know Heisenberg's real identity) shows up at Walt's school, confronts him about being Heisenberg and asks for a cut of the meth business.

During the first season of *Better Call Saul*, AMC published an online comic entitled, *Better Call Saul: Client Development*. In the comic, we see the entire DEA sting again, except this time, from Saul Goodman's investigator's perspective (RIP Mike). From his perspective, you learn he was actually staking out the entire sting operation himself, though you don't see him in the episode. It also tells how he ultimately finds out who Heisenberg really is, which leads to Saul Goodman confronting him at the school. Same story. One in the Micro-Series (the television show), the other in the Dispersed East Coast Extension (the comic book).

It's important to note, this opportunity only becomes valuable with Additive Comprehension, which means the other perspective you follow needs to be valuable and add to the story in a meaningful way. Another perspective just for the sake of another perspective is a recipe for an ill-effective East Coast Extension.

For example, take the scene from *Pulp Fiction* where Vince Vega and Mia Wallace are at Jack Rabbit Slim's and are having dinner. The scene is focused on the perspectives of those two characters. Technically, the scene could be told strictly from the perspective of Buddy Holly, their waiter and, technically, this would qualify as an East Coast opportunity. But would it add to the story at all or give us new insight into the characters or the plot? Probably not. It could, if you engineered it, but it doesn't pop off the page as a prime East Coast opportunity.

Now, take the scene where Jules and Vincent retrieve Marcellus Wallace's briefcase from Brett's apartment.

---

```
Grabbing the case and placing it on the counter.

                              VINCENT
            Got it.

Vincent flips the two locks, opening the case. We
can't see what's inside, but a small glow emits from
the case. Vincent just stares at it, transfixed.

                              JULES
            We happy?

No answer from the transfixed Vincent

                              JULES
                          (continuing)
            Vincent!

Vincent looks up at Jules.

                              JULES
                          (continuing)
            We happy?

Closing the case.

                              VINCENT
            We're happy.
```

---

Since we're given Jules' perspective in the scene, we don't see what's in the briefcase, though based on Vincent's reaction, it must be pretty amazing. Then, if you took Vincent's perspective in an East Coast Extension, it would be an Other Character Perspective East Coast Extension *and* an Unanswered Question East Coast Extension. Having it pull double duty actually makes it a really, really good East Coast opportunity.

Can you tell that I *really* want to know what's in that stinkin' briefcase?

## Character backstory.

Where did your character come from? How did he get that limp? Why does she dress like that? Who are their parents? Why was the character in jail? How did the main character learn how to do that one thing so well?

Backstory has always been a ~~maddening~~ ~~tricky~~ intriguing concept because writers are constantly tortured by how much backstory to include. Much like using seasoning when you cook, you're constantly asking yourself, "Is it too much? Too little? Just enough? What if it's just enough for me, but not for the reader? Or visa versa?"

Necessarily, backstory is the story before *the* Micro-Story. It's the events that transpire before the Micro-Story's events you've chosen to highlight and reveal and invite the audience into. The backstory is the cause for the events of the Micro-Story you ultimately put on the page or screen. Backstory covers motive, history and the roots of character personality.

However, while backstory gives reasons and excuses for events that happen in the *now* of your Micro-Story, backstory isn't that *now*. And if you dump too much of the past in at one shot, it slows the unfolding of the current story, and may even deaden the impact of the current action and event. It leaches the emotional power out of the story action that's unfolding on the page in the story's present.

Basically, backstory is part of the setup for plot and characters; it is not a substitute for unfolding events in your Micro-Story. So, it's valuable and many times necessary, but at the same time, the exposition of it cannibalizes your drama, which kills your story.

Thus, the debate.

You should be excited, however, to learn that (again) with a Super Story, you can have your cake and eat it too. In this model, you can have as much backstory as you want — just put most (or all) of it in an East Coast Extension of your Micro-Story. This way it won't stall or bloat the plot of your Micro-Story, but you still get the benefit of the audience understanding the backstory information — and you get to extend and/or innovate the experience with an East Coast Extension.

Put that way, it's like having your cake, eating it too *and* finding a $20 bill.

For example, in the AMC show *Turn*, there's a scene in the first season where the evil Lieutenant Simcoe holds a pistol to the protagonist, Abraham Woodhull's, head. The scene on television is quick; however, seeing an East Coast Transmedia opportunity, AMC released a comic series called, *Turn: Origins*. In these comics, it revisits the scene and actually shows Woodhull's life flash before his eyes. During this flash, we get a story of him as a child and see what happened to him that prepared him to be a revolutionary later in life.

The showrunners, admittedly, couldn't have included this in the television episode as they only have 47 minutes to pack in everything they need. Not only that, but every single one of those minutes is very expensive, which means if it's not *necessary* for the plot, it needs to go. Backstory is rarely necessary, so it's usually the first to go.

However, identifying and using the character's backstory as an East Coast Extension, allowed them to be efficient with their television, still communicate the character information, potentially open themselves up to a different market in comic book fans and extend the experience of the episode well past 47 minutes.

The Ridley Scott film, *The Martian*, utilized this same tactic when it released a 17-page Ares 3 Complete Mission Guide. The digital guide not only gives a nifty look at NASA's (fictional) mission statement, but it also offers great detailed bios and images of the astronauts. None of these backstories are (or should have been) included in them film, but with an East Coast Extension, they were able to not only extend the film in a valuable way, but also communicate the characters' backstories to the audience in a clever way.

*Overwatch* is a video game that is centered on gladiatorial battling and has zero narrative and character development, even though there are tons of characters included in the game. Instead of weighing down the game with backstory, exposition and narrative, *Overwatch*'s character-driven narrative is instead told *exclusively* in East Coast Extensions: genuinely endearing animated shorts, character-focused one-off webcomics, and website-bound character biographies.

Joss Whedon did a masterful job of this in his ill-fated *Firefly* series, specifically with his development of the character Shepherd Book. Shepherd Book seems to be a mild-mannered preacher; however, he inexplicably holds some sort of high-priority status within the Alliance and on numerous occasions demonstrates a depth of knowledge in a number of fields with which one would not expect a clergyman to be familiar. These include space travel, firearms, hand-to-hand combat, and criminal activity. In the fourteenth episode of Firefly, "Objects in Space," Simon berates the bounty hunter Jubal Early for assaulting a shepherd. Early replies, "That ain't a shepherd."

All of this worked masterfully to build a rabid desire for fans to find out more about the character and expertly incentivized the sale of the Dark Horse Comics series based on Shepherd Book's past, aptly titled *The Shepherd's Tale.*

## Storyworld exploration.

Another viable East Coast opportunity is the ability to explore parts of the Storyworld you didn't explore in the Micro-Story. For example, in *The Simpsons: Tap Out* mobile game, as you reconstruct Springfield after Homer destroys it during an ill-fated workday, you actually get to explore other parts of Springfield that aren't explored in the cartoon. In Taylor Swift's *Black Space Experience* app, you get to explore more of the Woolworth mansion that wasn't shown in the music video.

In *The Pretender*, the Centre has 27 sub-levels (26 official, the 27th a secret one tagged for nefarious use); however, not all the sub-levels are explored in the show or even in the novels. SL-18 is shown as having an Autopsy Room and is the level where JFK possibly was held as a "vegetable," SL-19 is where medical records are stored, SL-20 is the infirmary, and SL-22 is where a strongbox of cash is hidden behind a firehose. Nowhere in the show, though, do you find out what is actually on SL-21. Therefore, this is a great candidate for an East Coast Extension that simply explores that sub-level in a meaningful way. Maybe a VR experience? Maybe a digital comic issue that has something nefarious play out in SL-21? Maybe a website where you can somehow download the floorpan or schematic.

How about, in *Game of Thrones,* being able to explore more of the Great Pyramid of Mermen or to be able to explore the inner halls of the Iron

Bank? If you can't show it in the television show or in the books, both of those can be done as East Coast Extensions.

Of course, it bears repeating (as with all of these opportunities) if you're going to show a new part of your Storyworld that you don't show in the Micro-Story, it needs to be valuable and you need to reward the audience for traveling.

Show them something new, cool and amazing. Hide secrets in these places. Unveil something awesome about the Storyworld that, if you hadn't experienced the East Coast Extension, you wouldn't have known. Again, this is similar to the Storyworld Reveal Additive Comprehension for the Micro-Story so the same rule that applied in Unanswered Questions applies here: big reveals go in Micro-Stories, smaller (yet still significant) reveals go into East Coast Extensions.

### Narrative excess.

Unless you're writing a novel, there typically will be strict page-limit or time limitations to your Micro-Stories. Features need to be two-hours or 110 pages, songs need to be three and half minutes, television needs to be 47 or 21 minutes, single-issue comics need to be 24 pages, etc. With these limitations, you'll almost always find yourself cutting good parts from your story only to throw them onto the proverbial cutting room floor.

Typically, those parts are wasted, outside of languishing as a DVD special feature. However, in a Super Story model, nothing should ever be wasted. If you have to cut something from your story, simply shift it into a different medium or platform and release it as a Narrative Excess East Coast Extension.

For example, have you ever wondered why the terminators look like Arnold Schwarzenegger and speak with an Austrian accent? In *Terminator 3: Rise of the* Machines, a scene was cut that would have answered why Cybernet would ever create a race of ludicrously accented robots.

It happened within the Micro-Story, *Terminator 3: Rise of the Machines,* but wasn't necessary for the plot so it was cut. Nevertheless, it would still be rewarding to see since it adds a greater comprehension of not only the film itself, but the Storyworld as a whole. This is definitely a viable candidate for a Narrative Excess East Coast Extension.

How about the scene where Indiana Jones learns he can't look at the Arc? Or the bit in *Independence Day* when Jeff Goldbum's character actually manages to upload a virus to the alien mothership? Or how Nero was held captive in a Klingon prison for 20 years in J.J. Abrams *Star Trek*? Or when Yoda tells Luke Skywalker that he was the one who instructed Obi-Wan to hide the fact that Darth Vader is Luke's father? All of these scenes don't deserve to die in the Special Feature graveyard and should all be liberated as valuable Narrative Excess East Coast Extensions.

When Quentin Tarantino went to film *Reservoir Dogs*, a movie about a jewelry heist, he ran out of money and had to ultimately cut the jewelry heist sequence from the script. In the film, we see pre-heist and post-heist, but never actually see the heist. This is a perfect opportunity to use an East Coast Extension to tell that part of the story, which ended up being a victim of budgetary cuts. Maybe a comic that shows the heist? Maybe a mobile game where you can play the heist? Maybe a musical EP where you had a song from each of the character's perspectives and you see the heist through a host of different eyes? Fans of the film would love any (or all) of these — and it could be done without having to shoot one extra second of very expensive film.

Not too long ago, I was consulting with an author who had cut a chapter out of her book because it deviated too much from the main plot-line. It dealt with a young, female supporting, character who goes to Paris during the summer, finds love and then experiences heartbreak before coming back to the U.S. and rejoining the rest of the characters. She was simply going to delete the scene from her manuscript; however, I encouraged her to never hit delete ever again; only copy and paste because everything can be used.

I encouraged her to create an Instagram account for the young girl and actually hire actors in Paris to take pictures and tell the entire summer trip through photos, short videos and captions. It started with pictures of just the girl, then a guy shows up, then they're cuddling and kissing and sight-seeing, then she's alone again. For fans of the book, it's extra content that extends the story. For fans who find the Instagram feed first, it can be used to market the actual book. She got a great sub-plot without having to bloat her novel with extraneous detail *and* she created a great experience for the fans by using a cool, fun and engaging Narrative Excess East Coast Extension to extend the story.

## Tailor the suit.

When coming up with ideas for amazing East Coast Extensions of your Micro-Stories, be sure to tailor your East Coast Extensions to fit the demographic of your Micro-Story. Remember, East Coast Transmedia is meant to drill, deepen, extend and innovate the experience of the Micro-Story/West Coast component. Therefore, you need to make sure your East Coast Extensions are relevant and engaging to the Micro-Story audience. Otherwise, they won't want to explore, which defeats the purpose of drilling the story deeper.

For example, let's say you have a Micro-Story targeted to four-year-olds, another targeted to middle-aged housewives and another targeted to frat boys. Some of the East Coast Extensions could consist of a child's playmat for the four-year-old story, a recipe book for the housewives and a mobile game for the frat boys. Notice how each one of those East Coast Extensions are tailored for the target market of the relevant Micro-Story, which will make it more likely they will want to continue to explore the story through the extensions.

However, what if you paired the mobile game with the housewives, the recipe book with the toddlers and the playmat with the frat boys? They're the same stories and platforms, but because they are no longer tailored to the demographic, it's unlikely you're going to get the migration you want with your East Coast experience.

ALL THINGS ARE CONNECTED
LIKE THE BLOOD THAT UNITES US
WE DO NOT WEAVE
THE WEB OF LIFE, WE
ARE MERELY A STRAND IN IT
WHATEVER WE DO
TO THE WEB
WE DO TO OURSELVES

CHIEF SEATTLE

# 13. Dynamic Connections.

## All hail the Rat King.

In the age of 24/7 media, iPads, PlayStations, and Netflix queues, it's difficult to build incentive and overcome friction with repurposed material. This is why we built sufficient Additive Comprehension between Micro-Stories. However, is the use of Additive Comprehension enough incentive *per se*?

Possibly, but the deck may be stacked against you. This is especially true when you're trying to connect stories that are ultimately delivered across different mediums and platforms. Connecting a film, a comic, and a game in a way that feels like one big story is more of a chore than trying to connect three films in the same way. With that in mind, you're better off employing a "belt and suspenders" approach, which means if Additive Comprehension is your belt, then Dynamic Connections are most definitely your suspenders.

Simply stated, the more you connect your Micro-Stories, the more they'll relate to each other and the more the audience will get the sense they are actually working together to tell one big Macro-Story. Henry Jenkins refers to this as *radical intertextuality* — making your stories relate to each other in a way that is far beyond the norm.

You see, one man's radical intertextuality is another man's Rat King.

There's an old Russian folktale about something called the Rat King. Rat Kings are phenomena said to arise when a number of rats become intertwined at their tails and end up growing together to form one big, gross rat. As horrific, nasty, and nightmarish as this is, we want our creative projects to have so many connections they form the Rat King.

Admittedly, traditional franchising does employ some connections, primarily main characters and maybe some central locations. However, they're almost never enough to form the Rat King. We, as Super Story Architects, need to take it to the next level. We need more connections. We need connections that aren't passive and we need to connect our stories in new, different, more layered ways.

We need the Rat King.

## Types of connections.

In order to create the Rat King for your Super Story, you'll first need to familiarize with the six different kinds of Dynamic Connections at your disposal:

1. Plot Impacting Plot;
2. Character Connections;
3. Location Connections;
4. Object Connections;
5. Callbacks; *and*
6. Story Seeds.

Using these six types of Dynamic Connections, you'll be able to inextricably link your stories (Micro and East Coast) together in a knot of entwined narrative. Basically, think of these connections as freeways for the audience to travel between the Micro-Stories. Not the 405 freeway in LA, but one of those freeways in Texas where the speed limit is 85 mph. Ultimately, the greater use and variety of your Dynamic Connections, the faster, more comfortable and easier it is for the audience to migrate from story to story.

Let's take a few pages to explore exactly what these connections are, how they work, and how exactly you can implement them.

### Plot impacting plot.

Your Micro-Stories should always be both impacting and being impacted by other Micro-Stories in your Storyworld. A Micro-Story should never be set apart as a silo. If it is, it'll eventually dry up and fizzle away, its potential never coming to fruition.

With the Plot Impacting Plot connection, a Micro-Story will *be significantly impacted by another Micro-Story's plot.* Not only that, but *it will also significantly impact another Micro-Story with its plot.*

For example, in *Man of Steel,* Superman has an epic fight with Zod all over Metropolis, resulting in them destroying a good portion of the city. One building that is destroyed is owned by no other than Bruce Wayne. Superman saves the day, but innocent people end up dying in the wake of the super battle. This event directly impacts *Batman versus Superman: Dawn of Justice,* since it causes Bruce Wayne (who is Batman for those people who have been living in caves for 40 years) to label Superman as dangerous and seek to destroy him. If that event wouldn't have happened in the plot of *Man of Steel,* the plot of *BvS* would have presumably been much different.

Likewise, in *Batman versus Superman: Dawn of Justice,* Superman's sacrifice against Doomsday actually inspires Batman to want to find others like Superman so they can work together to protect the world, which directly leads into the *Justice League* film. Had that not happened in *BvS,* the Justice League may have never been formed (and we would have been robbed of Khal Drogo as a whiskey-swilling Aquaman — which would have been a crime).

Likewise, in the first *Avengers* film, the Avengers battle wave after wave of Chitauri descending out of the wormhole and into New York City. In turn, half of the city is destroyed. In the first season of the *Daredevil* digital series on Netflix, Union Allied Construction has construction contracts all across Hell's Kitchen. Because of all of its contracts, it is able to excerpt influence in powerful places, thus giving rise to the villain Wilson Fisk. What's interesting is that if the Avengers wouldn't have destroyed the city in the *Avengers* film, Union Allied wouldn't have to rebuild Hell's Kitchen, which means Wilson Fisk may have never emerged as the super villain, Kingpin, and become Daredevil's arch nemesis.

In *Star Wars: A New Hope,* Luke is living on Tatooine and Obi-Wan is an old hermit in the desert. This is the direct result of the actions and conversations that take place at the end of the *Star Wars: Revenge of the Sith* film.

Sticking with the *Star Wars* continuity, in *Rogue One: A Star Wars Story,* Jyn Erso leads a group of spies to steal the plans to the Death Star, which impacts *A New Hope* by giving the Rebel Alliance the information it needs to actually destroy the gigantic battle station. If Jyn wouldn't have been successful in *Rogue One,* the events of *A New Hope* would have played out very differently.

In Kevin Smith's *Jay and Silent Bob Strike Back*, Jay and Silent Bob travel to Hollywood to shut down the production of the *Bluntman and Chronic* movie that is starting production. In *Chasing Amy*, an earlier story in the *View Askewniverse* timeline, Banky Edwards starts to pursue more commercial goals for the *Bluntman and Chronic* comic series, which ends up being a bone of contention between him and Holden McNeil.

All of these show the plot of one Micro-Story impacting, altering and affecting the plot of another Micro-Story. This type of Dynamic Connection is, in my opinion, the strongest type of connection to forge since it has such an enormous butterfly effect throughout the Super Story. However, at the same time, it takes the most planning and coordination out of all the Dynamic Connections and is, thus, a little more difficult to execute.

Maybe you have an hour-long medical drama (ala *Grey's Anatomy*) where a penny-pinching Board of Directors takes over a hospital and ultimately shuts it down because it's no longer financially viable. Then, in a completely separate story, possibly a comic book series, a man is rushing his dying kid to a hospital, but because the local hospital is shut down, he has to drive an extra 20 miles to the next one. Predictably, the kid dies, leaving the father heartbroken and angry. Having nothing, maybe the father goes in a Punisher-esk rampage against all the members of the Board. The reason the kid dies is because there was no hospital in town. There was no hospital in town because the Board of Directors shut it down in a different Micro-Story.

Thus, plot impacting plot.

## Character connections.

Using Character Connections is another great way to link various Micro-Stories because the characters are our windows into the Micro-Story plots. This is simply *having the same characters show up in different Micro-Stories.* Using this kind of connection makes it more comfortable for the audience to migrate because they're familiar with the characters.

Think of it like getting invited to a party where you don't know anyone and then getting invited to a party where you know ten people. You're probably more likely to attend the second party simply because you're more comfortable with the crowd.

There are actually three different kinds of Character Connections, which break down into the following categories:

1. Personal Appearance;
2. Personal Reference; *and*
3. Family Tree Appearance.

**Personal appearance.**

This is when the same character *personally appears* in multiple Micro-Stories and is the most powerful type of Character Connection.

The fact that Obi-Wan Kenobi, R2-D2, and C3PO all make personal appearances in every single *Star Wars* film, multiple books, games and cartoons helps the series maintain a creative cohesion and makes it feel more like one, big saga than six separate stories. Likewise, Darth Vader actually showing up in *Rogue One,* helps make it "feel" like more of a *Star Wars* movie.

The constant recurrence of Jay and Silent Bob helps connect the six films of Kevin Smith's *View Askewniverse*, especially when the protagonists of the films almost always change.

Also, the Nick Fury character appearing toward the end of the Marvel superhero films works to bridge the gaps between all the *S.H.I.E.L.D*-related stories. Still in the Marvel vein, the fact that Sgt. Brett Mahoney, Jeri Hogarth and Rosario Dawson's character, Claire, all personally appear in *Daredevil* and in *Jessica Jones,* shows just how much those two series are connected.

In *The Pretender* universe, the fact that Jarod and Miss Parker are in the television show, show up in the books and personally make appearances on the concept album, help connect all those different Micro-Stories in a valuable way.

**Personal reference.**

This is when a character from one Micro-Story is *referenced* in another Micro-Story. While not as strong of a connection as a Personal Appearance Connection, it's still a valuable tool to have in your arsenal of connections.

In *Clerks*, we're personally introduced to the obnoxious Rick Derris, the consummate jock from high school who continues to brag about (and embellish) his sexual conquests. Then in *Mallrats*, Gwen Turner tells a story about a tryst she had with him at a party. Alyssa Jones does the same in *Chasing Amy*. So, even though Rick Derris doesn't actually appear in the other stories, simply referring to him works toward bridging the gaps between the films.

In the first season of Marvel's *Jessica Jones* digital series on Netflix, she references both Hulk and Captain America when she mentions "the big green guy" and the "flag waver." While neither one of them show up in the series, the fact they are referenced connects the *Jessica Jones* series to the superheroes' standalone films as well as the slate of *Avengers* films.

Moreover, if you read the *Spoon River Anthology* by Edgar Lee Masters, you'll see an expert example of how an author can connect a huge amount of characters. The *Spoon River Anthology* is a collection of short free-form poems that collectively describe the life of the fictional small town of Spoon River. The collection includes 212 separate characters, all providing 244 accounts of their lives and their deaths. In each poem, multiple other characters are referenced, tying them all together in a valuable way.

**Family tree appearance.**

This is when a family member of a character from one Micro-Story appears in another Micro-Story.

The character Heather Jones appears as a minor character in *Clerks*, while her sister Trisha Jones appears as a supporting character in *Mallrats* and her other sister, Alyssa, appears as a major character in *Chasing Amy*. Even though it's three different characters appearing in three different stories, the fact that they're family members adds an extra element of cohesion.

Similarly, the *Lord of the Rings* series wouldn't connect as well with *The Hobbit* if Frodo (the protagonist in the *Lord of the Rings* series) wasn't related to Bilbo (the protagonist in *The Hobbit*). There would still be connections, but this Family Tree Appearance definitely helps make the connection and synergy between the two Micro-Stories stronger.

This type of Character Connection is particularly handy when your Micro-Stories cross long times or distances. For example, the first act of *Captain America: The First Avenger* is set in the 1940's and includes Iron Man's father, Howard Stark. Because Tony Stark wasn't born until decades later, this was one of the only ways to connect the Iron Man stories to the Captain America film.

## Location connections.

Location Connections are a type of Dynamic Connection where the same locations show up in a variety of Micro-Stories. It's like Character Connections, just with locations and landmarks. Just like in life, you're most comfortable with your own hometown, not *just* because of familiar faces, but also because of the presence of familiar places.

As with Dynamic Character Connections, Location Connections can be utilized in a couple of ways.

1. Revisit; *and*
2. Reference.

### Location revisit.

This is when the exact same location physically appears in multiple Micro-Stories.

In *Clerks,* we're introduced to the infamous Quick Stop convenient store. Then in *Clerks II,* the Quick Stop is shown again. Kevin Smith's *View Askewniverse* is actually centered on the towns of Leonardo, Highlands, and Red Bank, all located in Monmouth County, central New Jersey. This simple creative decision made it so much easier for Smith to utilize multiple Location Connections.

Likewise, in *Star Wars: Revenge of the Sith,* the dune sea of Tatooine is shown at the end of the film and then it's shown again in *Star Wars: A New Hope*. Moreover, the appearance of the original Death Star is a Location Connection between the *fifty* different *Star Wars* Micro-Stories, including films, books, games, cartoons and comics.

In the DC universe, every time the Daily Planet is shown, no matter whether it is a Batman story, a Supergirl story or a Lois Lane solo adventure, it is a direct Location Connect to every other *Superman* story that ahas been produced.

### Location reference.

This is when a location from one Micro-Story is simply *referred to* in a different Micro-Story.

Again, in *Clerks,* we're introduced to the Quick Stop. Then in *Chasing Amy* (which is actually based in New York), when Holden and Alyssa realize they both grew up in the same part of New Jersey, Holden mentions the Quick Stop. This isn't as strong as having it appear in the story, but remains a good option, especially when one of your Micro-Stories is removed from the central location of the rest of your stories, as was the case in *Chasing Amy.*

In *The Pretender,* the Centre is a key, central location. In the first part of *The Pretender* concept album, the Centre isn't shown, but it's referred to, which still helps connect the album to the show.

So, if you can, actually revisit your locations in different Micro-Stories. But, if you can't actually revisit them, at least talk about them because when you do, your Micro-Stories will begin to feel like one big story.

## Object connections.

Object Connections are the exact same things as Location Connections, except instead of *places,* we're dealing with *things.* For example, Luke Skywalker's lightsaber is a great example of how to meaningfully link Micro-Stories with an object.

In *Attack of the Clones,* Anakin Skywalker constructed the lightsaber after losing his first one during an accident on Geonosis. Anakin uses this lightsaber throughout *The Clone Wars* cartoon series. In *Revenge of the Sith,* Anakin/Darth Vader was defeated by Obi-Wan Kenobi, who confiscated the lightsaber and kept it in his possession while in hiding on Tatooine. In *A New Hope,* Obi-Wan gave the lightsaber to Luke Skywalker who began his Jedi training. In *The Empire Strikes Back,* Luke Skywalker lost the lightsaber in a duel with Darth Vader in the Cloud City on the planet Bespin. Vader cut off Luke's hand at the wrist, and the hand (still holding the lightsaber) fell down the air shafts of Cloud City. In *The Force Awakens,* Maz Kanata has retrieved the lightsaber and gives it to Rey, who ultimately returns it to Luke.

So, not only does the same object showing up help connect five different films, but it also connects those films to *thirty* different stories across a multitude of platforms, including novels, games, cartoons and comics, in which the lightsaber appears.

As with Character Connections and Location Connections, objects can *reappear* in different Micro-Stories or they can simply be *referenced.* For example, even though the Tesseract isn't shown as it is in five of the MCU films, it is mentioned in the *Agents of S.H.I.E.L.D* broadcast television show. While that's not as strong as the Tesseract actually showing up, it's still a viable way to connect.

## Callbacks.

A *Callback* is simply a reference to an event that took place in a previous Micro-Story *and the audience has the ability to go to the previous Micro-Story and see firsthand the event that was referenced.* Again, "previous" simply means the Micro-Story is located earlier on the Macro-Story timeline and isn't referring to the order the stories are released to the public.

In *Chasing Amy*, Alyssa Jones mentions how her best friend, Caitlin Bree, had an unfortunate experience with a dead body and is now institutionalized. This actually occurs in *Clerks*, which takes place before *Chasing Amy* in the *View Askewniverse* timeline. If you hadn't seen *Clerks*, you could have gotten the DVD and watched the exact event to which Alyssa refers.

In the film, *Creed*, Adonis is told about how his father, Apollo Creed died in the ring 30 years earlier at the hands of Ivan Drago. At that point, the audience could actually go watch *Rocky IV* and actually watch Ivan Drago pummel Apollo Creed all the way to the pearly gates in all its '90's film glory (you should have thrown in the towel, Rock!). Because it was referenced and the audience could go back and find it, it's considered a Callback.

Also, in the *Jessica Jones* series there is direct reference to the "Union Allied corruption scandal." This is a direct reference back to the events of the *Daredevil* series. Because the audience can go watch *Daredevil* and see everything first hand, this is considered a Callback and a viable way to connect the two Micro-Series.

## Story seeds.

You can think of *Story Seeds* and Callbacks as first cousins. Like Callbacks, Story Seeds refer to events that take place in other Micro-Stories. However, there's one major difference between the two. Unlike with Callbacks, *the audience can't go and experience the referenced event because that particular Micro-Story hasn't actually been produced or released to the public.*

Because the audience members can't get their hands on the Micro-Story, the reference simply plants a seed in the audience members' minds (hence the name) and sets them up for a future story.

For example, in the first *Avengers* film, as Black Widow and Hawkeye are defending New York City from an alien onslaught, she says to him, "It's like Budapest all over again." He answers, "You and I remember Budapest very differently." As fans, we have no idea what they're talking about, but they're obviously referencing something very specific. However, since nothing has been produced showing this particular Budapest adventure, this reference is a Story Seed. If we could go and watch, read or experience whatever happened in Budapest, this would be a Callback. However, because this story hasn't been published or produced, it serves to simply pique our interest and plant a seed for a future story.

The most successful Story Seed in history was planted in 1977 by George Lucas when he wrote the line, "General Kenobi. Years ago, you served my father in the Clone Wars." When *A New Hope* was released, nothing existed about the Clone Wars. You couldn't find a book about them, a movie, a comic, a video game — nothing. But, it was provocative and it made you want to know who the clones were and why they were in a war.

Then, when Lucas announced he was going to release the Prequel Trilogy, the excitement for the film was off the charts, because that Clone Wars seed had been germinating for decades and was finally ready to harvest. Not only that, but he went on to release two more films, countless novels, video games, comic books, and an animated series — tens of billions of dollars of additional revenue — all from a single reference to a story that hadn't yet been written.

That, amigos, is a powerful Story Seed.

So, if Lucas can reap a harvest of this magnitude from one simple Story Seed, imagine what kind of harvest you'll reap if you sow at least one Story Seed in every single Micro-Story you write. Evangelist Jesse Duplantis once said, "If you plant year round, you'll always be reaping a harvest." This truth is equally applicable to spiritual law as it to creating a Super Story.

But check this out.

As soon as the prequel trilogy was released, the reference to the Clone Wars in *Star Wars: A New Hope* instantly changed from a Story Seed into a Callback.

Why?

Because the audience was then able to experience the event referenced in *A New Hope*. Why change the label? For the same reason we don't call a cornstalk a seed. Once a seed turns into a plant, it's no longer considered a seed. It's a completely different thing with a completely different function. Thus, the distinction in terminology will help you organize your project and differentiate between connections between actual Micro-Stories (Callbacks) and connections between potential Micro-Stories (Story Seeds).

## Keep feeding the rat.

Most of the discussion around Dynamic Connections, to this point, are centered around Micro-Stories. While it's most important to connect your Micro-Stories since their West Coast model dictates they standalone (and, therefore, run the risk to seceding from the whole and doing their own thing), you also want to utilize Dynamic Connections for your East Coast Extensions as well.

Your East Coast Extensions are already necessarily connected to their parent Micro-Story through plot, locations, and/or characters. Therefore, you'll want to focus your efforts on dynamically connecting them to other Micro-Stories or other East Coast Extensions.

Admittedly, it's easier to connect Micro-Stories to other Micro-Stories since they necessarily have more story with which to work (whole pie versus a slice of a pie — mmmmmmm pie). However, when you begin using Dynamic Connections in your East Coast, you truly see the Rat King begin to form.

## Recipe for a rat king.

Now that you know all the different ways to connect your Micro-Stories, let's figure out how to summon the Rat King. In order to achieve Rat King status, you need to make sure that:

1. Every Micro-Story plot is impacted by at least two previous Micro-Story plots;

2. Every Micro-Story plot impacts at least two future Micro-Story plots;
3. Every Micro-Story is connected to at least one East Coast Extension of *a different* Micro-Story in some way;
4. Every East Coast Extension is connected to at least one other East Coast Extension of a *different* Micro-Story;
5. Every Micro-Story connects to every other Micro-Story in some way at least three times; *and*
6. Every Micro-Story includes all six different types of Dynamic Connections.

Honestly, you may find it difficult to accommodate all of these connections. I encourage you, though, to dig in and figure it out. Get a white board and visually draw it out. Sure, it will cause some of your creative decisions to change, but when you embrace the Rat King, the process of connecting all the elements of your Super Story becomes one of the most fun and interesting parts you'll experience.

It's like a big, narrative puzzle. Sure, it's hard, but you and your Super Story will be better for it on the back end.

Not only that, but by creating the Rat King, you will ensure that your Super Story feels and operates like one, big timeless story and ultimately becomes a completely different entertainment experience for your fans.

I LOVE TO GO TO THE MOVIE THEATER ESPECIALLY WHEN THE MOVIE IS A BIG CROWD-PLEASER IT'S MUCH BETTER WATCHING A MOVIE WITH 500 PEOPLE MAKING NOISE THAN WITH JUST A FEW

STEVEN SPIELBERG

# 14. Platform planning.

## What's the holdup?

If a Super Story, at its core, means spreading a story into multiple mediums and platforms, why would I wait until Chapter 14 before ever broaching the subject? Admittedly, there are some really creative, successful folks who actually like to *start* with a plan of how to spread the story into multiple mediums. They decide they want to use certain mediums, such as a feature film, web videos, a video game, and a comic issue, early in the process and many times before the concept is ever fleshed out. Then, these creative, successful folks write stories to fit that plan and those mediums. I'm not saying that approach is wrong *per se*, just that at One 3 Creative, we do it differently.

I feel writing from the beginning for a specific medium or platform tends to limit your creative expression in a negative way because you're not totally focused on the story. You're halfway focused on the story and halfway focused on the functionality of the platform, and what almost invariably occurs is the lure of the bells and whistles of the platform leads you away from your focus like a siren on a cliff, making your story merely a secondary tool necessary only to show off your platform functionality.

Instead, at One 3 Creative, we like to initially design our stories to be liquid or, as some say, *platform agnostic*. We simply focus on telling really good stories. Then after the stories are outlined, we take a step back, figure out what medium/platform is the best match, and then start making the story fit the platform. Writing platform-agnostic stories gives you room to breathe and allows your stories to grow in meaningful ways you may or may not have anticipated.

The Super Story process inherently puts story first in the process. By this time, you will have decided upon a Soapbox, constructed a viable Storyworld, developed a Macro-Story for the Storyworld, and outlined multiple Micro-Stories and East Coast Extensions that are connected in numerous and dynamic ways. It's been story, story, and more story. Now, at this point, we'll allow the organically delivered stories to inform us as to what mediums and platforms are best to deliver them to the masses.

We like to say that if you focus on your fine china and ignore your cake, your cake will taste like feet. And if your cake tastes like feet, it doesn't matter how fancy the plate is.

## Playing matchmaker.

Have you ever heard there are certain types of people who shouldn't get married, such as two Type A personalities or a *Star Wars* fan and a *Star Trek* fan? Why? Because two driven, controlling, temperamental people will ultimately have a crazy, volatile relationship and the *Star Trek* fan will never get over the inevitable sense of inferiority that comes with, well, being a *Star Trek* fan (NERD BURN!). Ultimately, the differences are so inherent in the people that, outside of divine assistance, the relationships are all but doomed.

Likewise, there are certain types of stories that should never be put into certain mediums. Some stories make great films. Other stories make amazing video games. There are some that make terrific plays and even more that thrive as television shows. However, just because a story makes an unforgettable comic book, doesn't mean it will necessarily make a comparable film. Switching mediums and platforms is like switching spouses. When you switch, the relationship will almost always be different, sometimes for the good and sometimes for the bad. We call this phenomenon *platform potency*, referring to how certain stories are more potent in certain platforms.

Therefore, picking the proper medium and platforms to use for your stories (Micro and East Coast) is a critically important step that should be strategic, well thought out and informed. This process, in a sense, is like choosing a spouse for your child. You wouldn't just up and marry your kid off to someone without knowing whether there was a good chance of the relationship being a great one. If you wouldn't do it to your child, don't do it to your stories. Obviously, comparing a story to a human life you created breaks down on quite a few levels, but you get the point I'm trying to make.

Before we haphazardly throw our stories together with strange mediums and platforms, we need to pop the hood on these relationships and find out why certain stories fail in certain mediums and why others succeed. Why do certain stories take advantage of a medium and platform's unique characteristics when other stories can't?

Let's start, though, with some definitions.

## Mediums are not platforms are not mediums.

Throughout this entire book, you may have realized that I've used the phrase "medium and platform" probably thirty times rather amorphously without drawing a meaningful bright line between the difference between a "medium" and a "platform." Honestly, most people, even transmedia professionals, fail to make the distinction between the two. Making a proper distinction, however, will open up a world of creativity to you as a Super Story Architect.

At One 3 Creative, we define "medium" as *the creative and artistic method or style used to tell a story*. Conversely, "platform" is *the end-user technology used by the audience to experience the story*. Basically, stories are created in mediums and experienced in platforms.

For example, the medium of *The Force Awakens* is feature film, but the platform was the movie theater. Once it went to DVD, the medium remained feature film, but the platform shifted to television. If you download it on your iPhone, the medium stays feature film but the platform changes to a smartphone.

If you're reading a hardcopy version of this book, the medium is non-fiction book and the platform is printed book. If you're reading the Kindle or iBook versions, the medium is still non-fiction book, but the platform is a Kindle or iPad.

The medium of the new Bob Dylan album is music and the platform I experience it on is my phone. If I go to a Bob Dylan concert, the medium remains music, but the platform becomes a live concert.

To add a level of ~~complexity~~ nuance, sometimes creators choose the right medium for their stories, but don't choose the right platform. Conversely, sometimes they have the platform right, but drop the ball on the medium.

Ultimately, you need to look at the strengths and weaknesses of your story and match it with the medium that maximizes the strengths and minimizes the weaknesses *and* then match it with and tailor it to a platform that does the same. When all three are in alignment, your story can truly maximize its full potential.

## What's on the menu?

How can you consider strengths and weaknesses of mediums and platforms when you don't know just how many options there are for each? Well, you can't. So, being the nice guy that I am, I have compiled a list. Sure, it's almost certainly incomplete, but at least you'll have enough to get you going.

### Mediums.

When it comes to defining a list of mediums, my personal rubric was simply looking at a potential medium and asking the question, "Does the storytelling change?" If the structure, pace or rollout of a story changes, I listed it as a separate medium. If not, I didn't.

For example, the difference between broadcast television and a Netflix series isn't simply a difference in platform. Any television showrunner will tell they are forced to approach the actual storytelling differently for a normal hour episodic than for a 10-episode show that is going to be binged. Primarily, this is because the story of a binged-watched series needs to roll out like a 10-hour movie. However, when there's a week in between episodes — even on a serialized drama — the story can roll out a bit slower and the arc of each episode is more complete than in a binged series.

So, essentially, I've made a list of all the ways I can think of in regards to how to tell a story differently. Again, I'm certain this list is un-elegant and incomplete and I'll bet dollars to donuts that someone is going to complain that I didn't list all the nuanced sub-categories of each one. But, hey, you won't find another place that gives you a list of 90 different mediums (trust me, I looked for it), so ~~shut up and just be happy~~ sit back and enjoy. :)

- **Film**
  - Live Action Feature
  - Live Action Feature — 3D
  - Documentary Feature

    - Live Action Short Film
    - Made-for-TV Movie
    - Short Film Series

- **Television**
    - 30-Minute Multi-Camera Episodic
    - 30-Minute Single-Camera Episodic
    - Hour Drama - Episodic
    - Hour Drama - Serialized
    - Hour Drama - Binge Watching
    - Mini-Series
    - Reality Docu-Series
    - Digital Series
    - Reality Contest Episodic

- **Animation**
    - Animated Feature
    - Animated Short
    - Animated Episodic for Children
    - Animated Episodic for Adults

- **Music**
    - Single Song
    - EP
    - Full Concept Album

- **Publishing**
    - Novel
    - Novella
    - Short Story
    - Children's Book
    - Poetry
    - Interactive Book
    - Diary / Blog
    - Micro-Blog
    - Article
    - Encyclopedia/Wiki Resource
    - Adult Coloring Book
    - Children's Coloring Book

- **Comics**
    - Single Issue Comic — One Shot
    - Single Issue Comic — Series

    - Graphic Novel
    - Comic Strip
- **Games**
    - Platform Game
    - Shooter Game
    - Fighting Game
    - Open World
    - Social Game
    - Trading Cards
    - Sports Game
    - Endless Runner Game
    - Tabletop Roleplaying Game
    - Live Action Roleplaying Game
    - RPG Video Game
    - MMORPG
    - Tabletop Board Game
    - Party Game
    - Trivia Game
    - Alternate Reality Game
- **Performance**
    - Musical Theater
    - Immersive Theater
    - Spoken Word
    - Opera
    - Interpretive Dance
    - Theater in the Round
    - Puppet Show
    - Circus
    - Stand Up Comedy
    - Flash Mob
- **Fine Art**
    - Photography
    - Painting
    - Installation
    - Sculpture
    - Street Art
- **Tech**
    - iBook
    - 360° Experience

        - Augmented Reality
- **Audio**
    - Audio Drama
    - Audio Interviews / Podcast
- **Video**
    - Video Podcast
    - Vlog

**Platforms.**

Again, while mediums are the artistic style and method used to *tell* the story, platforms are the end user technology used by the audience to *experience* the story. So, while the choice of medium is more focused on the storytelling, the choice of platform is more focused on the experience the audience is ultimately going to have with the story.

Personally, I'm a big *Lord of the Rings* fan. In fact, *The Two Towers* is both my favorite book in the series as well as my favorite film. I love the cinematography, I love the action, I love the score, I love the scope of the storytelling, I love the sound design — I love everything about it. So, when I got my new iPhone, I downloaded it just in case I ever found myself bored (remember, we live in an age where boredom is optional). Finally that day came when I tried to watch it on my phone — and I got bored within ten minutes.

Here I am growing bored of a movie I love, that I saw multiple times in the theater and can watch it whenever it is on television. Why? Because on my iPhone screen, the cinematography isn't as epic, the sound design isn't as amazing through my ear buds, and, if I can't build some structure made of salt shakers and sugar packets, I have to hold my phone for three uncomfortable hours.

What this shows is that even when you have the same story (*The Two Towers*) in the same medium (feature film), the change of platform (movie theater to smartphone) completely changes my experience with it. Our experience with smartphones averages less than two *minutes*, while our experience with the theater is two *hours*. When we use our phones, we're usually in a mode of *doing*, not passive consumption. This, then, makes it awkward to be holding your phone and not fiddling with it in some way. Knowing this, you can't expect there to be a one-to-one transfer from the theater to the phone without the audience experiencing some level or type of frustration.

Moreover, the smartphone platform doesn't take advantage of all the amazing things about the move (cinematography, score, visuals, etc.), which means when you put the movie on that platform, all the strengths of the movie are stripped away. Likewise, the unique strengths of the smartphone is touchscreen interaction. That's what makes smartphones great and what separates them in the marketplace from other platforms. Therefore, by porting a story onto the smartphone platform that doesn't have any touchscreen interaction, you are also stripping the platform of its biggest and most unique advantage and simply relegating it to merely a tiny television.

And tiny TVs are un-American. #baldeagles

So, while you always have to factor in how both your medium *and* your platform will impact your story, when you're choosing a platform, you're really getting into what some people call "Experience Design," "User Experience" or simply "UX." In fact, a popular title for people who don't want to market themselves as traditional transmedia producers is "Experience Designer."

Once you have chosen the medium that best tells your story, what are your options for platform?

- **Traditional**
    - Standard Movie Theater
    - IMAX Movie Theater
    - Drive-In Movie Theater
    - CD
    - DVD
    - Blu-Ray DVD
    - Standard Television
    - Printed and Bound Book
    - Print Newspaper
    - Print Magazine
    - Video Game Consoles (Xbox, Playstation, Nintendo Wii, etc.)
    - Standard Stage Performance
    - Standard Concert
    - Radio
- **Digital**
    - Smart Television
    - Smartphone

        - *Web Video — Free (YouTube, Vimeo, Brightcove, Vzaar, etc.)*
        - *Web Video — Premium (Subscription, YouTube Red, Sling Orange, etc.)*
        - *Social Media (Facebook, Twitter, Snapchat, Instagram, etc.)*
        - *Music Streaming (Spotify, Apple Music, Tidal, etc.)*
        - *Blogs (Tumblr, Wordpress, etc.)*
        - *Email*
        - *Website*
        - *App*
    - Tablet
        - *Web Video — Free (YouTube, Vimeo, Brightcove, Vzaar, etc.)*
        - *Web Video — Premium (Subscription, YouTube Red, Sling Orange, etc.)*
        - *Social Media (Facebook, Twitter, Snapchat, Instagram, etc.)*
        - *Music Streaming (Spotify, Apple Music, Tidal, etc.)*
        - *Blogs (Tumblr, Wordpress, etc.)*
        - *Email*
        - *Website*
        - *App*
    - Personal Computer
        - *Web Video — Free (YouTube, Vimeo, Brightcove, Vzaar, etc.)*
        - *Web Video — Premium (Subscription, YouTube Red, Sling Orange, etc.)*
        - *Social Media (Facebook, Twitter, Snapchat, Instagram, etc.)*
        - *Music Streaming (Spotify, Apple Music, Tidal, etc.)*
        - *Blogs (Tumblr, Wordpress, etc.)*
        - *Email*
        - *Website*
        - *App*
    - Smart Watch
- **Non-Traditional**
    - Clothing

    - Outdoor (Billboards, Skywriting, Buildings, Pool Tables, Swimming Pools, etc.)
    - Human Body
    - Objects (Coffee Mugs, Magnets, Coffee Jackets, etc.)

- **Immersive**
    - Virtual Reality Platform (Oculus, Hive, Google Cardboard, etc. )
    - Dome and Planetarium
    - Immersive Live Performance
    - Immersive Live Action Games (Alternate Reality Games, Escape Room, etc.)

**Delivery platforms.**

You'll notice that the digital platforms of smartphone, tablet and personal computers have the same sub-platforms listed underneath them in italics. This, admittedly, can get tricky and is down the rabbit hole a bit; however, I think it's worthy of discussion and differentiation. For example, social media sites, such as Facebook, Twitter, Instagram and Snapchat are major vehicles of content distribution (text, video, pictures, etc.). In some ways, they can be considered to be their own unique platforms; however, I think that's an oversimplification.

Let's say I have a short film I upload to Facebook that someone watches on their iPhone. The medium is short film, but what is the platform? Is it Facebook or is it their iPhone? Personally, I consider the iPhone to be the *Experience Platform* with Facebook being a *Delivery Platform* that ultimately distributes, delivers and links the platform with the content of the medium.

Why not just consider it a regular platform like everything else and call it day? Because the experience of Facebook changes depending on whether you are on a phone, tablet, laptop or desktop computer. However, even though it's not an Experience Platform, it would be foolish to simply go from the medium to the Experience Platform without any sort of consideration into how these Delivery Platforms factor into your overall Super Story.

So, essentially, anytime you use the World Wide Web to deliver your content, you'll be adding a Delivery Platform into the mix.

## Pick a winner.

The process of matching a story with its ideal medium and platform isn't an exact science — yet. We're currently developing an application that will work as a veritable eHarmony for Super Story. It will audit the creative content of your stories and then recommend the perfect medium and platforms that will accentuate their strengths and minimize their weaknesses the most. Until that hits the market, the process of identifying the best matches consists of asking yourself a number of questions.

### Asking the right questions.

Again, we're attempting to examine both your Micro-Stories and East Coast Extensions, and based on the natural characteristics of the story, we're going to allow them to inform us as to which mediums are the best to implement. By looking at the narrative characteristics of your story and cross-referencing them with the characteristics of the platform, we should be able to arrange the perfect marriage or, at the very least, keep it from being a complete disaster Hollywood marriage. #RIPbrangelina

Here are nine considerations that should come into play:

1. **How visual is the Micro-Story?** If your Micro-Story is full of great visuals, you want to take advantage of it by pairing it with a visual medium and platform that show those visuals off in a big way. This would include mediums designed for the screen (film, television, web series, video games, etc.), art-based mediums (comics, paintings, photographs, etc.), or the stage (dance or stage play). Non-visual mediums (novels, short stories, songs, or poems) won't take full advantage of your Micro-Story's visual potential, so if visuals are important go another direction.

   In regards to platform, avoid platforms that minimize the visuals of your medium. For example, you may choose live action film as your medium, but then if you design it for the iWatch, the smallness of the screen will cannibalize any advantage you may have actually gained from your choice in medium.

2. **Is your Micro-Story high in action?** Your initial impression may be this question is the same as the last, but it's not. A Micro-Story can be extremely visual, but not be high in action, such as a story highlighting the majestic landscape of New Mexico. Likewise, your Micro-Story can be very action-oriented, but not rely on visuals. The visual mediums (*except* mediums such as paintings, photographs, or stage plays) will also work for this type of story. Also, non-visual mediums, such as a novel, can work.

3. **How long is the Micro-Story?** If your story is going to end up being really long, you're going to need a long-form medium that will accommodate. Obviously, a medium such as a short film or a song wouldn't be a wise choice. A novel or graphic novel would be a great choice for an extremely long story or even a television series. Feature films ideally run just under two hours or around one hundred pages in script form, so depending on how long your story is this may also be an option. The same goes for a stage play. Of course, you can always get creative with your Micro-Story and split it into parts and go with an episodic web series or comic series.

   In regards to platform, if your Micro-Story is long, be sure to port it in a platform that people are comfortable engaging with for long periods of time. For example, the smartphone is great, but the average interaction with a smartphone is less than two minutes, with half of people's interactions being less than 30 seconds. That's a platform where people have a lot of micro-interactions with it. Laptops and personal computers have longer interactions than smartphones, but are typically less than a television. Books are platforms that people are comfortable engaging with for multiple hours. So is television. Definitely factor this into your decision-making process.

4. **How complex is your plot?** Complex plots typically work best in mediums that allow for

multiple perspectives, longer length stories, and more exposition. Novels are great, as well as feature films, graphic novels, and television series. Conversely, songs, albums, and poems don't work as well due to the length and the limited amount of exposition you can include. Folk songs are known for their storytelling and if you listen to a few (such as Bob Dylan's "The Lonesome Death of Hattie Carol" and "Ballad of Frankie Lee and Judas Priest"), you'll see just how simple the plots and story beats need to be.

5. **What's the episodic potential?** If you know your particular Micro-Story has great potential for separate episodes, or if you were forced to take your Micro-Story and make it a Micro-Series, consider anything with "series" in the name — a comic series, a web series, a television series, a miniseries, or even a book series.

6. **Is your Micro-Story plot-centric or character-centric?** Character-driven stories work really well in mediums such as novels, films, paintings, and role-playing games, but not as much in video games or even comic books. There are examples of great, indie projects from the comic industry that are very character-driven; however, they typically are in graphic novel form and find difficulty piercing the core comic demographic.

7. **Is your Micro-Story dialogue heavy?** Certain mediums just don't accommodate dialogue as well as others. Mediums such as songs, poems, dance, paintings, and games would be an example of these. Films, novels, web series, and stage plays would be examples of good matches. Find a medium that will allow your dialogue to flourish and ultimately make Tarantino proud.

8. **How many characters does your Micro-Story have?** Lots of characters take up lots of space, so you'll need a big enough house to accommodate them all. Songs and albums aren't built for this.

Neither are short films or even a web series. You'll need to move toward mediums like novels, films, television series, or even role-playing games to find a medium that can house your motley crew.

9. **What's your overall project budget?** This consideration will narrow the field quicker than any of the others. While a console-based video game may be perfect for your Micro-Story, if you only have $5,000 in your project budget, it may not be a realistic option. Obviously, you can continue to develop the project and shop for future and additional investment, but the actual cost of the medium and platform should continue to be a factor (even an ancillary one) in your decision-making process.

It gets really interesting when you have multiple, competing considerations and sometimes, yes sometimes, you find you need to go back and tweak the story in order for it to find its home.

**Make creative combinations.**

Once you differentiate medium from platform, the calculus of how to pair what medium with what platform actually can become fun and open your mind up to some very creative combinations.

For example, you may want to pair a Micro-Story with the comic strip medium. If you're happy with the medium, now you need a platform. Your instinct is to simply slap it in a printed newspaper, which could very well be a viable route; however, there are more options out there. You could take your comic strip and deliver it to the audience directly through email. You could print them on business card-sized stock and leave them by the register of a coffee shop. You could rent a billboard and display it for the entire city to see.

I was working with a team of filmmakers who was shooting an independent series and, after talking with them, it was clear they felt like they only had two options: television or YouTube. However, once I started talking with them about all the different platform options out there, they quickly got excited about the possibilities. They could deliver the entire thing through Snapchat (selling ad space for revenue). They could make a deal with an independent movie theater and show one episode a week for eight weeks on the big screen. They could create an Apple TV or smartphone app and deliver their series that way.

Once they realized there were no rules they had to abide by and they could pair mediums with a variety of different platforms, a world of opportunity opened up to them — and they had fun while doing it.

**West coast or east coast?**

When choosing a platform for your Micro-Stories, try to use bigger, more traditional platforms because those typically drive the most revenue. Because your East Coast Extensions are focused on engagement and not revenue, try to pair them with platforms that are less expensive and can hit the market quicker.

Remember, though, that the critical question about whether something is West Coast Transmedia (and thus a Micro-Story) or East Coast Transmedia isn't platform-specific, it's whether the story stands alone as a complete, enjoyable, comprehendible experience. This being the case, technically, you can deliver a Micro-Story through any available platform.

For example, MTV's revamped *MTV Cribs* series is being completely delivered via Snapchat. Granted that's not a big, traditional platform, but it's still a West Coast Micro-Story because it stands alone. In the same way, there were a group of YouTube celebrities that created a project called *#spideymurdermystery* that was told completely via Instagram. If you wanted to experience the story, you had to follow all six characters on Instagram, where the story would collectively be told via photos, video and captions. Again, because it's a complete, standalone story, it would be considered a West Coast Micro-Story even though it's on the smaller Delivery Platform of social media.

The reason you want to try to use traditional platforms for your Micro-Stories, is that typically those are the platforms with the highest revenue potential. However, if you can figure out how to drive revenue with non-traditional platforms, go for it.

Nevertheless, because traditional platforms are so expensive to produce for, you *never* want to port an East Coast Extension in one. Think about it — do you really want to put millions of dollars and devote years of development into a film or console video game that people won't understand unless they see or read something else?

And even if you do, I bet your investors won't. It's simply too risky.

### Who's driving?

Despite the fact we're creating multiple points of entry into the project, not every entry point is equal. Inevitably, in every Super Story there will be one component that will stand out from the rest and act as the load-bearing wall or tentpole of the Super Story.

This is called the *Driving Platform.*

The major effect of a Driving Platform is it will ultimately pull in the most people and will thus be the main springboard for fans to jump off and experience other Micro-Stories. The other Micro-Stories in all the other mediums and platforms will also be working to send the audience to the other components, including the Driving Platform, but because the Driving Platform acts as the biggest door into the project, it will demand special care and attention.

The Driving Platform should be the cleanup hitter in your Super Story lineup, stand out as the strongest offering of the franchise, be the biggest doorway for audiences to enter into the Storyworld, act as the main jumping-off point for fans, and thus demand the lion's share of your marketing. It's a big role to fill, so make sure it lives up to the hype because if your load-bearing wall falls, the entire Super Story will be damaged — not irreparably, but enough that you want to avoid it.

The easiest way to decide which platform will be driving your Super Story car down the road is to simply look at revenue potential. A feature film has a greater revenue potential than your web series component, so between the two, the feature film would be a better candidate for a Driving Platform.

But how do you know which Micro-Story to port in this high revenue, high visibility platform?

The best Micro-Story candidate for your Driving Platform will always come out of the Act II of your Macro-Story. This is because the second act of your Macro-Story is where your High Concept thrives. Thus, because your High Concept is the most interesting part of your project, you want the Micro-Story of your Driving Platform to be firmly planted in it. Ask yourself, "Which one of my Micro-Stories shows off my High Concept the most?" Almost always, that will be the best candidate for your Driving Platform.

Once you have a great Micro-Story that shows off the High Concept of your Storyworld ported into a platform that has high visibility and high revenue potential, all the other components of the Super Story will be working as separate engines to drive the audience to it.

## Design for the natives.

Once you have arranged the proper marriage between medium and platform, it's important to be able to create, design and tailor your Micro-Story specifically to take advantage of the unique characteristics of the platform itself. While I understand your Micro-Story may eventually move to a variety of platforms (from the theater to DVD to streaming, or from physical book to Kindle, etc.), it's important to at first tailor it to the first platform it will actually premiere in — which is something I call the *Native Platform*.

For example, if you know you are putting your film into theaters, for the love of little baby Jesus, write it and shoot it to be a great theater experience — sound design, cinematography, high visuals, great score. Don't yet concern yourself with what it will ultimately look like on the mobile phone, because if you do, you'll end up trying to alter your compositions, sound design and other elements of the film to try to serve both platforms. When this happens, you'll be serving too many masters and will ultimately not leverage the unique characteristics of the Native Platform as best you should.

If you're going into theaters, make it an eye-popping, bone-rattling, soul-grabbing theater experience *first*. Then, after the theater, it may leave its Native Platform and go into a variety of Secondary Platforms, such as mobile and streaming. Once it goes into mobile, maybe consider re-cutting a mobile version? Or maybe even consider later adding in some features that take advantage of the uniqueness, strengths and power of the mobile platform.

If your Micro-Story is going to premiere on smartphones, don't write it or shoot like a theatrical experience. Actually design it for its Native Platform by composing the shots tighter, altering the sound design and adding in interactive, touch screen elements.

Again, it needs to shine in its Native Platform first. The only way to accomplish that is to initially ignore the Secondary Platforms and design specifically to leverage all the unique strengths and characteristics of the Native Platform.

## Differentiation.

Ultimately, you want all the narrative components of your Super Story to be differentiated in a good way — especially if you want PGA credit as a Transmedia Producer. If you recall, to earn Transmedia Producer credit, you need three storylines in three mediums/platforms. So, what happens if you have two movies, two television shows, three web series or even seven books? Are you disqualified from the PGA's Transmedia Producer credit? Not necessarily.

I work off this two-part rule:

1. **If two components are in the same medium, just shift the native platform of one of them.** For example, if you have two animated series, design one for broadcast and the other for the web. If you have two novels, make one a traditional bound book and the other an interactive book tailored for the tablet. If you have two coloring books, print one and deliver the second as an app.

2. **If two components are in the same platform, just shift the medium of one of them.** For example, if you have two broadcast television shows in your plan, make sure one of the shows is live action and the other animation. Same platform (traditional TV), but different mediums. If you have two stage performances, make one a musical and the other a spoken word piece.

Abiding by this rule will ensure your Super Story becomes extremely eclectic and is, at the same time, industry and PGA-compliant.

### New mediums, new platforms, new demographics.

One of the great by-products of shifting in and out of different mediums and platforms is your Micro-Stories will begin to target different demographics.

For example, if you have a printed, bound novel, it'll naturally lend itself to an older, male demographic. If you take it out of the bound book format and shift it into the platform of a tablet, it'll begin to skew younger even though it's still a novel. If you keep the tablet as the platform and then change the medium to a cartoon series, you'll skew even younger.

Keep this in mind as you try to engage different demographics with your Micro-Stories or as you try to tailor your East Coast Extensions to the core demographic of your Micro-Story.

**THE ONLY DIFFERENCE BETWEEN REALITY AND FICTION IS THAT FICTION NEEDS TO BE CREDIBLE**

**MARK TWAIN**

# 15. Media blurring.

## Verisimilitude.

Now that you have your Soapbox, Storyworld, Micro-Stories and their East Coast Extensions squared away, and have chosen the proper mediums and platforms, it's time to put a creative cherry on top of your Super Story by designing, what we call, Media Blurring. Media Blurring, essentially, is creating very specific creative architecture that makes your Super Story seem real by blurring the lines between fiction and reality.

More than 75 years ago, Orson Welles electrified the country with his *War of the Worlds* broadcast, in which the Mercury Theatre on the Air enacted a Martian invasion of Earth. The result was nearly a million people were actually convinced, if only briefly, the United States was being laid waste by alien invaders. The panic inspired by Welles made *War of the Worlds* perhaps one of the most memorable and notorious event in American broadcast history.

In the same vein, the creators of *The Blair Witch Project* took advantage of a very young World Wide Web by consistently presenting the film's central premise — that three students had gone missing in the woods of Burkittsville, Maryland while filming a documentary about a legendary local witch — as fact and manufactured online evidence to back up their claim. Nobody had seen marketing quite like this before, and nobody knew what to believe.

This was the first film to actually and successfully harness the power of the Internet, capitalizing on the fact no one was quite sure where to turn for trustworthy information. I remember seeing it with my wife (then girlfriend) on opening day, simply because we were intrigued by the poster. The rest of the day, we debated back and forth about whether it was real —

"The dialogue didn't seem like dialogue at all."

"Yeah, but why would they always hold the camera?"

"True, but it's not like they shot it like a movie — they shot it like a home video."

So, we went to the Internet as the final arbiter of our debate. And what did we find? A host of fake interviews, photographs and diary entries, courtesy of the official website, launched a year ahead of the film's release in 1998. Even the IMDB page for the film's main actors — Heather Donahue, Michael C. Williams and Joshua Leonard, all of whom shared their full name with their Blair Witch character — told us that they were "missing, presumed dead."

Today, audiences are too savvy to fool in such a way, but back in the late nineties, our inherent suspicion of all things internet wasn't quite so sharply tuned as it is now. The filmmakers even joined internet forums, to drip-feed further "information" to curious browsers and ensure the conversation surrounding their film was an ongoing one. Nobody and nothing was breaking character.

Again, in the age of social media, instant news and forced transparency, creators can't really fool fans in the same way. However, that doesn't mean they shouldn't create similar creative architecture. Just because you can't *actually* fool fans, doesn't mean the fans don't want to pretend. In fact, in an era of fanboy/cosplay entertainment, fans love to pretend their favorite stories are, in fact, real — they *want* to believe.

This, then, is the essence of "verisimilitude," which is the appearance of reality that then creates a willing suspension of disbelief by the audience. "Sure, I know that *Star Wars* isn't real. And I know that when I see Darth Vader walk into Comic-Con, flanked by the 501st Legion, that he's not really a Sith Lord and is probably just some dude that works at Burger King. But reality is boring, so I'm just going to have fun and pretend that it's really Darth Vader, okay?"

Growing up a professional wrestling fan, I always *hated* when people would say, "You know that's fake, right?" First off, it's not "fake." The outcomes are predetermined and the Undertaker really isn't an undead superhero who can summon the powers of the underworld to defeat his spandex-clad opponents; however, the stunts the wrestlers are doing are very real. When a stuntman flies off a five-story building while shooting the next *Mission Impossible* flick, it's not fake. Sure, he's not really getting chased by ex-KGB assassins, but he really jumped of an actual building. In the same way, these wrestlers are actually launching themselves in the air, hurling themselves onto each other, and diving onto concrete.

Beyond that, I don't sit next to you when you're watching *Game of Thrones* and say, "You know that's fake, right?" Of course, *Game of Thrones* is fake! Of course, I know that Sean Bean (the actor) didn't die when Ned Stark (the character) lost his head to King Joffrey. I know it's fake, but when I'm immersed in the story, I want to suspend my disbelief, and pretend, even for an hour, that this amazing world is real.

With the understanding that fans love to suspend their disbelief when engaging with entertainment, Super Story Architects can actually create multiple layers of architecture that extends the verisimilitude beyond just the main story.

This is the heart of Media Blurring.

## Like east coast transmedia, right?

Not really.

Media Blurring will resemble and feel like East Coast Extensions; however, strictly speaking, there's one salient difference — Media Blurring doesn't usually extend the story and there's typically no Additive Comprehension.

Wait, I thought that *everything* required Additive Comprehension!

The only time, in my estimation, that you can get away without extending your story and providing a unique, revelatory contribution to the unfolding narrative is when you replace it with the novelty of Media Blurring. When you strip away the Additive Comprehension, you strip away its value and contribution to the Super Story; you've necessarily made that particular component expendable. However, if you replace it with a Media Blurring element that blurs the line between fiction and reality and gives the audience a cool opportunity to suspend their disbelief and pretend your Storyworld is real, you actually replace the value that you lost with a different type of value — the novelty of verisimilitude.

While Additive Comprehension has narrative value (which I think is the strongest type of value in a Super Story), verisimilitude has a distinct novelty value that is worthy of Super Story inclusion.

## Some cool examples.

To give you a better understanding and illustrate how Media Blurring is used in practice, here are a handful of examples:

- ***Prometheus***: Ignition, RSA Films, and 20th Century Fox worked together to build a multi-phased effort that introduced fans and new audiences to the rich story world around *Prometheus* through a potent mix of social, traditional and transmedia storytelling. As a main component of their Media Blurring efforts, the team launched Peter Weyland's TEDTalk from 2023 at TED2012. Watching the TEDTalk, we all know Peter Weyland isn't real and that it's really just Guy Ritchie, but it's still awesome to see how they presented it *as if* he were real. The endplate of the video, directed fans to WeylandIndustries.com, which was executed as a fully-realized company website. The site spiraled out additional content, interactive experiences, and original videos, but above all, it presented Weyland Industries as a real company. In fact, through the site, users could access company financials, product intel, David 8 specs and a detailed Weyland timeline. At Wondercon, the team distributed Weyland business cards to eager fans, as if it were a real company. After calling the number on the card, fans received an exclusive look at a very Apple-esk product video announcing Weyland's newest android, David 8. Powered by Verizon, of course.

  Now, it's important to note there weren't any major story reveals in any of these pieces. If there had been, they would be considered East Coast Extensions of the film. However, because they supply the novelty of verisimilitude and make the world of *Prometheus* seem real, they still have value and are simply categorized as Media Blurring.

- ***District 9:*** For the release of *District 9,* the creators created Media Blurring architecture and debuted it well over a year in advance of the film's release. Signs prohibiting nonhuman use of restrooms surfaced at Comic-Con, and, by the start of the summer, the same type of signs were appearing on park benches, the sides of buses, and in a variety of other contexts around major cities. It didn't stop there. In fact, they also released a pseudo-public service announcement warning people to stay away from District 9 because the non-humans were dangerous. They also directed people to call Multi-National United (MNU) if there were any sightings of non-humans. Following that, they also launched an intentionally bad corporate MNU video (because all corporations have bad corporate overview videos) that presented the MNU organization as a real entity.

Of course, we know none of this is real, but fans of *District 9* loved the opportunity the Media Blurring components gave them to suspend their disbelief and pretend. Again, none of these components had major story information that was unique or revelatory. If they did, they would be considered East Coast Extensions. Instead, because they presented the novelty of verisimilitude, these are simply categorized as Media Blurring.

- ***The Exorcist* Television Show**: Ahead of its new television series, Fox brought Media Blurring into the real world by staging "surprise" exorcisms on the street in downtown San Diego. When the exorcisms began, no one near the commotion really knew what was happening. A space was cleared on the sidewalk and two seemingly random Comic-Con attendees, a guy and a girl, walked through it. The guy collapsed out of nowhere and he puked while his body was twitching and contorting in alarming ways. His friend freaked out and didn't know what to do. Then two priests stepped in to save the "possessed" guy in the staged flash exorcism. While it was shocking at first, by the end of the stunt everyone knew it was all for fun and the "possessed" person had been in on the ruse from the very start.

While there's no Additive Comprehension, this sort of flash mob-ish stunt, even just for a few minutes, made the world of *The Exorcist* seem real. Great example of Media Blurring, in my opinion.

- ***Batman versus Superman***: At Comic-Con, not only was the Wi-Fi sponsored by LexCorp, but *Fortune* magazine debuted an article that featured an interview with Lex Luthor, Jr. In the article, he speaks at length about his father's legacy, his vision of the company and what he hopes to achieve as its figurehead. Yes, I know that it's Jessie Eisenberg and that Superman isn't real, but I don't care because this gives me an opportunity to suspend my disbelief and pretend the DC Storyworld is real.

- ***The Pretender***: The Centre is the nefarious organization within *The Pretender*-verse and like any other organization, it has employees. So, as a Media Blurring opportunity, the creators published *The Centre Employee Newsletter,* which keeps its "employees" (read: fans) updated on the seemingly mundane internal issues — the menu in the cafeteria with a spotlight on any new recipes from the chef, Christmas parties for various departments, memos from annexed offices and employee awards. While the creators do a fantastic job weaving in and hiding tie-ins and clues in the newsletter, a major part of its value is that it makes The Centre seem like an actual organization, which in turn, gives the fans the opportunity to pretend *The Pretender* universe is real.

- ***Better Call Saul***: In addition to its official AMC website, *Better Call Saul* also has a site devoted to Saul Goodman, Esquire — as if Saul Goodman is an actual, shady plaintiff's lawyer. By going through the website, you're not going to find any Additive Comprehension. If you did, the site would be an East Coast Extension. Instead, you'll simply find fake advertisements, hilarious client testimonials, and even a "live" webcam. All of it is poorly designed — intentionally — because of course a shady plaintiff's lawyer in real life wouldn't have a nice website. They would have bad commercials, bad design and awful jingles. Because Saul Goodman's site includes all of these things, it makes him seem like a real lawyer, which is a heck of a lot of fun for fans.

- ***Super 8:*** J.J. Abrams is a master of Media Blurring. For *Super 8*, his homage to Spielberg, he littered YouTube with dozens of cellphone videos showing a mysterious container being shipped across country by the government. These videos made it seem like they were shot by regular people (not well-composed, shaky, erratic, etc.), which made it seem like this was a real occurrence and the government was actually transporting aliens across state lines.

- ***House of Cards:*** Ahead of the 2016 election season, Netflix released an "official" Underwood For President campaign video that not only makes it seem like Frank Underwood is a real person, but that he is actually running for president. Taking Media Blurring to the next level, Netflix even incorporated The Smithsonian's National Portrait Gallery, which features a gallery of portraits of the presidents. In the gallery, you see George Washington, Abraham Lincoln, Ronald Reagan — and Frank Underwood, as if he is a real president. You don't learn anything new when you see the portrait. If you did, it would be an East Coast Extension of the show, but instead it replaces Additive Comprehension with the novelty of verisimilitude.

- ***The Office:*** In addition to the official NBC website, *The Office* also had an actual DunderMifflin.com website that made it seem like Dunder Mifflin was a real paper company. On the site, you could see where the other branches were located, read newsletters from various branches, see the products they offered, etc.

- ***Entourage***: The creators of Entourage incorporated Media Blurring when they released the book, *The Gold Standard: Rules to Rule By*, "written by" Ari Gold. Of course, Ari Gold is a fictional character who can't actually write books, but even though we, as fans, know this, we don't care because, at the end of the day it's fun to pretend that Ari is a real guy.

- ***Independence Day:*** The creators of *Independence Day: Resurgence* blurred the lines between fiction and reality by releasing fake videos from the Las Vegas Tourism Board promoting the "ruins of Las Vegas" as a vacation spot. As you suspect, Las Vegas was destroyed in the original *Independence Day* film, but now it seems like some clever capitalists figured out how to turn the ruins into a tourism opportunity. Obviously, this is fake, but it's fun, so who cares?

I encourage you to look up all of these examples online because when you see the various videos, ads and articles incorporated into the ideas, the concept of Media Blurring really clicks into place.

It feels a bit like marketing (which most of the time it is), but it's marketing in a very story-centric way. This means it's difficult to simply leave your Media Blurring components to your traditional marketing team. There's a depth of knowledge about the project and the Storyworld required to truly blur the lines between fiction and reality, which means the best Media Blurring extensions are actually conceptualized ahead of time by the Super Story Architect.

## Creative Strategy.

So, now that you know how to recognize Media Blurring, as well as its intrinsic value to a Super Story, how do you create your own?

You start by identifying the following elements of your Storyworld:

- Main Characters;
- Organizations;
- Issues, Debates or Hot-Button Topics; *and*
- Locations.

Once you've made the list, ask yourself, "If these things were real, how would they manifest online, on social media and in the real world?" From there, begin to outline Media Blurring architecture that includes, but certainly isn't limited to, the following:

- Websites;
- Social Media Profiles (on major and minor platforms);
- Traditional Media (print ads, billboards, etc); *and*
- Live Events.

If you have a character who is a singer trying to break into the music industry, you can give the character an "official" artist website, a Twitter profile, a SoundCloud account, and a SnapChat account. You can have the singer take out a classified ad in the paper or on Craigslist looking for bandmates and possibly even book actual gigs at coffee shops and bars and even sing in persona.

All of this adds a valuable element to your Super Story in that it creates a layer of immersion and verisimilitude that is critical in having your Super Story stand out in an over-saturated entertainment market.

## Blurred merchandising.

Merchandising is indeed a major focus of large-scale entertainment projects; however, in the context of the conversation of Media Blurring, we're going to focus on *Blurred Merchandising.* Instead of simply slapping your project's logo on a t-shirt or making an action figure (which is traditional merchandising), Blurred Merchandising makes your world come alive by offering the audience *world artifacts* from your Super Story. I'm not talking about fossils, I'm talking about any objects or clothing that appear in your Super Story.

For example, there's a big difference between buying a hat with *The Walking Dead* logo on it and buying the hat Rick Grimes wears in the series. What are those pieces of clothing or jewelry your characters wear that you can provide the fans the opportunity to attain? Can you manufacture weapons or decorations from your world? Blurred Merchandising is all about reaching into your fictional universe, pulling out select pieces, and giving your audience the opportunity to physically hold onto them.

Blurred Merchandising includes items like the various wands from *Harry Potter*, the jelly beans from *Harry Potter,* the swords from *Game of Thrones,* Gandalf's staff from *The Lord of the Rings*, the DeLorean car from *Back to the Future*, the walking piano in *Big*, Wilson from *Castaway,* the cigarette holder from *Breakfast at Tiffany's*, and the adrenaline syringe from *Pulp Fiction* (okay, maybe not that one). By pulling out the content and items from the actual Super Story and merchandising them, a layer of verisimilitude is created for the fans.

A *Star Wars* wallet is cool merchandise, but being able to buy and wear Finn's jacket from *The Force Awakens* is cooler because it is actually bringing artifacts from the *Star Wars* galaxy into my world — and thereby helping blur the lines between fiction and reality.

Fox really capitalized on the concept of Media Blurring through Blurred Merchandising when they partnered with 7-Eleven to turn their stores into actual Kwik-E-Mart's ahead of *The Simpsons* movie. Not only did the stores look like the Kwik-E-Marts, but they also sold items from *The Simpsons* universe — KrustyO's, Homer's favorite donuts, and Duff beer were all sold. Even the famous Slurpee was actually sold as a "Squishee" for the month.

So, as you consider all of the merchandising for your Super Story, factor in what items you can pull out and sell as Blurred Merchandise. In fact, as you're actually creating your Micro-Stories, intentionally insert items into your Super Story you know ahead of time can be used for Blurred Merchandising purposes.

If you do it right, your fans will love the extra layer of immersion — and they'll be willing to pay for it!

## Blurred-*IP*.

Blurred IP is very similar to Blurred Merchandising, except that instead of manufacturing "items and artifacts" from your Storyworld, it involves *publishing actual content and intellectual property that already exists in your Storyworld in some way.*

For example, if you have a character who is an author in your Super Story, you can actually publish her books. If you have a musician in your Super Story, you can produce his music. If you have characters who have a podcast in your project, you can actually create and distribute their podcast. If your character is a painter, you can create the paintings and show them in exhibits.

This has proven successful for many projects. The creators of the television show, *Nashville*, record, produce and sell all of their characters' music from the show. In the show *Castle*, Richard Castle is an author of a line of mystery novels, so ABC used that as a Blurred IP opportunity and actually published his line of novels. In the television show, *Lost*, Sawyer reads an early manuscript of a book entitled, *Bad Twin*. In reality, that book didn't exist. That is, until the network actually had the novel written and published as a real book. *The Itchy & Scratchy Show* is a cartoon inside the cartoon of *The Simpsons* that the creators have been able to extract and actually use the intellectual property for its own shows, games, etc.

The faith-based independent film, *Fireproof*, is a about a man and woman who are experiencing marital difficulties. As a way to reconcile, they turn to a book called *The Love Dare,* which is a journal that helps them ultimately salvage their marriage. The film ultimately did very well, grossing well over their production budget. However, a few months after the film premiered, the filmmakers were contacted by representatives from Barnes & Noble, who were looking for *The Love Dare* book. The filmmakers explained to them the book wasn't real and that it was only inside the movie, to which the Barnes & Noble reps responded by telling them that thousands of people were actually requesting the book — and encouraged them to write it.

So, they did.

And while the movie was shot for $500,000 and made $33 million, the book itself grossed well over $75 million. Not only that, but the book help extend the *experience* (not the story) of the movie for fans of the movie and helped expose people who just needed a marriage counseling book to the movie.

When you publish or produce these components, they don't have any Additive Comprehension to the main narrative of the Super Story, else they would be either Micro-Stories or East Coast Extensions. However, because they help elements make the Super Story seem real, they're considered Media Blurring. Moreover, because Blurred IP is actual intellectual property itself (as opposed to Blurred Merchandising), you can actually go and turn the Blurred IP into its own Super Story. #itneverstops #mindblown #inception

## Blurred-*business.*

In addition to Blurred Merchandising and Blurred-IP opportunities, there can also be situations where you can use your Super Story to launch what we call a Blurred Business. A Blurred Business is where *you take a business or service that exists inside your Super Story, extract it and then use it to launch a dedicated, functional business that promotes real products or services in the real world.*

For example, in the film, *Forrest Gump,* Forrest ends up getting into the shrimping business and pursuing Bubba's idea of a shrimp-based restaurant. Starting as simply an idea for a potential *Forrest Gump* theme park, Paramount actually launched a single restaurant in Monterey, CA in 1996. Today, forty Bubba Gump Shrimp Co. restaurants operate worldwide. Twenty-nine of these locations are in the United States, four are in Mexico, three are in Malaysia, and one each in London, Hong Kong, Indonesia, Japan, and the Philippines.

It was really a brilliant move because one of the barriers for entry for new, small businesses is the lack of awareness, especially for restaurants. In this instance, the *Forrest Gump* film went ahead and created awareness for the brand and established a market for the restaurant before the restaurant was even launched. Now, the film acts as a tremendous marketing tool for the restaurant and the restaurant acts as marketing for the film.

There are so many opportunities out there, such as Pizza Planet, the popular family-friendly restaurant from Pixar's *Toy Story* series. This could be a legitimate kids-focused pizza chain, combining two things every kid loves: pizza and space. Or what about actually launching Los Pollos Hermanos from *Breaking Bad*? One in Los Angeles and one in Albuquerque. They could even have blue salt on the tables and an eternally locked or even guarded door to the basement. People would go simply because the novelty, but if they could actually have great food, it could be huge. I mean, who wouldn't go to Central Perk (from *Friends* fame) in favor of Starbucks?

Willy Wonka candy bars, the Mighty Ducks NHL franchise, Dunder Mifflin paper, and other Blurred Business have been launched, but really, this type of market remains largely unexplored.

In fact, I was just speaking with a woman who is the proprietor for a restaurant in Los Angeles who had a single, independent site that appeared in multiple episodes of *Entourage*. After the airings, she received multiple offerings to expand and actually franchise her restaurant. If the creators of *Entourage* would have understood Blurred Business and the overall power of Media Blurring, they would have created a fictional restaurant and promoted that instead. Then, they could have launched, expanded and franchised their own business instead of simply giving the opportunity to someone else.

So, what type of products, services or standalone businesses can you create inside your Super Story? When you identify those, make sure you highlight them in a great way, because, when you do, you may just have the opportunity to actually launch them into the real world.

*Part 3*

# Finishing Touches

WE'RE LIKE LICORICE
NOT EVERYBODY LIKES LICORICE
BUT THE PEOPLE WHO
LIKE LICORICE
REALLY LIKE LICORICE

JERRY GARCIA

# 16. Community building.

## The last leg.

Wow.

Congratulations.

Seriously. As Virginia Slim would say, "You've come along way, baby."

Going through the process of understanding the necessity of the Super Story approach, wrapping your head around the transmedia fundamentals, exploring your own soul for a great Soapbox, using that to inspire a massive Storyworld, developing an epic Macro-Story for the world, identifying Micro-Stories or series to tell within the world, finding ways to drill those stories with East Coast Extensions, pairing every component with the proper medium and platform and ultimately making your Super Story seem real using Media Blurring to blur the lines between fiction and reality — this was no easy breezy Sunday read. It's been a journey!

But it's not over.

This is the part of the race when you're close enough to see the finish line, so you simply have to use that as motivation to push through the last leg of this Super Story marathon.

Remember, toward the beginning of the book, when I mentioned that a Super Story has three essential elements? Here they are, by way of refresher:

- Transmedia storytelling principles;
- Powerful emotional connection with the audience that communicates a meaningful truth; *and*

- Online and offline community building, cultivation and community outreach.

We covered transmedia storytelling principles when we discussed West Coast and East Coast, converged and dispersed, and you put it to use when you outlined your Micro-Stories and their respective extensions.

First essential element? Check.

The powerful emotional connection with the audience that communicates a meaningful truth came by way of your Soapbox, which was used to inspire the entire Storyworld of your Super Story.

Second essential element? Check.

All we need now is the third essential element — *community*.

## Community, not audience.

In marketing circles, terms such as *fans*, *audience* and *community* are tossed around recklessly, making them seem synonymous even though they're not. An audience is a passive, non-participatory group of spectators. A community, however, is an active group of people who participate, work together and coordinate with each other to create common success. In fact, a fan community doesn't abandon a brand if it looks unsuccessful. Instead, they help, tweak, give input and are ultimately motivated to help generate success.

The fans, on the other hand, are individual observers who have a similar interest in success, but aren't working together to generate the success. Fans help achieve success on some broad level (more fans means more ticket sales, which means bigger budget to get better players or simply an intangible morale booster for the team) but they don't have the same unity as a team. Plus, when success isn't achieved, they'll stop coming.

A fan *community or Fandom*, though, will bridge the gaps between releases because the fire of excitement will continue to be stoked. While an audience will blast you on your Facebook page, a fan community will take up for you. When an audience will complain about price, a fan community will focus on why your project is worth it. Audiences only passively engage with each other (if at all), while the members of a fan community actively engage with each other even when you're not directing them.

Audiences are good.

But Fandoms and fan communities are soooo much better.

It's important to underscore that fan communities and Fandoms are not about mere numbers — it's about fervency. For example, the *Transformers* movies have made billions worldwide, but if Paramount announced they weren't going to make another one, nary a pen would be put to paper in protest. Meanwhile, *Community*'s audience has never tipped over five million, but nearly every viewer is a part of the fan community and all but stormed the NBC gates when the network decided not to renew the show for Season 3 and ended up keeping the show alive for another three seasons.

So, how do you go about building one of these types of amazing, supportive, slightly-crazy fan communities?

I mentioned earlier that one of my partners, Steve Mitchell, has a book he wrote with Jacci Olson entitled, *The Awesome Power of Fandoms: A How-To Guide to Engage, Grow, and Unleash Global Franchise Fanbases.* While many books about fans and fan culture are academic and sociological, Steve's book is born from experience and is rooted in practicality. Not only has Steve sat at the feet of the master when he worked with George Lucas on *The Clone Wars*, but also truly knows how to create something people aren't just interested in — but actually believe in.

So, while Steve's book is the gold standard of how to create community of not just fans, but brand evangelists, I'm going to cover some top-line community building methods that can go ahead and get your Super Story primed for a robust fandom.

## The nuts and bolts.

Building a fan community isn't something you should leave to just "happening." Building, cultivating and fostering an active and healthy fan community takes time, patience, flexibility, a thick-skin and perfecting not just the ability to create, but also the ability to listen. Like a garden, it doesn't grow overnight. Like a garden, if you ignore it, it will either die or become so unwieldy you can't control it. Like a garden, if you take the time to invest into it, it will not only be a beautiful reflection of your Super Story, but also the source of incredible, amazing, creative and powerful harvests.

So, what do you have to do to get your own Potterheads, Browncoats, the Colbert Nation, the Bee-Hive, Phans, Swifties, Whovians, Bronies, Hulkamaniacs, Buffistas or Trekkies?

## The project hub.

In order to have a fan community, you need somewhere for it to live. Above all, this should be the official website of your Super Story or, what we call, the Project Hub. Keep in mind this is different than any websites you may have developed as East Coast Extensions or Media Blurring components. This means for *The Pretender*, the Project Hub will be the official ThePretenderLives.com website, not the fake website for The Centre.

Minimally, the Project Hub should accomplish the following four purposes for your community members:

1. **News and Updates**: Fan communities love even the smallest morsel of news and updates, which means this is a great way to maintain consistent traffic for the Project Hub. Knowing this, your Project Hub should have a news feed, news ticker or blog clearly posted on the front page — don't make them work too hard just to find an update. Also, it's worth noting the news can both be posted by you and also aggregated from other sites (articles from the trades, rumors from gossip blogs or even from your fans themselves — deputize them as reporters!).

2. **Roadmap and Direction**: Your Project Hub should be a veritable Grand Central Station that clearly and easily connects your fan community to every single component of your Super Story (Micro-Stories, East Coast Extensions, Media Blurring components, etc.). This helps ward against audience fracture. Beyond that, go ahead and show connections between stories, tease Additive Comprehension and actually entice them to explore.

3. **Access**: Your Project Hub shouldn't just be a one-way street. Give them access to email you, submit things, post work. Give them the ability to actually participate in the community in a way that allows you to use the Project Hub to validate their various contributions to the Super Story.

4. **Collaboration**: Not only should your Project Hub give the fan community access to you, but it should also give them access to each other in a way that allows them to collaborate.

If you're able to build this functionality in your Project Hub, you will optimize it for community management. It's worthy to note that it's good to have other outside branded channels for your Super Story, such as a Facebook page or a Reddit thread, but those should only be entry points for fans to ultimately be led back to your Project Hub.

Also, let me just say that if you don't create a Project Hub or neglect your Project Hub, your fan community will create their own and then it will be nearly impossible to eventually migrate them back to yours as the main hub for your Super Story.

## Feed the beast.

Though creating a Project Hub is a necessary step in cultivating a robust fan community, once you have it created, you can't simply walk away and expect the fan community to self-organize and thrive on its own. Therefore, you need to have an actual plan of how to continually engage the fan community in a meaningful, valuable way. After examining some of the best practices from some of the best fan communities in pop culture, here are seven ways for you to continually "feed the beast":

1. Top-Down Dialogue;
2. Exclusive Access;
3. Content Creation;
4. Cross-Talk;
5. Live Events;
6. Cosplay; *and*
7. Fandom nickname.

### Top-down dialogue.

This is where you give your fan community access to the main stakeholders of the Super Story, primarily, yourself as the creator. Though this was unheard of just a couple of decades ago, Fandoms love to engage with the actual creators of the stories they consume. As soon as they realize you, the creator, are nowhere to be found on your Project Hub or branded channels, they become less important. So, give your fan community access to yourself, to other writers, to actors and producers.

Be sure to participate in Google Hangouts, Reddit Q&A's, Twitter interviews and anything that actually connects your fans to you.

**Exclusive access.**

Fan communities love to feel special, so through the Project Hub, give the members of the fan community access to *valuable* content "outsiders" can't get. This can include behind-the-scenes specials, deleted scenes, lost chapters, project secrets and breaking news. If the general population has access to all of the same information as the fan community, where's the benefit of actually being in the Fandom?

**Content creation.**

This is where you empower the fan community to not just consume, but to actually create things and validate the best. This includes fostering fan fiction, art, graphic design, games, films, music and anything else that allows the members to actually invest their talent and their creativity into. Another popular Content Creation strategy is to tap into what Henry Jenkins calls the "remix culture" and allow the fans the opportunity to re-edit scenes, remix songs or rewrite dialogue. An important element of Content Creation is for you, as the creator, to continually validate it by posting the best creations on the Project Hub or possibly even adopting parts into the actual Super Story canon.

**Cross-talk**

This is where you encourage the community to not just create individually, but actually connect and collaborate collectively. You can help foster these opportunities by creating fan forums (especially ones reflective of your Social Segments) or even giving them "assignments" to work on together. For example, after the first *Avatar* film, Lightstorm Entertainment encouraged their fans to work together to actually finish the Na'vi language that was started in the original feature film. For two years, the fan community collaborated on a book for the entire language and Lightstorm eventually published it as canon. Another opportunity is to have your fans collaborate on maintaining the official Wiki of your Super Story. Honestly, it may get to a point your fans know more about your Super Story than you do, so this is definitely very helpful.

**Live events.**

It's great to have a robust online presence for your fan community, but it's also good to have them connect in person. Therefore, try to organize events for them to participate in, such as when *Star Wars* has the "May the Fourth Be With You" Celebration in Anaheim every year or the *Star Wars* Half Marathon where people dress up as their favorite characters and run a race together as fans. Which brings me to the next way to feed the fan community of your Super Story...

**Cosplay.**

Cosplay is a huge part of Fandoms and, for those who are unfamiliar, is a shortened form of two words — costume and play. The early '90s saw the rise of cosplay into popular culture, although it probably originated initially in Japan. Essentially, it is the practice of portraying a fictional character and, at times , even completely identifying as that character while in costume. Honestly, I could probably write an entire chapter on cosplaying, but you simply have to go to Comi-Con or *Star Wars* Celebration to see how popular and powerful this is within fan communities. As a creator, you need to first design your Super Story characters on the front end in such a way that lends itself to cosplay — unique clothes, uniforms, and dress, distinct looks, interesting objects they carry, cool weapons, etc. — and then help encourage and validate the cosplay for your fan community on the backend.

**Fandom nickname.**

Lastly, almost all great fan communities have a moniker or a nickname that unites them and labels them in a good way, such as Cheeseheads, Deadheads, Truebies, and Marshmallows. Honestly, the fans will almost always choose the nickname for themselves, but you can still encourage them to create it — possibly even as a contest or poll on the Super Story Project Hub.

If you *consistently* feed the members of your fan community in these seven ways, you'll see the community begin to grow both in numbers and devotion.

As an aside, just because this is Chapter 16 doesn't diminish the importance of an engaged and participatory fan community. In fact, you should *always* be thinking in these terms. Brainstorm ways of getting your fans involved early, even during your creative development, financing (this is especially true if you're using crowdfunding resources to back your project), and even your production process. The more engaged and plugged in your fans are, the more likely you'll be able to form the fan community you need.

## Devotion to the larger good.

Now that you have your online fan community organized, well-fed and happy, it's time to turn your attention to your actual, physical, offline community. At this stage, I want you to begin strategizing how to use your Super Story to make a positive, lasting impact on the actual lives of real people.

As you may recall, many moons ago, I quoted a recent *Forbes* article talking about the importance of this, saying:

> *"Within a global society increasingly vexed by problems, the only smart long-term business move is for a brand to* ***demonstrate a tangible commitment to the larger good.*** *Consumers are increasingly inclined to support brands best known for making a* ***positive impact in the community.*** *The future opportunities are breathtaking for those* ***brands that seek the larger good*** *in meaningful, demonstrable ways."*

With an understanding of just how powerful and necessary corporate social responsibility is for a 21st century brand (consumer or entertainment), you can't simply limit the scope of community building to cosplay and fan fiction. If you do, the growth of your Super Story will ultimately be stunted.

Let's be real — you're inheriting a world on fire. Our children? God help them. It's not an abstract problem. The world needs help. People need help. In this day and age, simply shoving a piece of entertainment into the marketplace and walking away — even if it has a good message — shows a deep-rooted distancing from the struggle. Instead, as Super Story Architects, let's take it to the next level.

If you're as passionate about your Soapbox as you should be, you'll want to get it to as many people as humanly possible and do whatever it takes to help them implement it in their lives. If you actually believe your Soapbox is a good, important message for people to hear, to simply walk away after you slap a book on the shelf or get your movie on Netflix is, in my opinion, a little selfish. #crabssaydontbeshellfish

A regular, simple story asks, "How can I *entertain* the world?" However, a Super Story asks, "How can I help *change* the world through entertainment?"

For example, Mattel's *Monster High* IP features the teenage children of legendary monsters facing the awkward struggles of high school. Armed with their Soapbox of "be comfortable with yourself and each other even though we all may be different," they teamed up with the creators of the Kind Campaign, a grassroots movement that offers an empowerment solution to bullying. Together, they went on a national anti-bullying tour and used the *Monster High* IP as the catalyst for a solution-based approach to what is becoming a serious problem in American culture. Annually, they visit over 300 schools and organizations and speak to thousands of young people about this issue.

According to one Mattel executive, "We balance profit with a sense of social responsibility. I don't see any reason why we can't legitimately reach both of these goals simultaneously."

Similarly, The Harry Potter Alliance, or the HP Alliance is an organization that uses online organizing to educate and mobilize *Harry Potter* fans toward being engaged in issues around self empowerment as well as social justice by using parallels from the books. With the help of a whole network of fan sites and Harry Potter themed bands, they reach about 100,000 people across the world.

The main parallel they draw on comes from *Harry Potter and the Order of the Phoenix* where Harry starts an underground activist group called "Dumbledore's Army" to wake the Ministry of Magic up to the fact that Voldemort has returned. The HP Alliance strives to be a Dumbledore's Army for the real world that is waking the world up to ending the genocide in Darfur. Recently they have expanded their scope, discussing human rights atrocities in Eastern Burma, and they're going to be incorporating Congo into their vision soon.

The Inspire USA Foundation, the organization behind the teen mental health site ReachOut.com, partnered with The HP Alliance and ran a campaign using the "Horcruxes" from the *Harry Potter* books as metaphors for issues. They partnered on the issue of "fighting depression" and asked fans to share their "patronuses" with the world through art.

Participant Media is a leading media company dedicated to entertainment that inspires and compels social change. They have produced more than 75 films, including *Spotlight, Contagion, Lincoln, The Help, He Named Me*

*Malala*, *The Look of Silence*, *CITIZENFOUR*, *Food, Inc.*, and *An Inconvenient Truth*, and have collectively earned 50 Academy Award® nominations and 11 wins, including Best Picture for *Spotlight*. Participant's digital hub, TakePart, serves millions of socially conscious consumers each month with daily articles, videos and opportunities to take action on issues dealt with in their films and series.

One of their films, *Beasts of No Nation*, highlights the horrors of child soldiers in Africa. Using the film as a platform to raise awareness of the plight, they are also using their content as a way to empower the millions of youths around the world who are trapped in a cycle of violence and conflict. They are also mobilizing teams to help connect with African youth and showing them how to help their communities shift toward stability.

For the film, *The Beaver*, which is about a once-successful toy executive and family man who suffers from depression, Participant created a social action campaign that addressed the effects of mental illness and depression on individuals, their families and their relationships. Furthermore, they sought to de-stigmatize mental illness and depression, and provide tools and resources for families to support loved ones battling with an illness.

## How do you make an impact?

Inspired by what these other projects are doing to make the world a better place? I certainly hope so, because you can accomplish the same thing with your Super Story — possibly even more.

Here are three basic steps that can set your Super Story on a path toward real-world significance:

1. Teaching Materials;
2. Supply Truck; *and*
3. Frontline Action.

### Teaching materials.

This strategy is where you use your Soapbox to create value-based materials that help people apply it to their lives and their communities. Keep in mind, though, you're not creating stories — you did that already. Instead, you'll be creating materials specifically about the topic of your Soapbox.

For example, let's say your Soapbox is, "If you're depressed, don't isolate yourself because the only way you improve is to lean on and find hope within the people in your life that love you and support you." Your Driving Platform may be a film about a depressed man who finds hope and help in a beaver hand puppet, as in *The Beaver,* or a stage play about a housewife diagnosed with bi-polar disorder like in *Next to Normal.* However, when you're designing community outreach with your Teaching Materials, you want to squarely deal with just the actual, real-world topic of depression.

Maybe you can publish a self-help book like *Laughing in the Dark* or *When the Darkness Will Not Lift?* Or possibly a YouTube series focused on the different ways to help someone with depression? How about an app that helps people monitor their moods and provides several resources aimed at educating people about thought patterns that may be worsening their depression? Maybe you should consider creating them all?

Moreover, throughout the Teaching Materials, be sure to use your Micro-Stories and your various Super Story components as a way to illustrate your teachings. The more you draw parallels between your Soapbox and your stories, the more people will understand and emotionally relate to your Teaching Materials.

**Supply truck.**

Once you've created all of your Teaching Materials, identify organizations already using the Soapbox to reach out to communities. Once you identify them, supply them with various components of your Super Story that help them achieve their mission, including produced Micro-Stories and your Teaching Materials.

As I mentioned, The HP Alliance partnered with the Inspire USA Foundation, Mattel partnered with the Kind Campaign and for *The Beaver,* Participant Media partnered with Kristin Brooks Hope Center as well as the National Alliance on Mental Illness.

Non-profit organizations are always looking for any and all support they can receive, including methods of becoming more widespread and effective in their mission. Therefore, try to identify those organizations that align with your Soapbox and help supply them for their fight.

**Frontline action.**

While the Supply Truck step has you partnering with existing organizations, this step actually has you using your Super Story material to *directly* reach out to the community. It's great (and needed) to equip other people or organizations in order for them to achieve their missions and help spread your Soapbox; however, that shouldn't give you a license to *completely* shift that missional responsibility to someone else.

It's good to physically get on the frontline and actually look into the faces of the people who are impacted by and are living your Soapbox. Plan an event, even a small one, in your community. Screen your materials, discuss your books, play your games. Above all, create real conversation and actually connect with people in a meaningful, human and authentic way. I know that sometimes this is difficult for introverted writers to do such things. Trust me when I say that when you do, it'll not only change the people you're connecting with, but it will also change you as a creator.

At the end of the day, if you want to achieve that third element of a Super Story, you need to not only build a robust online fan community, but also reach out to your actual community through a devotion to corporate social responsibility and the larger good. By using your Super Story to not just entertain people, but actually make their lives better in a meaningful way, your entertainment brand will be on a path of attaining not just success, but significance — and significance is always better.

# EVERYBODY WHO IS SUCCESSFUL LAYS OUT A BLUEPRINT

KEVIN HART

# 17. The blueprint.

## Get it all down.

By now, you more than likely have amassed quite a bit of creative output. Now it's time to start putting it all together in one, stinkin' big document. Some folks call this document a bible, story canon, or a production guide, but we like to call it a "Super Story Blueprint" since it not only details and memorializes the creative canon of the Storyworld, but it also outlines all the practical plans and strategies for the entire project, including functionality, marketing promotions, and social outreach initiatives.

Take every description, every story treatment, every connection, every character breakdown, every dispersed this and converged that, every creative decision, every chart, every graph, every bullet point, and every immersion and community strategy you design and lay it all out in a clear, coherent production document. Collectively, it will all form the Super Story Blueprint.

Once finished, the Super Story Blueprint will help guide you and/or others as you begin to write and produce the content. It will literally have everyone working on the project on the same page.

If a screenwriter or novelist has a question about a story, it'll be in the Super Story Blueprint.

If a film producer has to change a location in one of the stories, the franchise blueprint will tell him all the ways the change will impact the other stories.

If a fan calls you out on a continuity question, the Super Story Blueprint will tell you how to set him straight.

It'll act as a guide and a built-in project manager as your Super Story goes from development, to writing and implementation, to production and ultimately to brand managing.

There isn't any one perfect way to create your Super Story Blueprint, as the order and layout will be dependent on your particular project. However, based on my experience, here's a suggested order or table of contents:

1. **Table of Contents:** It should go without saying that this is always helpful, especially with big documents.

2. **Quick Description:** Lead off the Blueprint with a pithy summary of your entire project. Think of it as a veritable "logline" for your Super Story that efficiently represents the project and gets a potential reader interested in checking it out. Don't worry about conveying every story, medium, platform and connection. Instead, simply focus on writing a a sentence or two that sells the basic idea of the Super Story, rather than the intricacies of the stories themselves. Pro tip: The most effective way to do this is focus everything around your High Concept.

   If you have a perfectly constructed logline that genuinely taps into the essence of your Super Story, then its meaning should resonate on every page of your Blueprint. If you're ever stuck writing a scene, coming up with a story idea, or developing an East Coast Extension, you can always look to that logline and it will push you in the right direction. It helps you maintain focus on what the core of the story is really about and ultimately, your Super Story Blueprint should be a detailed extrapolation of it.

3. **Soapbox**: Follow the Super Story logline with a thorough explanation of your Soapbox and how your Super Story is not just cool, but important. Explain in detail the problem

you're attempting to solve or issue you're focused on tackling and then detail how your Super Story will help contribute to the larger solution. Done right, this section will build a powerful emotional context for the rest of your Super Story Blueprint.

4. **Storyworld**: Whereas the Soapbox section creates an emotional context, detailing your Storyworld early in the document will create a creative one. Go through all the elements of a viable Storyworld and be sure to include maps, visuals (if you don't have custom art, just pull art from Google Images for inspiration — *you won't get sued because you don't publish your Blueprint*), character concepts, flora, fauna, etc. Also, in this section, I typically include the Macro-Story for the world.

5. **Visual Table of Contents:** Because, admittedly, there are quite a few moving parts in the Blueprint, it helps to give people a simple visual of the story architecture you're getting ready to introduce. Without going into descriptions of your stories, you can simply use icons or other types of simple art to create a veritable Table of *Creative* Contents.

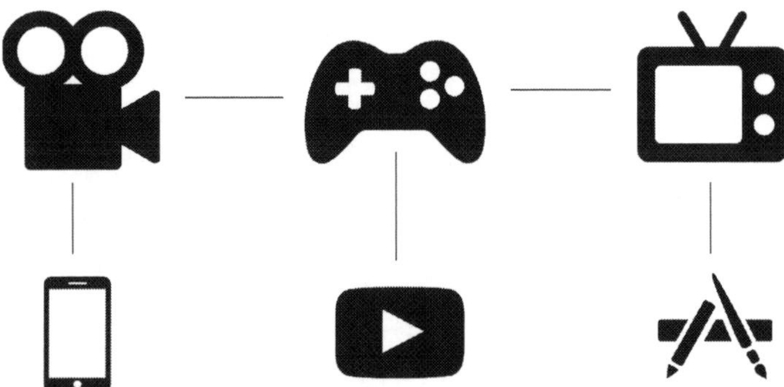

Trust me, a simple map of your West Coast stories and their East Coast extensions (like the one above) will help organize everything in your readers' brains and act as a quick reference in times of need.

Many times I like to actually include the icons on a Macro-Story timeline of the world so everyone can see where they appear in the continuity of the Storyworld.

6. **Driving Platform:** Regardless of your suspected release order, go ahead and establish your big, tentpole Driving Platform. Create a longline for the story, detail your cast of characters (protagonist(s), antagonist(s), supporting characters), describe the Additive Comprehension that is going to make people want to experience it, and detail how it dynamically connects with the other stories, etc. Once you have the core information about the Driving Platform, then you can begin adding outlines, treatments, reference art, and anything else you want as you continue to develop the project.

7. **East Coast Extensions of the Driving Platform:** Go ahead and begin breaking down the East Coast Extensions of the Driving Platform itself, detailing the stories involved, how it extends the story or experience of the Driving Platform, the mediums and platforms to be used, etc.

8. **Other Micro-Stories and Their Extensions:** After the Driving Platform, begin doing the exact same thing for your other Micro-Stories. Some may be extremely developed and others may be a simple longline or idea, but because the Blueprint is a living document, you'll be able to add and develop them later.

9. **Dynamic Connections:** Even if it's just the West Coast stories, I like to visually depict

how all the stories connect (see a basic example below).

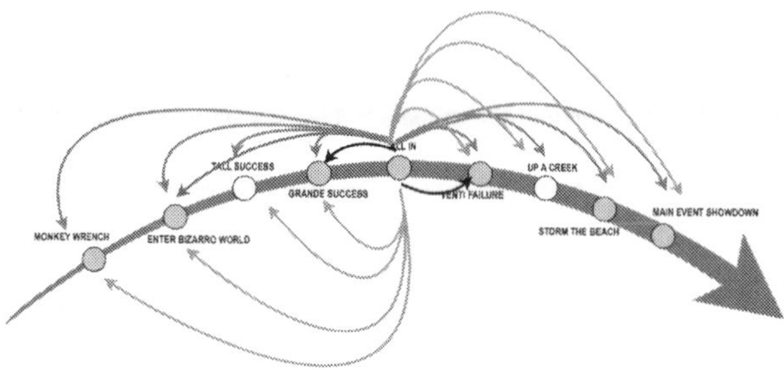


10. **Media Blurring:** Detail how you intend on blurring the lines between fiction and reality, including descriptions of Blurred Merchandise and even Blurred Businesses.

11. **Community Building:** A cohesive breakdown of your community building strategy and how you're going to grow your fanbase over time.

12. **Advancement Campaign:** This isn't discussed in this book, but an Advancement Campaign is a grassroots, promotional strategy that ties back to and actually strengthens the narrative. I'll probably cover this in a future publication of some kind. #storyseed

13. **Appendix**: This is a bit of a miscellaneous/ hodgepodge section, but in the appendix, you can include all the full character breakdowns of all your various characters, more detailed maps of various locations, etc.

Depending on the project, a Super Story Blueprint may run hundreds of pages. Sure, it's hefty and takes a lot of work, but this is the document that will guide you and your teams through years of content creation. Looking at it that way, you can't realistically expect it to just be a handful of bullet points pasted into a simple ~~Word~~ Pages document (I'm a Mac guy #sorrynotsorry).

Once you have a healthy draft of the Super Story Blueprint, the vision of your project should be crystal clear to anyone who sets eyes on it. Communicating your vision and the depth of the project is one of the most important parts of gathering partners, investors, and collaborators, which makes your Super Story Blueprint one of the most valuable tools in your arsenal.

*Part 4*

# The gravy.

TRY NOT
DO OR DO NOT
THERE IS
NO TRY

YODA

# 18. Some parting words.

## And here we are.

Finally.

At the end of the book.

No more macros, no more micros, no more arcs or explorations.

Let me take a moment to compose myself...

Ultimately, you may need to read through this book ~~fifty~~ a couple more times to fully absorb all the intricacies of the Super Story approach. As I said before, let this book be a continual resource for you as you go through the development process. Highlight passages, flag pages, tweet quotes (#superstory) — keep coming back to it time and time again. I'm honestly convinced I've given you the tools to truly create a quality narrative that is pervasive, participatory, sprawling, and most importantly, can withstand the rigors of being stretched and expanded for years to come. Accomplishing such a feat will clearly and automatically set you apart in a hyper-competitive, over-saturated entertainment landscape.

A great transmedia project may start with a single logline, but as you apply this Super Story process, and even put your own spin on the process, you'll be able to watch as it becomes a growing, living, breathing entertainment experience right before your eyes.

Just remember, even though others may have more money, more experience, or better technology, it's your *stories* that will allow your project to evolve and grow into something that will affect people's lives for decades. It's your stories that will motivate fans to help you improve and refine your project as time goes on. It's your stories that will hook them. If you don't have great stories, you're sunk, no matter how much engagement you provide, how many cool mediums you can take advantage of, or how innovative your technological elements are.

So, above all, become a master of storytelling and create from your soul. When you do these two things, your foundation will always be strong and your direction will always be true.

## Some sage advice.

At this point, I know you feel like I've been talking to you for ~~hours~~ ~~days~~ ~~weeks~~ months on end, but allow me to formally introduce myself.

Hi. I'm Houston.

Like the city.

Though, I was born in Ohio, grew up in Kentucky, graduated from college in West Virginia, went to law school in Virginia, and live in California.

Curious, I know.

A few things about me to get started:

- My full name is made up of three first names — Houston. Joe. Howard. For some reason, this has been the cause of an inexplicable amount of confusion for people throughout my short life;
- I have a peculiar aptitude for creating board games;
- I have been called by some a "serial hobbyist," which seems to be the pejorative version of the preferable "renaissance man," "hyphenate" or "polymath";
- I exploited a loophole in my undergraduate program and saved myself from a full semester of classes (a feat that I honestly don't get enough credit for — pun intended);
- I've likely heard the whole "Houston, we have a problem." joke well over two thousand times throughout my life;

- I love Cincinnati sports (Go Reds/Bengals!), but root for the University of Kentucky in basketball (C-A-T-S, Cats, Cats, Cats!); *and*

- I'm a huge fan of timely and well-placed analogies.

I went to law school at Regent University School of Law in Virginia Beach, VA, and loved every second of it. I never had the whole "I'm completely overwhelmed, I have no life, I'm drowning in a sea of briefs and dissenting opinions" feeling that so many law students have. Honestly, law school came easily to me. God helped me through and showed me how to do very well. Heck, I even won the Virginia Trial Lawyers award for the best blue chip, up-and-coming trial lawyer. Don't think I'm saying this to brag about myself — I'm not that kind of guy.

I'm merely telling you this to set up what a big decision it was for me not to continue to practice law, and instead, pursue a career in entertainment.

The last semester of my third year, my wife and I began seriously praying about what God needed us to do for the rest of our lives and shockingly, it wasn't being a lawyer. Not that my degree was a waste by any means. Thankfully, a Juris Doctor is a wildly versatile degree. We simply examined what we would do if we had all the money in the world and failure was out of the picture. For me, it was making movies. I could do that all day, every day and it would never feel like work. So, we sold everything we had, packed what we could in our Jetta, and drove to Los Angeles.

The only problem was that when we arrived to the sunny West Coast, I realized I didn't *really* know how to do anything. I mean, I had a good idea of what to do, but the difference between having a good idea of what to do in the film industry and *really* knowing what to do in the film industry is as big as the Grand Canyon (which we saw on our cross-country trek).

So, I was left with a decision: go to film school and incur another round of student loan debt or spend a couple hundred dollars reading books. Lots and lots of books.

I chose the books.

I went to the bookstore and devoured every film book I could find — producing books, writing books, directing books, dialogue books, character development books, production management books.

William Indick's *Psychology for Screenwriters,* Stanley D. Williams' *The Moral Premise,* Paul Chitlik's *Rewrite,* William Akers' *Your Screenplay Sucks,* Pamela Douglas' *Writing the TV Drama Series,* Jennifer Van Sijll's *Cinematic Storytelling,* Tom Malloy's *Bankroll,* Maureen Ryan's *Producer to Producer,* Blake Snyder's *Save the Cat* series, Martin Roth's *The Writer's Partner,* and Christopher Riley's *The Hollywood Standard* became just a select few of the books that acted as my personal film school curriculum.

However, even after filling my head full of industry knowledge, it was still tough to find a footing. Hollywood is a competitive place. Not literally Hollywood the city — it's just kind of dirty and weird, but "Hollywood" the industry. Tens of thousands of scripts are registered with the Writers Guild every single year. Every day studios and agents are bombarded with every idea, concept, and pitch imaginable — all from really smart, capable people who were probably the most artistically-gifted folks from their hometowns. Literally, you have 50,000 crazy-talented people all running for one doorway.

Trust me, it's bananas.

I don't say this to scare you away from the industry. Not at all. For me, quitting was not an option. I was called here for a reason, so I'm staying until I achieve everything I'm supposed to achieve. However, that doesn't mean I have to follow the herd of people running for that one, lucrative doorway inside the industry.

And you don't have to either.

For me, I chose (and am still choosing) to sneak in through a side window by thinking slightly differently. I didn't just go by the industry's status quo. Instead, I looked at where culture and media were heading. I looked at the shift that is happening in how audiences consume content and the democratization of content creation. I saw how new, interesting distribution channels were popping up and I endeavored to be a Swiss Army knife rather than a machete.

Enter Super Story.

This process has allowed me and the team I've assembled to not only continue to develop content in the area that's closest to our hearts (film), but it's also allowed us opportunities to navigate a competitive industry in a recessive economy. It's led us into not just meeting with studio heads and independently pursuing our own productions, but also into helping other people and companies with their projects through consulting and partnership. Also, it's allowed us to expand in ways we never dreamed of, such as using our Super Story process to work in the music industry, facilitate corporate branding initiatives, and even work with school systems on both getting literature-averse students to love to write, and overhauling their writing standards.

This process has diversified us brilliantly so we can now leverage our success in the education space to get meetings with producers and then use our success in the film space to get meetings with potential corporate clients. It really has been a cool journey.

So, while so many people will tell you that it's folly to pursue a career in entertainment (especially in the current economy), I say simply do what you were put on this planet to do and don't let outside influences sway you from your path. If that's not entertainment, but you want to try the entertainment industry anyway, you'll more than likely burn out within a couple of years.

But if it *is* entertainment, know that you really need two things to compliment your talent: perseverance and the ability to understand the times in which we are living. I can't teach you to be talented and I can't teach perseverance, but I'm being truthful when I say this book can help with the last one.

People are changing. The economy is changing. The industry is changing. We're living in a time where marketing, technology, and entertainment are merging like never before.

Therefore, as professional storytellers, we need to stay light, efficient, and versatile in the way we communicate with audiences. We not only need to create differently, we need to *think* differently.

Why were the Wright brothers the first to fly? They didn't have the most cutting-edge technology or an economic advantage over any one else. In fact, there were other teams more advanced, more financed and more credible than themselves. So, how did they do it?

They changed the way they looked at the problem.

Everyone else was trying to solve the problem of building the best fixed wings in order to produce lift. The Wright brothers, however, began to focus on how to control an unstable aircraft in flight. You see, up until that time, the concepts of aileron's, rudders, vertical and horizontal stabilizers were not envisioned and all the other airplane inventors were still designing fixed wing aircraft.

Through the paradigm shift of visualizing an unstable aircraft the Wright brothers began thinking about the technical requirements to give an aircraft controls. Indeed, innovation for the next level requires the understanding that the flip-side of every problem is opportunity.

Sure, audiences consume entertainment on a zillion different devices. Sure, they demand engagement and interaction above and beyond what is reasonable. Sure, they never want the same story twice and have a never ending entertainment appetite. Instead of trying to fix all these problems, let's just embrace them and have them actually inform us, as creators, how to adapt.

I truly believe a Super Story can help you do just that.

So, go ahead, get to work and make awesome things.

Seriously.

You don't have all day.

# I LIKE GOOD STRONG WORDS THAT MEAN SOMETHING

LOUISA MAY ALCOTT

# 19. Glossary of Terms

## What dem words mean?

I know, I know — there are quite a few (149 to be exact) funny-sounding, complicated or downright bizarre terms thrown around in this book. In a way, this is a good thing, as it shows how this particular space is developing and progressing — since one of the signs of a maturing industry is the development of industry terms and unique trade vernacular. However, I admit, it's difficult to keep them all straight.

So, I thought I would help by creating a Glossary of Terms for you to reference for clarity and comprehension.

Enjoy.

1. **Act I:** The first act within the Three Act Structure, which typically introduces the "normal world" before the High Concept is realized in the story.
2. **Act II:** The second act within the Three Act Structure, which typically shows the "bizarro world" where the High Concept is thriving and ultimately creates an adventure for the protagonist(s). Act II is where most of your "trailer moments" come from as well as your key art for marketing.
3. **Act III:** The third act within the Three Act Structure, which typically shows the "resolution" of the story. The hero usually takes the natural strengths from Act I, adds the lessons he learned in Act II and then is able to accomplish the "need" of the story toward the end of Act III.
4. **Act of God**: This is a way to apply a High Concept to a Storyworld. It's when you, as a creator, apply a large-scale, sociological, biological, technological, political, environmental or meteorological change to the Storyworld in such a way that it impacts the entirety of the Definable Location as well the lives of *every* Character Group residing there.
5. **Adaptation**: Taking a story that exists in one medium/platform and duplicating it in another medium/platform. See Multimedia.
6. **Additive Comprehension:** Literally, "adding to the understanding" of the audience. It consists of the new, unique and valuable information that only exists in a single story. This decreases friction and therefore incentivizes Audience Migration.

7. **Alignment**: A method of creating designations for your Character Groups that will inform you as to the ethical and moral perspectives of the groups, their motivations, outlook on life and generally how they should act in a given situation.
8. **All In:** The midpoint beat in the Six Stage Story and one of the Fence Post Beats for the Macro-Story. Specifically, in a Macro-Story, this is the point in the Storyworld's history where the world has learned to accept the Bizarro World as reality.
9. **Alternate Reality Game:** Also known as the "ARG." A type of narrative experience that uses the "real world" as a platform and creates an extremely participatory, engaging scavenger hunt where the audiences are actually characters in the story.
10. **Ancillary Narrative:** A type of Micro-Story where the plot doesn't have to move the Macro-Story forward in any meaningful or major way. Rather than advancing the Macro-Story, it simply "colors" it.
11. **Anticipated Showdown:** A type of Additive Comprehension for a Micro-Story that lures audience member with the promise of seeing a long-awaited face-off between two main characters, groups or factions.
12. **Audience Migration:** This is when the audience travels to and fro, from one story component to another.
13. **Augmented Reality:** Also known as "AR." A type of experience where a digital device is used as a "window" into the real world while also augmenting the world with digital overlays. *Pokemon Go!* is a popular example.
14. **Badge Brand:** A brand that acts as a reflection of their customers themselves to the point that the customers proudly wear the brand logo as a symbol of their lives.
15. **Blurred Merchandising:** Both a type of merchandising and Media Blurring where objects, clothing and artifacts from your story are pulled out of the narrative and produced as merchandise in the real world.
16. **Blurred Business:** A type of Media Blurring where businesses or services in a story are actually created and launched in the real world as standalone ventures.
17. **Blurred IP:** A type of Media Blurring where any fictional, created content that exists in a story is actually produced or published in the real world.
18. **Brand Evangelists:** Fans that not only purchase a brand's products, but actively, openly and proudly promote the brand.
19. **Broad Geographical Boundaries:** One of eight elements of an optimized Storyworld. Specifically, it deals with the process of stretching the geographical bounds of your Definable Location so as to maximize the narrative potential of your Storyworld.
20. **Call to Action (CTA)**: One of the elements of a Soapbox where you take your Opinion of a Topic and turn it into actual, actionable advice for the audience.
21. **Callbacks:** A specific reference to something that happened in another Micro-Story where the audience members can actually go and find the other Micro-Story and see the event to which the character was referring.

22. **Cartographic Continuity:** Maintaining the geographical consistency of your Storyworld across multiple narratives.
23. **Character Archetype:** Part of your Character Breakdown. Specifically, this is the classic role of your character, as discussed by Christopher Vogler in his book, *The Writers Journey: Mythic Structure for Writers.*
24. **Character Backstory:** A narrative opportunity where you explore a character's past in an East Coast Extension rather than in a Micro-Story.
25. **Character Breakdown:** This is the comprehensive outline for a character where you define a character's personality, sociology, archetype, secrets, motivations and other interesting aspects of the character's life.
26. **Character Connections:** A type of Dynamic Connection that connects multiple stories through the use of characters.
27. **Character Groups:** One of eight elements of an optimized Storyworld. Specifically, the nine groups of characters (as opposed to individual characters) defined by Craft or Soapbox that inhabit the Definable Location.
28. **Character Reveal:** A type of Additive Comprehension for a Micro-Story that lures audience members with the promise of learning something interesting and important about one or more of the main characters.
29. **Chewy Transmedia:** Either a project that didn't start as pure transmedia, but began to purely transmediate at some point midstream or a project that has a mix of both multimedia and transmedia components.
30. **Compounding Revenue:** A value proposition of a Super Story where you don't just create additional revenue streams, but use Additive Comprehension and Audience Migration to *exponentially* increase ROI.
31. **Content Creation:** This is where you empower the fan community to not just consume, but to create different parts of the project, such as fan fiction, art, graphic design, games, films and music.
32. **Converged East Coast Transmedia:** A type of East Coast Transmedia where the East Coast Extension takes place *during* the West Coast story, thereby innovating the overall experience in some way.
33. **Core Narrative:** A type of Micro-Story that deals directly with events in a Fence Post beat and works to move the Macro-Story forward in any meaningful or major way.
34. **Corporate Social Responsibility (CSR)**: This refers to a brand's sense of responsibility toward the community and environment (both ecological and social) in which it operates. It also refers to the brand's devotion to the larger good.
35. **Cosplay**: The practice of portraying a fictional character – at times completely identifying as that character while in costume. Also, one of the various ways to Feed the Beast while cultivating your Fandom.
36. **Definable Location:** One of eight elements of an optimized Storyworld. Specifically, the physical boundaries and setting of your Storyworld.
37. **Delivery Platform:** A web-based, intermediary platform that works as a go-between for a Medium and an Experience Platform. Social media platforms would be considered Delivery Platforms.

38. **Dynamic Connection:** Meaningful, narrative ways to connect the variety of stories appearing in a Super Story.

39. **East Coast Extension:** Using East Coast Transmedia to extend a West Coast story where the East Coast Extension doesn't make sense, isn't enjoyable or isn't valuable without experiencing the West Coast component. Can be Dispersed or Converged.

40. **East Coast Transmedia:** A style of Transmedia that uses stories that depend on other stories for context, meaning or value. East Coast Transmedia is focused on engagement over revenue and is characterized by low-cost, quick-to-market platforms.

41. **Emergent Narrative:** A term coined by Scott Walker that refers to an audience's participation in the overall narrative of a story. Mainly, this includes the creation and writing of fan fiction.

42. **Enter Bizarro World:** A beat in the Six Stage Story where the plot moves forcefully into Act II and into the High Concept. Also, it is one of the Fence Post Beats for the Macro-Story. Specifically, in a Macro-Story, this beat shows the people of the Storyworld making an affirmative decision to move into not only uncharted territory, but a world that is the exact opposite of the one from which they came.

43. **Essential Services and Critical Infrastructure:** The vital information the U.S. military defines before invading. They are the elements critical to a location's survival and existence. In turn, when creating our Storyworld, we need to define these same elements in much the same way.

44. **Essentials:** One of the elements of Essential Services and Infrastructure that specifically defines what it takes for the Definable Location to minimally function. Also, it defines where the people actually get these things.

45. **Exclusive Access:** Part of the Feed the Beast initiative of cultivating and nurturing a Fandom. Specifically, it's where you give the members of the fan community access to *valuable* content that "outsiders" can't get.

46. **Experience Platform:** The end user technology on which the audience experiences the story. This is specifically differentiated from the Delivery Platform.

47. **Family Tree Appearance:** A type of Character Connection where the same character doesn't appear in multiple stories, but rather his or her family members do.

48. **Fandom**: An active, engaged community of superfans.

49. **Fandom Nickname:** The cool, catchy moniker the fans give themselves — Trekkies, Potterheads, etc.

50. **Fence Post Beats:** The seven most important story beats in the Six Stage Story. Consider these the load-bearing walls of the narrative structure for your story.

51. **Forever Franchise:** An IP that can continue to persist and even thrive across multiple mediums and platforms for generations.

52. **Four-Quadrant Storyworld:** A Storyworld that can attract and entertain any and all audience demographics.

53. **Friction**: The psychological resistance to a given element of your franchise that causes pause, aggravation, fatigue or confusion. Or, basically, any reason someone doesn't want to do something.

54. **Frontline Action:** This is were a brand takes its Teaching Materials and actually goes into its physical community and actually helps better the lives of real people.

55. **Gamification**: The concept of applying game mechanics and game design techniques to engage and motivate people to achieve certain goals.

56. **Grande Success:** A beat in the Six Stage Story that takes place in Stage 3/Act II of a story. Also, it is one of the Fence Post Beats for the Macro-Story. Specifically, in a Macro-Story, this beat shows something good happening in the Storyworld that makes the residents feel better about living in the High Concept and Act II.

57. **Grow the Group:** A method of applying a High Concept to a Storyworld where the size of a High Concept Character Group is increased to the point of becoming systemic.

58. **Hard Transmedia:** A project that was meant to be total, complete and pure transmedia from inception.

59. **High Concept:** An entertainment concept steeped in irony that is immediately interesting and doesn't rely on execution to to be compelling or arouse curiosity.

60. **Homophily**: A sociological tendency of individuals to closely associate and bond with others who are similar to themselves.

61. **Hyperdiegesis**: Literally, "super story." Refers to the art of world building whereby you build a robust world even though you may only show "the tip of the iceberg."

62. **Infrastructure**: One of the elements of Essential Services and Infrastructure that specifically defines the minimal, yet essential infrastructure system of the Definable Location — bridges, railways, roads, tunnels, sewers, etc.

63. **Irony**: Experiencing the opposite or something you least expect. This is the essential ingredient in forming a High Concept.

64. **Leadership**: One of the elements of Essential Services and Infrastructure that specifically defines the leadership structure of the Definable Location.

65. **Live Events:** One of the various ways to Feed the Beast while cultivating your Fandom. Specifically, the practice of planning and producing meet-ups and occasions where your fans can connect with each other in person.

66. **Location Connections:** A type of Dynamic Connection that uses locations to connect multiple stories in meaningful ways.

67. **Location Reference:** A specific type of Location Connection where a location from another Micro-Story doesn't show up, but is simply referenced.

68. **Location Revisit:** A specific type of Location Connection where a location from another Micro-Story actually appears.

69. **Macro-Story:** The narrative history of your Storyworld as told through a well-structured, story arc.

70. **Main Event Showdown:** A beat in the Six Stage Story that takes place in Stage 6/ Act III of a story. Also, it is one of the Fence Post Beats for the Macro-Story.

Specifically, in a Macro-Story, this beat shows the epic showdown between the heroes of the world and the villains that ultimately decides whether the world remains on its path, goes back to its original form — or worse.

71. **Major Death:** A type of Additive Comprehension for a Micro-Story that lures audience member with the promise of seeing the death of a main character or faction.
72. **Media Blurring:** The use of digital, web and real world media to blur the lines between fiction and reality, thereby making your Super Story seem real.
73. **Medium**: The artistic style and method used to create a story.
74. **Meraki**: An old Greek concept that means, "soul creativity or the essence of yourself that is put into your work."
75. **Micro-Series:** A Micro-Story that has enough narrative potential to actually be turned into a series of stories. A Micro-Series is also structured by the Fence Post beats.
76. **Micro-Series, Anthology:** A Micro-Series that has different protagonists for each episode and that shifts every single episode into both a different medium and platform.
77. **Micro-Series, Episodic:** A Micro-Series that has the same protagonists throughout and largely maintains the same medium and platforms. Nonetheless, a select few episodes of the series can, in fact, be shifted into other mediums and platforms as long as they follow the same protagonists.
78. **Micro-Series, Serialized:** A Micro-Series that maintains the same protagonists and the same mediums and platforms throughout the entirety of the series.
79. **Micro-Story:** A standalone West Coast story that takes place somewhere along the Macro-Story timeline.
80. **Monkey Wrench:** A beat in the Six Stage Story that takes place in Stage 2/Act 1 of a story. Also, it is one of the Fence Post Beats for the Macro-Story. Specifically, in a Macro-Story, this beat shows the unexpected event that throws the Storyworld out of its normal world and thrusts it toward the High Concept world of Act II.
81. **Multi-Modality:** The ability for stories to be successfully, effectively and meaningfully spread into multiple mediums.
82. **Multimedia**: Taking a story that exists in one medium/platform and duplicating it in another medium/platform. See Adaptation.
83. **Nano-Series:** This is when a story within a Micro-Series can't adequately be told through a single story and needs its own series. A Nano-Series can adhere to the Fence Post beats or simply be told as a trilogy.
84. **Narrative Excess:** A narrative opportunity where you take story content that was "cut" from the final version, shifting it into another medium and ultimately using it as an East Coast Extension.
85. **Narrative Space:** The narrative time between Micro-Stories that have yet to be filled or developed. See Negative Space and White Space.

86. **Nathan Model of Storytelling:** A Biblical storytelling model where you take a helpful truth, deliver it in a relevant story and then do personal outreach to draw parallels between the audience and the characters.

87. **Native Platform**: The platform on which a Micro-Story is specifically designed to premiere or debut.

88. **Negative Space:** The narrative time between Micro-Stories that have yet to be filled or developed. See Narrative Space and White Space.

89. **Object Connections:** A type of Dynamic Connection that uses objects or clothing to connect multiple stories in meaningful ways.

90. **Opinion**: One of the three essential elements to a Soapbox where you give your personal view, judgment or thoughts on a particular Topic.

91. **Origin Story:** A type of Additive Comprehension for a Micro-Story that lures audience members with the promise of seeing how a character, organization or a historical event came to be.

92. **Other Character Perspective:** An East Coast Transmedia opportunity where you tell a piece of the Micro-Story again, but this time from a different character's perspective.

93. **Other Micro-Story Reveal:** A type of Additive Comprehension for a Micro-Story that lures audience members with the promise of finding out valuable information about something that happened in another Micro-Story.

94. **Personal Appearance Character Connection:** A specific type of Character Connection where a character from another Micro-Story actually appears.

95. **Personal Reference Character Connection:** A specific type of Character Connection where a character from another Micro-Story doesn't show up, but is simply referenced.

96. **PGA**: The Producers Guild of America.

97. **Phenomenology**: A philosophy or school of thought that posits that the greatest achievement of an artist isn't the art itself, but the experience that an audience member has with the art. It encourages creators to always be focused not just on their own artistic vision, but on the people for whom they are creating.

98. **Pico-Series:** This is when a story within a Nano-Series can't adequately be told through a single story and needs its own series. A Pico-Series can adhere to the Fence Post beats or simply be told as a trilogy.

99. **Platform**: The end user technology on which the audience experiences the story. Synonymous with Experience Platform.

100. **Platform Agnostic:** The process of creating and developing stories without regard for Platforms or Mediums.

101. **Platform Potency:** How well a story performs in a given platform based on the strengths, weaknesses and unique characteristics of both the story and the platform itself.

102. **Plot for Inspiration:** Using the plot of an established story as a muse and template for an Ancillary Narrative.

103. **Plot Impacting Plot:** A type of Dynamic Connection where something so significant happens in a Micro-Story that it dramatically impacts the plot of another Micro-Story.

104. **Plural Perfection:** A philosophy that states that one product can't reach and satisfy everyone's needs and desires so instead of pursuing one perfect product, create multiple products that collectively achieve this goal.

105. **Population**: One of the elements of Essential Services and Infrastructure that specifically defines the people who inhabit the Definable Location.

106. **Portmanteau Transmedia:** A style of transmedia that exclusively deploys East Coast components that don't rely on a West Coast component for context and meaning, but rely on other East Coast components. Only when you experience *all* the East Coast components is the experience enjoyable.

107. **Primary Character Group:** The *main* Character Group out of the nine that inhabit your Definable Location.

108. **Project Hub:** The official website of your Super Story.

109. **Protective Forces:** One of the elements of Essential Services and Infrastructure that specifically defines the security forces employed by the Definable Location.

110. **Radical Intertextuality:** The relationship between stories and the shaping of a story's meaning by another story.

111. **Rat King:** The subject of Russian folklore that is a metaphor for connecting your stories in such a way that it feels like they're telling one, big story.

112. **Recipe for a Rat King:** The specific formula for using Dynamic Connections to achieve the Rat King.

113. **Remix Culture:** A term coined by Henry Jenkins referring to fans' love of altering entertainment, including re-editing scenes, remixing songs or rewriting dialogue.

114. **Room for History:** One of eight elements of an optimized Storyworld. Specifically, this refers to how much narrative history your Storyworld has to explore. Typically, the more Room for History, the better.

115. **Six Stage Story:** The proprietary story structure system design by One 3 Creative. It breaks a story down into three acts, two stages per act, and four specific beats that take place in every stage. This brings the total to three acts, six stages and 24 total story beats.

116. **Soapbox**: The thematic, personal mission of your Super Story. It is made of a Topic, Opinion and a Call to Action.

117. **Social Segments:** Horizontally dividing your Character Groups based on personality, geography or other unique identifiers.

118. **Soft Transmedia:** A project that was never meant to be transmedia; however, the creator allows licensees or fans to unofficially extend the story in a transmediated way.

119. **Special Sauce:** One of eight elements of an optimized Storyworld. Specifically, this refers to the unique twist you give your Storyworld that separates it from other, somewhat similar concepts.

120. **Status Ladders:** Within the Social Segments, there should be different vertical levels of statuses held by the characters that are also achieved by the audience through gamification during community building.

121. **Story Seeds:** A specific reference in a Micro-Story to something that happened in the past; however, the audience members can't see the event to which the character was referring because the Micro-Story hasn't been produced yet.

122. **Storyworld**: The imaginary world that is inspired by your Soapbox and is where all your stories are set.

123. **Storyworld Exploration:** An East Coast Transmedia opportunity where the audience explores parts of the Storyworld not explored in the West Coast Micro-Story.

124. **Storyworld Reveal:** A type of Additive Comprehension for a Micro-Story that lures audience members with the promise of learning something new about the Storyworld.

125. **Super Story:** A proprietary storytelling system and business model that combines transmedia storytelling principles, powerful emotional connections with the audience that communicate meaningful truths, and online and offline community building.

126. **Super Story Blueprint:** The comprehensive development and production document that memorializes your entire Super Story.

127. **Supply Truck:** This is were a brand takes partners with a non-profit that has a core mission similar to the Soapbox and supplies it with its Teaching Materials and various entertainment components.

128. **Systemic High Concept:** A High Concept that is so pervasive in the Definable Location that it affects everyone and no one can escape its influence or impact.

129. **Tautology**: The ability to continually say the same thing in different ways.

130. **Teaching Materials:** This is when you create Soapbox-centric, value-based materials that help people apply the Soapbox to their lives and their communities.

131. **Three Act Structure**: A dramatic storytelling model created by Aristotle that divides a narrative into three distinct parts.

132. **Top Down Dialogue:** This is a community building strategy where you give your fan community access to the main stakeholders of the Super Story through interviews, Google Hangouts, panels, etc.

133. **Topic**: The theme or subject matter of your Soapbox.

134. **Transmedia**: The art of telling a story across a variety of mediums and platforms in a way that forms a cohesive whole and creates an entirely new experience for the audience.

135. **Transmediate**: The *verb* version of transmedia.

136. **Unanswered Questions:** An East Coast Transmedia opportunity where you intentionally don't answer a question in a West Coast Micro Story, only to eventually answer it in an East Coast Extension.

137. **Unfamiliarity**: One of eight elements of an optimized Storyworld. Specifically, this refers to making your Storyworld seem foreign or strange so as to create a desire by the audience to explore.

138. **Unfamiliarity, Fictional:** This is a type of Unfamiliarity that is achieved by creating a completely fictional Storyworld.

139. **Unfamiliarity, High Concept:** This is a type of Unfamiliarity that is achieved by making the High Concept systemic within the Storyworld.

140. **Unfamiliarity, Past and Future:** This is a type of Unfamiliarity that is achieved by shifting the Storyworld into the past or into the future.

141. **Unfamiliarity, Real World:** This is a type of Unfamiliarity that is achieved by finding a place in the real world that most people haven't explored or with which most people are still unfamiliar.

142. **Urtext**: A central place or entertainment component that holds all the information about an IP. This should *not* exist in a transmedia project.

143. **Value Propositions:** All the reasons and wisdom to support or justify a particular creative or business approach.

144. **Venti Failure:** A beat in the Six Stage Story that takes place in Stage 4/Act 3 of a story. Also, it is one of the Fence Post Beats for the Macro-Story. Specifically, in a Macro-Story, this beat shows how a betrayal leads directly to one, big, whopping failure that makes it seem like the Storyworld should have never embarked on this new path.

145. **Verisimilitude**: The appearance of reality that creates a willing suspension of disbelief by an audience.

146. **Virtual Reality:** A digital storytelling genre that takes the audience out of the real world and immerses their senses into another world where they typically have some level of agency or control.

147. **West Coast Transmedia:** A style of Transmedia that uses independent, standalone stories.

148. **White Space:** The narrative time between Micro-Stories that has yet to be filled or developed. See Negative Space and Narrative Space.

149. **World Artifacts:** Items that exist in your Storyworld, such as objects, clothing and artifacts, that are pulled out and actually produced as merchandise in the real world. See Blurred Merchandise.

# About me.

As the Chief Storyteller and Co-Founder of One 3 Creative, Houston has been a recognized thought leader in the entertainment and branding communities because of his unique and proprietary transmedia approach to story. Advising entities such as Mattel, Disney Imagineering, Reliance Media Works, West Coast Customs, McKinsey and Company, Unilever, Samuel Goldwyn Films and Harper Collins Publishing, as well as designing a number of transmedia-focused projects for Fox, Slinky, the writers of Toy Story, independent authors, music artists and a number of other professionals, Houston has an impressive amount of experience designing projects that are primed for the 21st Century.

When he's not outlining a new slate of transmedia design books, setting up international co-productions for current transmedia projects or leading a wildly diverse creative team, Houston is educating professionals on how to adapt to an ever-changing entertainment landscape. This has included leading workshops for the Television Academy of Arts and Sciences, the Producers Guild of America, the National Association of Broadcasters, Act

One, Storyworld USA, The Greater Los Angeles Writers Conference and the Swedish Chamber of Commerce. Additionally, Houston is planning a series of international transmedia masterclasses across Brazil, Australia, Africa and China throughout 2017.

His first book — *Make Your Story Really Stinkin' Big: How to Go From Concept to Franchise and Make Your Story Last For Generations* — has been a go-to manual for creative professionals on how to leverage a variety of media platforms, maximize revenue potential and engage audiences in new and innovative ways. His second book, *You're Going to Need a Bigger Story: The Essential Guide to Not Just Telling a Story, But Telling a Super Story*, builds on that success and takes his teachings about Super Story to the next level of professional, entertainment education.

Learn more about how Houston builds projects that exist at the intersection of branding and entertainment at **superstory.works**.

# About us.

## Who the heck are these guys?

Simply put, One 3 Creative is a collection of diverse creative professionals committed to telling stories that cause positive changes in people's lives.

You see, there's work and there's your calling.

A calling is the kind of work that never actually feels like work. The kind of work you'd never compromise on. That you'd sacrifice for. The kind of work that has your fingerprints all over it and adds up to something. Something big. Something that couldn't happen anywhere else or with any other group of people.

That's the kind of work we do at One 3 Creative.

We believe that storytellers, especially in the entertainment industry, have a social responsibility to move beyond mere entertainment and create a lasting, indelible impression on the culture-at-large. Stories, even ones that pose difficult questions about life, can help promote progress. By nature, stories give us a connection to our past, an inspiring vision for our future, a tangible human experience to share, and a forum for discussing solutions to tough problems.

The Shakers have a philosophy of furniture-making that states:

> *"Make every product better than it's ever been done before. Make the parts you cannot see as well as the parts you can see. Use only the best materials, even for the most everyday*

> *items. Give the same attention to the smallest detail as you do to the largest. Design every item you make to last forever."*

That's the kind of work we engage in at One 3 Creative when we build our Super Stories. In fact, we consider ourselves architects and craftsmen just as much as we are storytellers, because we build intricate, emotional machines that don't just entertain, but connect and engage.

Throughout history, the paradigm of a craftsman has represented man's ability to create — physically, creatively, and intellectually. In fact, we believe we don't just have the ability to create, but are hardwired and *called* to create to add to the world. Patterned after the Great Creator, we are *homo faber* — man the creator. Instead of just passively consuming and allowing the world to shape his life, the craftsman creates and proactively shapes and influences it. Ancient philosophers, both in the East and in the West, have used the craftsman as a symbol of someone who contributes to his or her community in an impactful way.

It seems as if over time, the connotation of the craftsman has solely become a picture of a lumberjack or a mason, toiling away with his tools in a workshop. The Greeks, however, had much more of an inclusive idea of the craftsman. In addition to potters, carpenters and masons, they included doctors, legislators, administrators, even parents — anything that required great care and attention to detail. Among that list, they also included — you guessed it — storytellers; primarily storytellers who told stories focused on engaging the community in a powerful way.

When you emotionally engage people with a story in a positive way and intentionally harness its deep-rooted social, emotional, psychological and spiritual potential, you've accomplished much more than entertaining an audience. What you've actually done is plant the seeds of a vibrant, mobilized community that is engaged not only with your story, but with each other.

That, my friend, is what we call the Nathan Model of Storytelling

We've assembled a light and efficient team that shifts in and out of being music producers, board game designers, screenwriters, editors, directors, marketing professionals, comic writers, actors and singers. However, no matter what we're doing, we all understand the times in which we live and are committed to using our combined talents to tell powerful stories that leave an endurable mark on today's culture.

Armed with that overall philosophy, we have a threefold approach to our business:

1. **We Create:** We develop original intellectual properties (IP's) with the focus and intent of independently producing the projects as Super Story franchises. We also develop original Super Story-ready IP's with the intent of shopping the project for acquisition or license from a studio partner or another stakeholder entity;

2. **We Help:** We consult with other content creators in a variety of industries on the best way to diversify and grow their projects to have maximum commercial and mainstream impact; *and*

3. **We Teach:** From going into high schools (check out **superstory.academy**), to building college curriculum at The Los Angeles Film School, to running intensive masterclasses and workshops for industry professionals, we feel the more we can teach and empower people with the tools we've developed, the better the industry will be as a whole. A rising tide lifts all boats. We want to be the tide.

Moreover, we are centered on six distinct values, which act as our unique fingerprints in the marketplace. They support our vision, shape our culture and reflect what we believe both corporately and individually.

- Have purpose;
- Think big;
- Create well;
- Be positive;
- Come through; *and*
- Go further.

In everything we do, we ask ourselves whether we're accomplishing these six values. If so, our work is reinforced. If not, we're immediately informed on how to improve.

These values also help us know what type of team members to hire and even who to promote. Ultimately, our six values should be found in the DNA of every scene we direct, story we write, song with produce and Super Story we design.

If you would like to stay updated with what we're doing at One 3 Creative, including receiving tips, tricks, news and updates on our live events and workshops, email us by scanning the code below.

I promise to never spam you. :)

# UPCOMING BOOK RELEASES

THE SUPER STORY WORKBOOK

The official companion to *You're Gonna Need a Bigger Story* that allows you to take an idea and walk step-by-step through the entire Super Story process.

Start with a concept and end with a fully-mapped out Super Story!

This includes a Super Story Quick Reference Guide as well as a downloadable PDF for future ideas.

THE AWESOME POWER Of FANDOMS

A HOW-TO GUIDE TO ENGAGE, GROW, AND UNLEASH GLOBAL FRANCHISE FANBASES.

STEVEN LONG MITCHELL
& JACCI OLSON

HOUSTON HOWARD & CHRIS HOFFMAN

SUPER STORY SUPER BRAND

BRAND INNOVATION THROUGH MULTI-PLATFORM ENTERTAINMENT

# AMPLIFY

USING THE POWER OF SUPER STORY TO GROW YOUR MUSIC INTO A MASSIVE ENTERTAINMENT BRAND

**HOUSTON HOWARD**
WITH TRAVIS CARTER AND KEITH GIONET

THE **SIX STAGE STORY**

**AN INTERACTIVE STORY STRUCTURE GUIDE TO DEFEATING THE BLANK PAGE**

HOUSTON HOWARD

WITH BRAD LUSHER

THE AWESOME POWER OF
Soul Stories
HOW TO USE EMOTIONAL CONNECTION TO CAUSE
YOUR ENTERTAINMENT TO STAND OUT

84655836R00208

Made in the USA
San Bernardino, CA
09 August 2018